ALARMING REPORTS

Anthropology of Media
Series Editors: John Postill and Mark Peterson

The ubiquity of media across the globe has led to an explosion of interest in the ways people around the world use media as part of their everyday lives. This series addresses the need for works that describe and theorize multiple, emerging, and sometimes interconnected, media practices in the contemporary world. Interdisciplinary and inclusive, this series offers a forum for ethnographic methodologies, descriptions of non-Western media practices, explorations of transnational connectivity, and studies that link culture and practices across fields of media production and consumption.

Volume 1
Alarming Reports: Communicating Conflict in the Daily News
Andrew Arno

Alarming Reports

Communicating Conflict
in the Daily News

Andrew Arno

Berghahn Books
NEW YORK • OXFORD

First published in 2009 by

Berghahn Books

www.berghahnbooks.com

©2009 Andrew Arno

Library of Congress Cataloging-in-Publication Data

Arno, Andrew.
  Alarming reports : communicating conflict in the daily news / Andrew Arno.
    p. cm.
  Includes bibliographical references and index.
  ISBN 978-1-84545-579-8 (alk. paper)
  1. Social conflict in mass media. 2. Discourse analysis—Social aspects. 3. Mass
media—Social aspects. 4. Mass media and anthropology. I. Title.
  P96.S63A76 2009
  302.2301'4—dc22

                                       2008053761

British Library Cataloguing in Publication Data

A catalogue record for this book is available from the British Library

Printed in the United States on acid-free paper.

ISBN: 978-1-84545-579-8 Hardback

Contents

Figures

Acknowledgements

The origins of this project grew largely from my participation as a faculty member of the Department of Communication (currently the School of Communications after a merger with the Department of Journalism) at the University of Hawai'i. I am indebted to my colleagues there for their encouragement and inspiration, particularly Majid Tehranian and Richard Vincent, and especially to John Bystrom, who always made talking about news at all levels a great pleasure. More recently my greatest debt is to my anthropology colleagues, especially Jack Bilmes and Matt Tomlinson, for their generous and constructive criticisms of successive drafts. On the domestic side, I would like to thank the scholars in my own family, Letitia Hickson, Claudia Arno, and Samuel Brenner for their encouragement and suggestions.

CHAPTER I

News and the Anthropology of Conflict Communication

Studying mass mediated news as conflict communication, charting the social career of an alarming report as it moves off the page or screen and into the flow of social life, poses significant methodological challenges for anthropology. News is often an important part of conflict talk in a community, and anthropology clearly has staked a distinctive, if only incipient, claim on news as an object of study through the ethnographic literature on conflict talk and disputing in cultural contexts. For example, in the 1980s, Donald Brenneis and Fred Meyers presented a collection of essays by Pacific anthropologists in which language and disputing—topics that had each received considerable anthropological attention on their own—were brought together with an explicit focus on the interaction between the two (Brenneis and Meyers 1984). Karen Watson-Gegeo and Geoffrey White edited another substantial collection of work on this topic in their book, *Disentangling: Conflict Discourse in Pacific Societies* (1990), and several monographs have provided detailed ethnography of conflict talk in the area (e.g., Bryson 1992; Arno 1993). Studies of this kind, at the village community level, do not pursue mass mediated news as an object of study, but they lay the groundwork for the investigation of news as I define it in this book—not merely as newspaper or television content, but more broadly as a speech genre. My goal in this book is to explore the mass media dimension of news from the perspective of language theory, which will provide a bridge to established ethnographic work on conflict communication as well as language based theories of law. Within a more inclusive anthropology of the media, the study of news promises a particularly well-focused and politically salient area of investigation.

Mass media anthropology is an exciting, newly developing field, and it may in some sense point the way to an expansion, if not a redefinition of basic anthropological ideas and practices such as ethnography, participant observation, and "the field" in the future of anthropological research (see Rothenbuhler and Coman 2005; Peterson 2003; Askew 2002; Herzfeld 2001; Spitulnik 1993). Regarding the prospects for an anthropology of news, Michael Herzfeld makes the interesting observation that news may have been initially neglected by media anthropology because journalism proclaims itself to be factual and may seem to lack the expressive, cultural aura that tends to attract anthropological notice (2001: 299). Similar claims to a fundamental grounding in observable fact, however, may link anthropology and journalism as sister disciplines, and the interest of anthropologists in understanding their own techniques of representation (e.g., Marcus and Fischer 1986) may have spurred a parallel interest in news production (e.g., Pedelty 1995).

Daniel Boorstin (1962) points out that many items reported as news are in fact pseudo-events that are simply created for the media and would not otherwise have taken place. More generally, Jean Baudrillard investigates the relation of real events (events that exist independently of the media) to media representations and argues that hyperreality, in which there is no real event (only representation), dominates a putative "age of simulacra and simulation" (1988: 171), which we can begin to see around us. For Baudrillard, "ecstasy is that quality specific to each body that spirals in on itself until it has lost all meaning, and thus radiates as pure and empty form," and just as "fashion is the ecstasy of the beautiful: the pure and empty form of spiraling aesthetics, … simulation is the ecstasy of the real." Baudrillard asserts that "to prove this, all you need to do is watch television, where real events follow one another in a perfectly ecstatic relation, that is to say through vertiginous and stereotyped traits, unreal and recurrent, which allow for continuous and uninterrupted juxtapositions" (1988: 187). Baudrillard's observation seems to apply perfectly to cable news channels, with their steady stream of events, pseudo-events, and "news" about the parent companies' entertainment shows. News, like ethnography, however, insists on an anchoring reality. Demanding reality, the aesthetic of news is sharply differentiated from that of fiction, but the reality of news is to be found in the totality of the news process, not just in the relations between event and story. When news—the report of an actual event—goes off the page into the news community, it discovers, by meeting up with its interpretation, its reality in the lives of the news consumers. Even the fluffiest pseudo-event or the most ecstatic simulacrum has the potential to be news if it raises (or quells) real alarm in the reader. If a media company promotes its "reality" programs (a category that illustrates Baudrillard's observation well) by inserting promotional stories into its news shows, those stories are not news to the great majority of the viewers—some of whom may be interested or amused, however—but it is at least conceivable that it could be news to someone. Something factual in the promotional message might be relevant to a particular viewer's financial, litigation, or other "realistic" interests. For example, the media company may insert a story about an exciting new plot development on a popular show: a gay marriage will take place. The factual element is not that it happened (it did not), but that it will be shown on television. Two viewers are watching the show together; one is fervently religious, the other an aspiring author. One shouts, "they are destroying the Godly way of life!" and the other shouts, "they stole my idea!" Only by using ethnography can one map the news process and indicate the sites of reality with which it engages.

Specifically with regard to future developments in ethnography, Douglas Holmes and George Marcus (2005) explore the concept of paraethnography: ways that professionals such as economists engaged in forecasting and regulation have developed to form sensitive representations of unfolding social reality, and how such techniques may be related to anthropological ethnography. Journalists and their editors, I argue, engage in a two-tiered form of paraethnography, one directed at the objects of their reporting, and the other at the structure of the readership's knowledge, beliefs, and anxieties. Several media studies by anthropologists have combined, without labeling it as such, paraethnographic analysis of media production with ethnographies of media content reception.

For example, in *The Cell Phone: An Anthropology of Communication* (2006), Heather Horst and Daniel Miller directly address the challenges that mass communication technologies present for the development of an anthropology of communication. A major methodological issue concerns moving beyond the traditional anthropological focus on face-to-face interaction in small scale communities to include the *mass* dimension of mass communication. Horst and Miller demonstrate that when members of a cultural community communicate by way of telephone—whether cell phone or land line—the technological device is by no means a transparent medium, but instead is an active element in the construction of social reality. Accordingly, Horst and Miller combine the macro perspective—accounts of the ways in which national and transnational economic trends, corporate strategies, and government regulatory policies shape the social reality of the cell phone—with the micro perspective afforded by close ethnographic observation of cell phone use by relatively nonaffluent Jamaicans in rural and urban communities. In Horst's and Miller's anthropology of communication, technology and culture are seen to define one another dialogically—

neither one unilaterally determines the other—but the process does not occur simply two-ways. Rather, the cell phone defines and is defined by culture in multiple, recursive layers of interaction that are ordered by hierarchies of power. The technology as it confronts Jamaican users has already shaped and been shaped by business and government, for example, and the uses that the Jamaican poor make of it will in turn alter the meaning of the cell phone to business and government. In situations of this complexity, typical of mass mediated communication processes, anthropology must find ways of documenting the interrelations of macro and micro processes of meaning. Michael Agar (2006) has discussed this general problem as one of fractal recursivity in relating the transnational political economics of the drug trade to street level ethnography of the drug culture, noting that although awareness of the larger, global pattern enriches understanding of each local reality, the researcher cannot derive the macro reality from fine-grained ethnography. Both levels must be studied with methodologies appropriate to each.

When an element of material culture, such as a cell phone or a package of cocaine, is the central object in the investigation—that is to say, the investigation of the social relations that center on such an object—the great and small patterns that structure the social reality are typically looked at as relations of production and reception. The production and distribution of the modern technology or consumable commodity takes place on a mass scale and is best described by economic, political, and regulatory studies, integrated by macro sociology. The reception of the product, however, is more effectively captured by ethnographic observation in specific cultural contexts. In terms of scientific logic, the empirical observations of ethnographic fieldwork do not establish hypotheses or propose grand theory but rather act as a test that puts the brakes on broad generalizations offered by macro sociology and futures studies (Flyvbjerg 2001). Manuel Castells's vision of what he calls the emerging network society in the information age (e.g., Castells 2004) and the predictions of development economists, for example, make persuasive predictions about the uses and cultural consequences of the cell phone. In the network society, the cell phone and other mobile communication technologies that allow instant, intimate conversations across the globe should, theoretically, shift importance away from local, kinship based social units, and small scale entrepreneurship should blossom, freed from the constraints of office rents and land lines. The cultural realities of cell phone use that Horst and Miller document among the Jamaican poor, however, are infinitely richer than the theoretical accounts and suggest quite different directions.

The research strategy of studying relations of industrial production at the mass scale and reception at the individual and cultural community level can also apply to news, even though it is an object of intellectual, intangible property. Scholars in the fields of communications and cultural studies as well as journalism have frequently looked at news as the product of the journalism industry, producing critiques of such issues as concentration of media ownership and subservience to commercial and political interests. This salutary body of critical literature, examining the productive practices of journalists and their bosses as well as government and business policies, has been paired with studies of reception as well. Denis McQuail (2003), in a survey of mass communication theory and research, documents the importance that has been given to the reception side of mass communication products, including the news. There is a large literature on "effects" in mass communication research in which the mass dimension of reception is sought by statistical techniques of random sampling of a presumably homogeneous mass audience. At the same time, however, mass communication theorists have also long recognized the social complexity of the reception arena, such as when Paul Lazarsfeld (1944) discovered a "two-step flow" in which media content was inflected by opinion leaders around whom interpersonal communication about the media content was organized. Elihu Katz and Jay Blumler (e.g., Katz et al. 1974) explored the idea that audience members actively shaped reception, as motivated by their own "uses and gratifications" in relation to the media product. More recently, media scholars have been attracted to ethnographic approaches to mass communication media reception, and David Morley (1996) describes the tides in research ideology that have energized a movement back and forth between views of the audience as culturally autonomous interpreters or, on the other hand, as passive targets of hegemony. Virginia Nightingale's (1996) trenchant critique of audience research demonstrates the powerful attraction as well as the complexities and potential for confusion about issues of agency and structure that have characterized attempts to find a place for ethnography, variously defined, in the cultural studies tradition. Studying an active audience has often been seen as requiring ethnography along the lines of the familiar anthropological paradigm of counterposing mass production on the one hand, with de-massified, cultural particularist reception on the other.

One problem with applying the production-reception model to news and other mass media products is that they are continuously produced. When a news story exits the "factory" as a product of the journalism industry, it continues to be under production all of the way to the end users in a culturally segmented news community. By contrast, although cell phone users continue to construct the social meaning of the machine, they do not, except for some after market tinkering, reconstruct the material product. A news story, however, is a configuration of social meaning from the start, and its continuing production off the page or screen can be a total reconstruction of the object. It is essential, then, to study the continuing processes of production in the arena of reception. This approach, which must rely on theories of language and discursive practice to explain the continuing processes of narrative production and circulation, can serve as a way of confronting a basic paradox inherent in mass media anthropology: how can the diversity of individual and small group meanings be studied on a mass scale?

Studying the discursive formations that "receive" news reports as intermediaries within the audience—much like the opinion leaders that Lazarsfeld identified in his two-step flow theory of reception—provides a connection between the local and the mass levels. The Lazarsfeldian opinion leader, of course, was a person—the foreman at the factory, or an especially cool teenager with a developed sense of fashion, depending on topic and community—but discursive formations are immaterial entities. Bruno Latour in his Actor-Network-Theory (2005) argues that nonhuman entities like computers or automobiles must be considered avatars of agency, *actants,* in social assemblages in order to achieve a more realistic understanding of the social than the traditional Durkheimian definition of the social fact affords. From this kind of perspective, the social actor can be regarded not as an entity, but rather as a function of complex relations among material and immaterial actants. Webb Keane (1997) in an innovative ethnography of ritual performance on Sumba Island, Indonesia, shows how moving agency out of individuals and into the ritual scene enables the analyst to recognize the powerful, active role of material objects in ritual. Of course, ideologies, clothed in words, are also essential participants in the distributed agency of ritual as social action. In this book, I will argue that conflict discourse systems—ways of defining, talking about, and acting in regard to conflict—are prime actants in the news process.

While conflict discourse systems and their interrelations of opposition and alliance can be identified in individual conversations about news, it is more effective to concentrate on media content as an indirect method of observation because of the uniquely fast moving feedback involved in daily journalistic production. As with, surely, most academics interested in studying news, I have often puzzled over the way to design a study that would mobilize a large team of participant observers who would instantly begin to record natural conversations about a breaking news event as soon as it hit the media. For example, in April of 2007, a few days after the Virginia Tech shooting in which 32 people were killed by a student gunman, other students and I in a graduate seminar discussed the idea that distinct conflict discourse systems were being attracted to such an event and that their involvement could be traced in media content as well as in natural conversations. I mentioned that, without having closely studied the coverage, I had the impression that pro-gun and anti-gun discourses had mobilized to corroborate themselves by explaining the meanings and the lessons to be taken from the attack, but I felt there were many missing conflict discourse systems that I had not yet seen reflected in media coverage—for example, feminism. One of the students then reported that on the afternoon the news broke, she had been in a popular lunch spot across the street from the University of Hawai'i campus, and she overheard people talking in an animated way about the gender implications of the shooting. Another student said that she herself had told her husband in a discussion of the event at home that evening that, "of course it had to be a guy—a woman student would never have done it." Her husband objected at first, but in the end he had to agree with her interpretation, she said.

This anecdote points out the limitations of media content studies of conflict discourse. There are always missing dimensions, some of which might even be actively suppressed in the media coverage, but rampant in certain face-to-face communities. Still, a single overheard conversation in Volcano Joe's restaurant or a researcher's own home, while valuable in themselves, are very limited in scope. Conflict discourse systems that are discernable in media coverage, especially over the range of an extended series of stories as a news narrative develops in the community, carry a certain presumption of mass significance. A question for the discipline, of course, is whether or not some connection between the data and actual people in specific physical and social contexts is obligatory in anthropological research. Horst's and Miller's cell phone study ranges widely into the areas of government policy and transnational business models, but it also presents participant observation data such as direct quotes and concrete scenarios from Jamaican communities. Is this the aspect that marks it as anthropology of communication rather than sociology? In another excellent example of mass media anthropology, Purnima Mankekar (1993) visited lower middle class homes in New Delhi, watched television with the family members, and recorded the individual comments of men and women about their interpretations of state-produced serial dramas with nationalist and gender identity themes. She also investigated the production side, interviewing writers and describing the institution of state television, but the specifically "anthropological" part of the study might be seen as the reported information from, for example, Selepan and Padmina, a married couple whom Mankekar interviewed in depth. But clearly the study is not really about Selepan and Padmina; instead, as mass media anthropology, it is about the discourses of gender and nationalism that they articulated in conversations with Mankekar and each other. Selepan and Padmina can be seen as elements in the Latourian social assemblage of Indian television. In the present work, I am focusing on conflict discourse systems as immaterial actors in the social process of news. My first step, then, is to define news in a way that is realistic in terms of common sense and also that makes it amenable to analysis as a form of institutionalized communication about conflict.

Defining News: A Bold Claim

A central argument of this book is that news, according to my functionally and historically grounded working definition, is always about threats—whether from social conflict or natural forces—to the vital interests of the news consumer. For example, shipping news, a staple of the earliest American newspapers, might seem a boring topic—the routine comings and goings of merchant ships—but it was information fraught with the potential for financial disaster to the papers' subscribers. The safe arrival of a ship is good news, but it is *news* only in relation to, and proportionate with, the anxiety that is relieved by it. Absent that emotional hook, it is simply routine intelligence, which, I will argue, may be new information without being news in the full sense. Commenting on the origins of the commercial trade in news in early seventeenth century Europe, John Thompson observes that "there was growing interest in the Thirty Years' War and this provided a major stimulus to the development of the fledgling newspaper industry" (Thompson 1995: 66). Almost four hundred years later, wars still boost mass mediated news consumption. From my perspective, good news is epiphenomenal. Good news is news—that is, talk possessing the particular kind of narrative energy marking news as a distinctive genre—only because it draws its energy from a necessary precondition of threat. Peace in the Middle East is news; peace in Switzerland is not. One could object that peace in Switzerland is not news only because it was already peaceful, while peace in the Middle East is "new." But current events constituting continuing unrest in the Middle East *are* news—although nothing "new"—while fresh instances manifesting peaceful relations in peaceful regions are not newsworthy.

The definition of news, and particularly the line between good news and bad news, is by no means a merely academic or philosophical issue.

In April of 2007, Russian journalists employed by the Russian News Service, a major private company that provides newscasts for the Russian Radio network, began to struggle with a new rule according to which "50 percent of the news must be positive, regardless of what cataclysm might befall Russia on any given day" (Kramer 2007). The rule was articulated by new managers who were selected by the owners of the news service who were businesspersons loyal to the current government who evidently felt that too much bad news was not politically healthy. A news editor with the company, interviewed by Andrew Kramer for the *New York Times,* said that in the case of difficulty in deciding exactly what constituted good news for the day, they were instructed to ask the new leadership, and "we are having trouble with the positive part, believe me" (Kramer 2007).

Bold claims such as that news is necessarily bad are always over simplified, of course, and the news media are full of stories that blur the lines of any definition. Some stories are clearly big news, and others are relatively trivial, although still news to a degree. Evidently, then, news is not an all or nothing category, but more like a sliding scale. It seems to be an aspect of the specific story and can vary in importance from huge to almost nothing. At a minimum, I think one can maintain that news is keyed to the present and refers to actual events—things that really happened. Fictional events are never news, and everyone involved, editors, reporters, and readers, hates to be fooled by them. That news consumers *are* sometimes fooled, of course, can be news when it happens. Fakery in news is itself news because it represents a threat to the integrity of the process, which is a vital one in social life. What we call fake news on the cable TV comedy channel, on the other hand, is not fake at all, but real news to the extent that it refers to actual events that are of concern to the audience. Stylistics—whether the report is cast as sarcastic parody or delivered with pious objectivism—is merely the vehicle of news, not its essence.

Furthermore, news has to be of interest to someone—it has to be news *to* somebody. The specific nature of that interest, its intensity, and the number of people it engages are important elements in the definition of news that I am proposing to explore in this book. It is the particular *kind* of interest that separates news from other kinds of interesting information. My argument in essence is that news is about disorder—disruptions to the standard expectations that obtain in the news community. At the most basic level, humans rely on a benign or at least manageable order in nature. Disease and dangerous weather, although part of natural order, represent disorder to people and are newsworthy because of the threats they pose. A favorable weather forecast is nice information to have in planning a picnic, but it lacks something—news value within a mass media news community—that is central to the report of an impending hurricane. Social disorder, of course, is an even larger source of news, and it also concerns threats to the vital interests of individuals.

Social order, experienced as the normal course of everyday life, supports, and in an important sense is constructed of, the identities of the community members. Social identities can be conceptualized as bundles of rights and duties, which is to say that identity in action—not just as abstract labels—consists of the social rights and obligations that are acted on and demand respect in everyday life. While some standardized personal interests are recognized and protected by law in modern societies, others, although strongly felt and jealously guarded against infringement by individuals, may be open to negotiation in other forums, such as the mass news media. A lot of news reports, which might be disparaged as mere "human interest" stories, bear on the validation of social identities about which individual readers have anxieties. News stories can participate in the institutionalized systems of managing conflicts in the intimate spheres of life—family and interpersonal relations—as well as be integral to the management of public conflicts in politics and law. In this book, by looking at news as a speech genre and as a form of communication about conflict, I want to include the subjective and interpersonal aspects of news as they are functionally integrated with the public, political, and societal aspects.

Disorder of virtually any kind can represent an open threat to individual and group interests. If an account of disorder conveys an *immediate* threat to *vital* interests, starting with the fundamental interest of physical integrity and progressing up the ladder of a hierarchy of needs, it provokes a response of alarm that, in its intensity, is the index of newsworthiness to the individual or collectivity. Abraham Maslow (e.g., 1970) proposes a theory of human motivation according to which the more basic needs trump the less basic. An immediate threat to air, water, or food supplies can erase the usual concerns for physical safety, and only when basic needs of physiology and safety are somewhat satisfied can an individual go on to concentrate fully on sex, love, and family. Issues of self-esteem and reputation represent a still higher level of concern, according to Maslow, capped by a rather open category he calls "self actualization," which includes creativity and morality. From a comparative perspective, however, it is clear that the hierarchy of concerns is culturally highly malleable (see Douglas and Ney 1998). In a given community, and in certain situations, honor, social solidarity or some other high level ideological construct may be assigned basic priority over concerns for comfort or even life itself. Viewed in terms of cultural and situational complexity, then, a Maslovian theory of relative salience in motivation translates directly into a theory and practice of newsworthiness. The successful reporter, news editor, or blogger gauges the relative power of alarm among available stories based on a shrewd knowledge of the target news community's current hierarchy of motivation. One can criticize a news medium for preferring to print or air a story about celebrity love affairs rather than an essay on the history of Middle East politics, but an editor with any pretension at all to journalism would certainly bump the celebrity story for news of a major terrorist attack or a natural disaster. The successful editor knows the thresholds of alarm that define his or her target news community at different stages in the flow of events. The political slogan, "9/11 changed everything," in reference to the terrorist attacks on US targets on 11 September 2001, may not be literally true, but at least it can be said that 9/11 suddenly and drastically altered the thresholds of alarm in the national news community.

One corroboration I can offer, then, for my definition of news as inherently conflict-centered—given that conflict is defined by actual or perceived threats to the interests that define personal identity or physical safety—is that *big* news stories are often easy to link to basic and obvious threats such as war, epidemic disease, hurricanes, or bursting economic bubbles. Of course, it is true that the news media are filled with all kinds of stories that do not have such obvious links to threat. This is where the argument for news as conflict has to become subtler. Because news has an essential subjective component, one cannot just dismiss as non-news stories that the analyst does not consider news, but that many others in the news audience do. For example, over lunch recently (2005), a colleague offered this example of a news item for discussion. "As I was leaving the house," he said, "I noticed that a 'Fox Alert' flashed on the TV screen. The TV was on mute, but the caption said that Madonna fell off a horse." Neither of us felt that this was newsworthy, particularly, but, given that it was a real event and not a publicity stunt, I think we both felt a slight twinge of discomfort in speaking of it ironically. "Well, anyway, I hope it wasn't serious" my companion said, "like that actor"—we quickly came up with the name, Christopher Reeves—"who fell off a horse and was paralyzed."

This episode illustrates several points I would like to make about news. For one thing, news stories on the screen, page, or air are not in themselves the news. They are potential news, and as such they represent the often-accurate estimates of editors and reporters about the uptake among audience members that will realize that potential. Conversations about the news stories, even ironic ones, are an essential component of the news as a social process. Another point is that the calculus of threat to one's interests in determining newsworthiness is by no means completely rational and literal. Social identities form a system within a community, which means that they are interdependent and interconnected. The interrelationships are not only functional but also encompass shared identities and feelings of empathy. We can identify with victims of murder and accident, at times simply because we share identity categories like "parent," "spouse," or even "pedestrian," and this makes their stories newsworthy—that is, shocking or scary in personal terms— even if any actual danger to ourselves is highly remote and unrealistic. The point is that once a link of shared identity is established, any reported injury, even on the remote outer fringes of personal identity represented by strangers in a broad, shared category, is a personal threat.

Celebrities are a special case because, although remote objectively, they are far from strangers, and the events of their lives are enmeshed with the motivational gears of their fans' lives. Like works of art, celebrities can be the focus of a special kind of *einfühlung* aesthetic in that their fans experience emotions *through* them. In 1984, John L. Caughey, an anthropologist whose fieldwork ranges from Micronesia to Pakistan to the United States, initiated an important line of research in his book, *Imaginary Social Worlds: A Cultural Approach*. One of the topics Caughey writes about is fans' social relations with media figures, and social psychologists and media sociologists have continued to explore the kind of one-sided but very intimate and intense *parasocial* relationship between fan and celebrity. Such relationships, like conventional real life social relationships, can be important to the fan's own sense of identity. The so-called "relationship" problems—in the sense of the management of intimacy—of the celebrities can merge with or even displace those of the fan, thereby evoking genuine feelings of anxiety and threat (see, e.g., Thompson 1995).

To follow up on the Madonna story, I typed "madonna horse" into an Internet search engine after lunch, and I found a number of references. Some online newspapers from the UK played up the parasocial angle of fan identification with punchy, rhythmically interesting one-sentence paragraphs like, "singer came a cropper on her 47th birthday," and supplied information such as that the horse had been gift from her husband. Each personal detail offers the fan an avenue of identification with the celebrity and her misfortune. On the other hand, a BBC online story, which appeared the next day and was segregated under the heading of "entertainment," took a more practical, business oriented stance and reported in the lead that the accident would not delay production of Madonna's new CD. The allusion to a possible, but thankfully averted, disruption in the orderly flow of commerce would constitute news of a mild sort to readers who are players at some level in the music trade. One also could imagine that the story "someone fell off a horse in England and broke her collar bone," even without the celebrity aspect, would ring a bell of vague newsworthiness with a parent whose child had been asking for riding lessons.

Clearly, news stories hold different meanings for different segments of the—in that sense de-massified—audience, and the stories themselves have narrative elements indexing those interpretations. Another point that arose from my lunch conversation about the Madonna story—which as a real event had a certain force that transcended our reference to it as an *example* of news and made us consider it, however tangentially, as news per se—concerns the automatic linkage to the much more prominent, long running US news story about actor Christopher Reeves, ultimately connected to his remarkable advocacy activities in the larger public controversy about stem cell research in the treatment of nerve damage. The Reeves story has broader and deeper newsworthiness than the Madonna story because of its connection, beyond the celebrity/fan element, to the ongoing political conflict over the role of religion in US government. The connection to the Madonna story was only fleeting, of course, but potentially all news stories can share intertextual relations with certain other stories, especially major stories or very recent ones. These relations can pump up the newsworthiness of a minor story.

Admittedly there are some classes of stories appearing in the media as "good news" that are very hard to link convincingly to threatening issues. Wonderful new technologies that will make life better or more fun are sure to evoke wide interest, and people will be eager to hear and talk about them. The anodyne effects of something like 3-D TV, for example, would no doubt outweigh any threats that it might pose, but I think in a consumer society that reports of such advances more properly belong in the category of *advertisement* (incitement to consumption, generally) than of hard core news. The dangers, however unlikely but possible, of exciting scientific advances like nanotechnology or bioengineered crops are more likely to be the central focus of news stories about them than are the consumer benefits. The key difference between advertising and news genre, elements of which are often mixed together in a single media report, is the specific tenor of the reader's reaction. They are interesting to the reader for different reasons.

Speaking of nanotechnology, *The Wall Street Journal,* in its 25 August 2005, edition ran a story headed "Nanotechnology Hits the Tennis Court: Latest Rackets Use Magnets, Tiny Crystals, to Add Power; A 54% Bigger Sweet Spot" (Sheng 2005). The story appears in the "Personal

Journal" section of the paper, characterized across the top of the page as concerning "Personal Finance * Cars * Health * Entertainment * **Home & Family** * Leisure & Arts" (emphasis in original). Is this story news? According to my proposed definition, it might well be news—of greater or lesser intensity—to readers who make a living from playing tennis or selling tennis rackets. Another kind of interest, more in the nature of entertainment, is engaged in readers who like to hear about neat gadgets, or, more abstractly, the interface between science, technology, and everyday life. For most readers, I believe, the impact of the story is not alarm—"what should I do about this?"—but rather consumer desire—"where can I get this, and how much will it cost?" This example raises a crucial methodological issue in the study of news when subjective impact is central to the definition. The answers to "is this news?," and "to what *degree* is this news in the news community?" are empirical, ultimately, but impossible to measure directly. Ethnography, listening to people talk about news stories in natural situations, provides the highest quality answers, but of course it cannot cover a mass audience. Fortunately, the feedback relationships among publishers, editors, journalists, and readers are uniquely sensitive and fast moving in news as a publication genre. Narrative elements of the stories index the reader interests for which they are reaching out, providing a cybernetically informed professional estimate of presumed reception, a window on the paraethnographic resources of the industry. Discursively focused content analysis, then, together with the analyst's own participant observer knowledge of ambient conflict discourses in the community, can form a picture of what is happening in the news process.

News Definitions and Cultural Diversity

The meaning of the term *news*—in the sense of what people mean when they say *news*—is determined by how the word is actually used in a community of speakers and only indirectly by formal definitions that people might or might not pay attention to. Philosophers and language theorists since the early to mid years of the last century have moved away from metaphysical study and toward interactional objects of study. If Plato had been interested in studying news, he might have sought an eternal ideal of the concept, only imperfectly realized in the understanding and practices of society.

Wittgenstein, however, would turn the classical process of definition upside down by asking instead how people in a news community use the term *news*, rather than seeking a metaphysical ideal beyond everyday talk. This is a much more feasible and productive approach. The extent to which my working definition runs counter to actual American usage, then—which it clearly does in some ways—is an issue for me. In justification, I would argue that *news* in the contemporary US setting that is my area of study displays a pattern of usage having a loose and very general periphery arranged around a more sharply delineated core. In peripheral usage, "news" can indicate any kind of current, surprising, interesting information, but the core meaning among journalists and news consumers is linked to conflict and threat. They may not *say* that it is, but their practices, as I will demonstrate in this book, confirm it. I am concerned, then, with the *form* of the news genre in my definitional statements, not the *content*. The content will vary from person to person and from one cultural community to another, and in this book I am looking at specific American news communities associated with media organizations such as the *New York Times, Honolulu Adverstiser,* and *C-SPAN*. As for possible broader, even transcultural generalizations about news, patterns of kinship—cross cutting family resemblances—among news genre in India, Fiji, China, and so on, are open to empirical investigation, and one can speculate that forces of globalization will operate to make observations in one news community more and more relevant to other culturally distinct news communities. That is to say, every community can be expected to have communication institutions centered on the production and distribution of alarming reports. Some will be configured by corporate structures and mass media, others by interpersonal relations and small, point-to-point media, and the mix of news bearing communication practices will continually vary as forces of modernization, technological change, and cultural resistance movements contend with one another.

Criticism of News Media

In the spirit of anthropological reflexivity—that is, the acknowledgement that the interests and motivations of the author are an important part of any description or analysis—I must say that my interest in news as conflict is motivated by a broader academic orientation to the general topic of communication about conflict in diverse cultural and social settings. That has a lot to do with my conflict/threat definition of news. But I certainly am not saying that the more traditional definitions of news developed and used by professionals and academics in journalism are misguided. As an avid consumer of news, I have found the historical and sociological insights of journalism scholars and reflective practitioners engaging and enlightening. I particularly enjoy the sometimes passionate criticism of the press in the US, and I intend this book as a contribution to some of the ongoing debates from a language theory perspective. Criticism of the press implies a policy position, and part of my motivation in writing is to counter the often-heard argument, articulated by readers, pundits, and even journalists, that news is too negative. This is what Cindy Crawford, of Morristown, New Jersey, wrote to the editor of the *New York Times:*

> I am only one small voice in this country, but I feel confident that people want to be optimistic about their lives and their country.
>
> As I watch this country become so divided over the war, I wonder why the news media will not come together and support what our country is doing for another country. How long will our young brave individuals in our military continue to volunteer for all of us, given the constant barrage of negative information?
>
> I remember September 11 so very well and feeling that if there was ever a time we could depend on our neighbors, it was after those attacks. It was one of the only times I truly felt that this country was united.
>
> This is again a time to unite, regardless of our political preferences.
>
> *Letters, The New York Times*
> 8 August 2005

Ms. Crawford's letter has the impact of a sincere and eloquent statement about a serious political situation—bitter divisiveness in a situation of crisis—and her misgivings about the news media are widely shared. I strongly feel, however—and I am sure a majority of serious students of, and participants in, the news process would agree—that the notion that the news media should "come together and support our country" and avoid providing a "barrage of negative information" is exactly counter to the reality of properly functioning news media. To the extent that this widespread but misguided pro-social news policy position is based on a "good news" theory, it needs to be countered by a theory that defines news as reporting what is *wrong* with a given situation, and only by way of contrast what is right.

In summary, definitions of news are not so much right or wrong as suited or not to the research questions that are being pursued. News can be usefully defined as the content of the news holes of print or broadcast news media. That definition suits an investigation of journalistic practices—what do editors and reporters define as news? Journalists' definitions, of course, reflect a judgment about what readers are motivated to accept as news, and that is a valid indirect way to approach this basic question. However, if news is viewed in larger context as a fundamental, possibly universal, speech genre, a wider array of questions can be asked. News in this broad, generic sense may or may not appear in a conventional news medium. The path of news through interpersonal communication is an important dimension of the social process in general and the workings of journalistic institutions as well. From this perspective, the connection to mass news media is important, but not essential to the definition of news. Likewise, the quality of containing new information is necessary, but it is not sufficient to mark out a particular report as news—there are many other kinds of new information, historical, technical, and so on, that are not received as news. Immediacy—that is, proximateness in time, space, and interests—is another necessary but not sufficient dimension of news. Factuality or objectivism—the quality of being grounded in reality and not fiction or distorted by ideology—represents, again, an aspect of news that is essential, but shared with many other kinds of reports, such as historical or scientific accounts. The key factor that ultimately defines an account as news, I argue, is its capacity to stimulate the consumer's interest through an association of the narrative with anxiety and threat. A story that is new information, accepted as factual, is immediate rather than remote in potential impact, that may or may not have been selected by journalists for inclusion in a news medium, *and* is alarming or draws its energy from association with an alarming issue, is news.

The political level of news media critique—examination of the role of the news media in specific historical contexts of power struggle and domination—is essential, and I argue that such criticism should be complemented by a deeper level of analysis. Anthropology and language philosophy provide a way of getting at the deeper structure of news as a social process, and in the following chapters I will explore the application of speech act philosophy to news, suggesting a fundamental "news act" underlying not only modern news media, but many other forms of communication, such as law and policy talk, about conflict in diverse societal and cultural settings. Following the lead of Walter Lippmann, in his 1922 classic, *Public Opinion,* I apply Peircean semiotics to the analysis of news, addressing the inter-linked issues of *meaning, truth,* and *communication* as emergent from structural interactions between the points of a news triad formed by *event, story,* and *reader.* Charles Sanders Peirce, a founding exponent of pragmatist philosophy and the field of semiotics, argued that the fundamental element of meaning, the sign, not only stands *for* something, it also stands *to* someone, engendering another sign in the mind of its interpreter. Lippmann argues, in parallel terms, that a news story stands for—is an image or representation of—a news event, and it stands *to* the reading public, thereby creating a public opinion based on the "pictures in our heads" that result from news stories. From this perspective, news as a communicative process has an essentially dialogic character in that what M.M. Bakhtin refers to as the "active role of the other" (1986: 70)—in this case, the news consumer— is fundamental. For Bakhtin, speech, including complex written speech genres such as novels and scientific treatises (and, we may add, news stories), is not merely expressive in the sense of representing the ideas and intentions of the author, but finds fruition in the rejoinder, expressed or not, of the person addressed.

My strategy is to approach news as a quintessential form of communication about conflict, located theoretically within the anthropological tradition of the ethnography of communication and, in the broadest sense, following from the basic theme in cultural anthropology of culture as communication. This broad communication perspective allows a conceptual bridge between the classic first amendment vision of the press in the public sphere and the contemporary cultural studies understanding of news in the context of identity politics.

CHAPTER 2

The Dark Side of the Media

News as Control Communication

In Volume I of his trilogy, *The Dark Side of the Dialectic,* Alvin Gouldner discusses the relationships in modern society among ideologies, social movements, and the news.

> Movements are those sectors of the public responsive to the mobilizing efforts of ideologies; they share an ideology that, on the one side, interprets the news and, on the other, provides an awareness of their own social identity from reports in the news media. News generates ideology-centered social identities which, in turn, are now media-constructed and defined. Thus social movements in the modern world are both ideology- and news-constructed. (Gouldner 1976: 100)

Gouldner states in a concise way the basic perspective on news as a social process that I explore in this book. But from a language theory, discursive practice perspective, the terms *movement* and *ideology* seem too heavy and solid as constructs to capture the intricate cultural dynamics of the news. *Ideology* and *social movement* represent important dimensions of mass media news analysis, but in this project I see them as referring to the ideational precipitants or solidified sediments that sometimes result from a much more volatile, highly agitated, cultural process. News is a high-speed social phenomenon. Stories can explode onto the social scene and then disappear from sight overnight. The rarified discursive reality from which ideologies and ideologically driven political action emerge—and into which they are ultimately dissolved again from their margins—is a free-wheeling arena of communication about conflict in which news plays a central role. My argument is that news is one among many institutionalized forms of communication about conflict, and it is uniquely important in modern society as an anchor that connects competing conflict discourse systems to a shared sense of extra-discursive reality. Conflict discourse systems are ways of thinking, talking, and acting with regard to issues that threaten key interests central to imagined (utopian) or actual ways of life in the news community. Some conflict discourses are highly ephemeral, others deeply rooted and enduring, and they are constantly interacting, reinforcing or diluting one another in everyday conversations about news events and are, to an important extent, observable in the text of mass media news reports.

In this book, I am approaching mass media news as a participant, critic, and anthropological observer. A well-socialized anthropologist, of course, might reject such a claim. A person sitting on a couch watching C-SPAN or reading a newspaper is not doing ethnography! Michael Herzfeld (2001) and Mark Allen Peterson (2003) are persuasive champions of face-to-face, in the field participant observation as the distinctive contribution that anthropology can make to media studies. Content analysis of news stories is a method typical of conventional communication studies and, although important, it is not central to anthropology. Fair enough, but an anthropological sensibility can be brought to bear in such activities. An essential dimension of the anthropological sensibility is concern for different organizing perspectives or systems of meaning assignment—cultures in a broad sense—shared by collectivities. Such collectivities in the mass audience are not marked by co-residence, kinship, and so on, but rather by ephemeral narrative allegiances that can be studied as conflict discourse systems. The other distinctive characteristic of anthropology is holism, the consideration of social institutions not in isolation, but in relation to one another. Studying the interdiscourse dynamics of conflict discourse systems in news media content provides a way of relating news to other important forms of communication about conflict in the larger society, such as law. In this sense, at home in a virtual field site of enormous scale, the conflict discourse system analyst is operating on the outer limits of the ethnographic participant observation research model. From this inside/outside position, news criticism, which is clearly part of the total news process, as well as social or anthropological theory per se, poses research questions for anthropological inquiry.

Criticizing the News

The news media attract criticism. Not only that, news media criticism itself also attracts criticism, and the intensity and even vehemence of all of that criticism is a genuine tribute to the importance of news media in modern life. The idea of public or civic journalism, for example, is a news critique that is itself heavily critiqued (Glasser 1999). Although it is more of a yearning than a program—not yet, but potentially a movement in Gouldner's sense—public journalism is centrally concerned with the effects of journalism on community. There is a deep historical relationship between journalism and community in the US, but, as John Paul Nord argues, both the notion of community and that of journalism are complex, and press criticism needs to recognize the tension between utopian goals and empirical reality (Nord 2001). Both are important, of course. The utopian ideal of group harmony and consensus—whether rhetorically grounded in rationality or piety—as well as the pursuit of unvarnished universal *fact* in the journalist's utopian ideology of objectivism, are as much a part of the reality as are the countervailing realist, critical notions of interest group pluralism, divergent imaginations, and perspectival truth.

In this book, I pursue two related questions from an anthropological, cultural, and holistic perspective. First, how are the modern news media, print and electronic, related to broader, more fundamental forms of social control and conflict management? Second, to paraphrase Greg Urban (2001), how does news move through the world? The first question speaks to the debate over negativity in news, often cited as detrimental to community problem solving. The second examines the movement of news off the page or screen as it enters into the life of the community, a topic that is basic to an understanding of the nature of community as social process.

The role of the news media in creating social reality has been discussed over the years in a large, often stimulating literature. Newspapers and television news have been looked at in context of broad social and historical currents (e.g., Lippmann 1922; Boorstin 1964; Schudson 1978; Schiller 1981; McChesney 1999; Hackett and Zhao 2005), but much of the debate about the nature and role of news media has retained a media-centric stance that tends to invite a view of the news media, particularly the newspaper, as a unique species among social institutions. The approach to news taken by the British cultural studies school, however, in which news is seen as one among many instruments of ideological domination in the context of class conflict, is an exception to media exceptionalism (e.g., see Hall 1973; 1977). In British cultural studies, a basic social process is invoked that applies to many social institutions and practices, and mass media news is understood as a constituent element in the larger process of political hegemony. Nightingale, citing Halloran, Elliot, and Murdock (1970), observes that this perspective supported "alternative reportage—an academic account of what 'really' happened and why" in the coverage of political protest demonstrations, intended "to counteract the perceived totalitarianism of the mainstream manufacture of news" (Nightingale 1996: 25).

I am proposing an alternative, discourse dynamic perspective that retains a conflict, ideology, and rhetoric focus, but does not privilege class or any other "actual" root source of conflict in society. Instead, I want to look at the rich and colorful fabric of conflict talk in the news, and I am employing the term *discourse dynamics* in two senses. The term focuses on the interactions among distinct conflict discourse systems as they oppose, complement, or reinforce one another in the larger context of societal conflict exacerbation and management, and it also refers to the integration of social and psychological processes through which conflict discourse systems shape social life. The print or broadcast news story represents a feeding trough to which the emerging and the established conflict discourse systems of a news community flock, elbowing and jostling one another. Looking at conflict discourse systems as active entities depending on news consumers as their carriers and their means of reproduction and growth parallels Richard Dawkins's notion of the *meme*, the ideational counterpart of the gene in evolutionary theory. In his *The Selfish Gene* (1976), Dawkins portrays seminal ideas that are passed from one person to another as replicating and evolving entities, memes, within the ecology of human culture. News stories represent a striking example of replication and growth as they move through a news community, but they move only as they are configured by conflict discourse systems to make sense to individuals who are initiated into—one might almost says "infected" by—those patterns of talk, reasoning, and interpretation. This theoretical perspective of shifting attention from individual agents to systems of communication and identity is also broadly consistent with Michel Foucault's foregrounding of discourse formations in understanding history and society. But as John Fiske, describing his own approach to news as discourse, puts it, Foucault in his early writings "was concerned with the dominant discourses by which power was applied in post-Renaissance Europe, but the contemporary United States is a far more highly elaborated and socially diversified society than any that he studied, so its discursive circulation is more complicated, more contradictory, and, in particular, more contestatory than the discourses he analyzes" (Fiske 1996: 3–4). Fiske's own critique of the role of media, especially visual media but also including print and radio, in US politics and popular culture demonstrates how news as a social process is not confined to the narrow traces of the news media, but runs through a wide range of entertainment and other genres. In these separate but interconnected genres discourse dynamics—how relatively coherent discourses merge, separate, form alliances, and strive to eradicate one another—can be observed.

Foucault's later work, for example, his celebrated discussion of power and knowledge in *The History of Sexuality, Volume I,* moves away from the common sense idea of power as a monolithic force potential that can be cumulated at structural sites in society, such as the state or giant capitalist enterprises, and deployed in one-way, top down impositions. Instead, he argues that:

> power must be understood in the first instance as the multiplicity of force relations immanent in the sphere in which they operate and which constitute their own organizations; as the process which, through ceaseless struggles and confrontations, transforms, strengthens or reverses them; as the support which these force relations find in one another, thus forming a chain or system, or on the contrary, the disjunctions and contradictions which isolate them from one from one another; and lastly, as the strategies in which they take effect, whose general design or institutional crystallization in the state apparatus, in the formulation of law, in the various social hegemonies. (Foucault 1978: 92)

Power in this sense is of the essence in conflict discourse; Foucault's comments about the dynamics of force relations—forming cumulating connections as well as schisms that sharpen system identities through contrast—apply directly to conflict discourse systems. Force relations, the impositions of will against actual or potential resistance, are inherent in and specific in content to every institutionalized social practice. They constitute the cultural dimension, identified in Durkheimian terms as *constraint,* which is everywhere in social life. For example, the intimate arena of family authority generates force relations that may become discursively aligned with those that define the organization of large institutions like the church or the state, especially when religious dogma, legal rules, or state policy statements are invoked or implied in reasoning, justification, or category formation within household conflict discourse. When church, state, and indigenous culture become aligned, forming a discursive chain, the force relations invoked in family conflicts can achieve considerable weight. The power that might be exercised— expressed as a definition of the situation and sanctioned statements of how members *ought* to act—might appear to emanate from one of the organizational sites, church, state, or tradition, but actually it is co-generated and draws its strength from multiple points of origin. This alliance aspect of discourses called into play in conflict situations is a constant source of vulnerability and challenge. In this or that particular family—just to stick with this one example of an interactional site of conflict—new forms of discourse alliance or schism can contend with one another. Changes in political ideas, religious doctrine, science, medicine, or social science can make conflict discourse highly volatile. News, bringing word of these changes, is an important force in the dynamics of power and knowledge in specific discursive sites.

In another sense of *dynamics,* as outlined in chapter 4, I include the individual agent in a theory of the news process, incorporating a psychodynamic view of narrative pleasure as the source of discourse energy. Actually, I do not *include* the individual agent—something I take to be impossible in theory—but I suggest a methodological (Miyazaki 2004) rather than theoretical solution to the problem of agency in news. Hirokazu Miyazaki, in *The Method of Hope: Anthropology, Philosophy, and Fijian Knowledge* (2004), recounts the struggle of philosophy to encompass hope. The difficulty with such a project—constructing a philosophy of hope—is that hope is an ideational creature of the future, and philosophical knowledge is oriented to the past; the two are discontinuous. In his own attempts to develop a framework for analyzing the production of hope in Fijian ritual, Miyazaki came to understand the discontinuity between his own analysis and its object, however, as a "methodological opportunity" (2004: 23). He explains that,

> it was precisely at that moment of incongruity that hope emerged as a driving force for my own inquiry. At the moment when I apprehended the temporal incongruity between my own analysis of the ritual production of hope and Fijians' hope, in other words, I replicated Fijians' hope on a methodological terrain ... In the method of hope, this hope for synchronicity is a "representation" of the hope to which it is deployed. Moments of hope can only be apprehended as sparks on another terrain, in other words. The sparks provide a simulated view of the moments of hope as they fade away. (Miyazaki 2004: 23–24)

In analyzing news as it moves off the page and into social interaction, I argue that individual subjectivity in discourse exists only at the exact interface between the psychological space that can be thought of as interior to the self and social, intersubjective space, which is exterior. This social/psychological discontinuity presents another methodological opportunity, in Miyazaki's term, and what is required is a binary pair of theories—a social theory of intersubjective discourse and a psychological theory of narrative energy. In the untheorizable space between them a sort of stereographic image or representation of other's subjectivity can emerge, overlapping that of the analyst's. Henri Lefebvre (1991), in his theoretical exploration of what he calls the *production* of social space, for example, the urban space of cities, argues for the recognition of the integrated co-production of space, time, and energy (power) in social reality. News stories, I argue, move between and across both social and psychological space, spaces saturated respectively with narrative and psychic energy, and Greg Urban's work suggests a way of conceptualizing that kind of movement.

Urban addresses the broad topic of cultural change and continuity in *Metaculture: How Culture Moves through the World* (2001). The notion of culture moving through the world, and specifically *how* it moves, allows Urban to reach important questions about the conditions that govern the path, acceleration, and deceleration of a cultural element. Metaculture is *about* culture, and it influences the way members make judgments about—and valuations of—the sameness or change of culture as it is encountered over time, fixed and re-fixed in various kinds of material media. The basic question of culture's movement in time and space, of course, has been addressed in the many anthropological theories of cultural diffusion that have waxed and waned in the development of the discipline, and Urban's attention to the metacultures of tradition and change evokes the foundational distinction in classic social theory between traditional societies that value continuity with the past, and modern societies that value newness and change. But Urban brings a fresh linguistic, semiotically informed technique as well as an orientation to the future rather than to the past to the understanding of culture as a thing in motion. In this book, from a variety of angles, I address the question of how news moves through the world, with attention to acceleration, friction, and countervailing orientations to past and future. Mapping what I call the extra-textual terrain of news—the social and psychological spaces in which the news story finds its legs—I argue that the news story characteristically makes use of a variety of communicative techniques to grease the channel of uptake, accelerating the progress of the story into the readership community. These techniques include linking the current story with other stories that frame the readers' understanding and recognition of news worthiness either because they are *big* stories historically—Pearl Harbor, Watergate—or have formed a chain of recently reported news events and constitute an ongoing storyline. Another central technique of communication in news narrative is linking the story to master narratives, such as the evil empire, war on terror, racism, hypocrisy and corruption in politics, and so on, that are central to conflict discourse systems that link significant numbers of readers in the target audience. In this regard, the recent work on delineating the mythic dimensions of news (Lule 2005; Coman 2005), and of the media generally (Peterson 2003), explore the ways that news narratives engage with and move through audiences.

News as Control Communication

The term *control communication* (Arno 1985) evokes a cybernetic view of social process that implies a systems, functionalist model of society. Structural-functionalism, in which the structure of an institution or practice is explained in terms of the way it works in concert with other institutions to accomplish a social end, is consistent with the orientation of many empirical studies of news, such as the powerful critical interventions of McChesney (e.g., 1997; 1999), Bagdikian (e.g., 2000), Galtung and Vincent (1992; 2004), Keever (2004), and others. In this book, by concentrating on the social function of conflict management, I explore the idea that the news media are integrated parts of a larger social control process associated with societal conflicts. For example, news media and law are tightly integrated in US politics. The collections of interacting conflict discourse systems that I examine in the following chapters have the effect of creating, restoring, or maintaining order in the ways of life that they emerge from and regulate. In that sense, each is engaged in control communication to the extent that it attempts to repair shattered expectations or modulate perceived threats.

The notion of control communication as I use it, although functionalist and empirical in perspective, implies a central focus on the way communication *creates* social reality rather than just reports on it. Anthony Giddens argues that viewing language as merely descriptive and transparent—which he calls an "outmoded and defective philosophy of language" (1979: 245)—is a major shortcoming of earlier forms of structural-functionalism. As a more current perspective on language, J.L. Austin's speech act philosophy (Austin 1962) provides a useful way to look at the creative power of language in social life, and Austin's definition of the perlocutionary force of speech—as referring to the actual psychological impact of a speech event on the hearer—is a good starting point from which to define news. My argument is that news is defined on a person-by-person basis—except to the extent that people's shared interests and identities are coordinated as members of distinct conflict discourse systems—by its relation, positive or negative, to a sense of alarm, which is the characteristic psychological effect of news.

In his *The Theory of Communicative Action* (1984), Jürgen Habermas looks at perlocutionary speech acts as instrumental and manipulative.

He observes that "the perlocutionary aim of a speaker, like the ends pursued with goal-directed actions generally, does not follow from the manifest content of the speech act; this aim can be identified only through the agent's intention" (Habermas 1984: 290). For Habermas, then, "perlocutionary acts constitute a subclass of teleological actions that must be carried out by means of speech acts, under the condition that the actor does not declare or admit to his aims as such" (1984: 292). I am using the term perlocutionary, however, as Austin does in parts of his analysis, to refer to a kind of force inherent in every speech act, and as such it simply describes an actual—whether conventional or not—effect on the hearer, without reference to the speaker's intent. News (except when it is disguised propaganda) is not a perlocutionary act in the sense of having a concealed agenda of manipulation, and this is precisely because the overt content of the message is conventionally understood to convey alarming information related to threatened interests of the hearer. But that conventional understanding does not mean that each person who hears the news will be affected in the same way or to the same degree. By insisting on a perlocutionary definition of news as pertaining exclusively to a *subjectively* perceived threat to individual interest, the conflict discourse system approach, which I develop in chapter 3, deals in a relatively unforced way with the role of the individual actor in the news process. A theory of conflict discourse systems suggests a way of aggregating individuals' participation. As I use the two terms in this book, then, *control communication* refers to the cybernetic process of regulation and conflict repair at various levels of social or communicative integration (not necessarily constrained by territoriality) from global to national to local. *Conflict discourse system*, on the other hand, refers to the mechanism of aggregation that integrates the individual news consumer into the group level control communication process.

Mass media news has a central defining characteristic in common with other institutions such as law, religion, philosophy, and social science, and many others. They all, in varying degrees and circumstances, are ways of communicating *about* conflict, and each can play a specific role in the management of the conflict it focuses on. Like Gregory Bateson's *metacommunication*, control communication is *about* communication. In Bateson's seminal account, metacommunication is parallel to ordinary communication and tells the receiver how to interpret message content—how to know that a playful nip is not a serious bite (Bateson 1972). But control communication, on the other hand, is metacommunication that takes as its object the repair and reordering of broken down communication patterns, managing the threat of conflict that is inherent in disorder. Every society has a variety of institutionalized control communication forms—some explicit, well-defined, and narrowly focused, others subtle, amorphous, and pervasive.

Structural—as contrasted with control—communication is the normal pattern of meaningful exchange that constitutes accepted social reality (Arno 1985). Control communication comes into play when some sort of problem has occurred at the structural communication level, and it functions to repair and refashion structural patterns of message exchange. In short, control communication is a response to conflict, and conflict can be thought of as a potential property or state of any social relationship. Conflict arises, for example, when some or all parties to an established, "normal" (i.e., not objected to) interaction pattern no longer accept the terms of the exchange. For this reason, major innovations in social relations often encounter turbulence. The problem presented by this situation is how to reach a new understanding (see Habermas 1984) that creates the framework for a new form of structural, nonconflictual, harmonious, well-synchronized, and unremarked upon communication. At the societal level, the news media play a key role in the process of creating shared understanding in this sense. News, from this perspective, is clearly a special case, with a specific ideological force, of what linguistic anthropologists Michael Silverstein and Gregg Urban have termed *entextualization,* the formulation of a text drawn from, and then reinserted into, the ongoing discourse of social life (Silverstein and Urban 1996). As a text genre, news has a well-developed text ideology dimension. That is, the production and reception of news is framed by a set of beliefs about the nature and force of news text—it must be firmly keyed to intersubjective, objective reality, and it is a warrant for social action.

Control communication need not be accomplished through language-based text alone, however, and it need not be of a peaceful nature. Physical violence, for example, might be employed with the intent of dealing with conflict and establishing acceptable interaction patterns. Any theory of the *just war* defines combat by those in the right not as aggression per se, but as *about*—that is, in answer to—previous aggression. At early English law, trial by combat was a recognized form of control communication in which the sword or axe spoke for the parties to a previous conflict and settled the issues of contention (Lea 1967).

But in the normal range of modern civil life, talking about conflict in some way is the expected response. Two businesspersons, a husband and wife, or a professional and client may "have a talk" about their relationship, they may call in a trusted third party to mediate, or they may take legal action. Each of these latter two alternatives is simply an elaborated way of talking about the conflict—a conflict discourse system. The mediator facilitates the message exchange using the specific communication rules and practices developed within the craft of mediation (e.g., Fisher and Ury 1981; Raiffa 2001), and the legal system provides an even more elaborate and highly structured way of talking about conflict. The challenge I am undertaking in this book is to explore the role that news media play in accommodating less explicit, but pervasive, systems of conflict talk.

In its more subtle forms, control communication is part of virtually every human activity. Reduced to its most basic elements, it is the representation of an object of concern in a secondary medium, and the act itself of representation implies control, in a certain sense. But while the original naming of an object of anxiety might be considered an exercise of control communication, once the use of the word becomes habitual—when the original gulf between the signifier and the signified has been obliterated through habit, and the two are unified—another level of representation is necessary to reassert control. Measures are often instituted by society, such as invoking notions of sacredness, fear, and veneration, for example, to prevent the habituation and familiarity that negates the effectiveness of control communication.

Perhaps the earliest records of control communication text are the 20,000-year-old paintings in the caves of Altamira and Lasceaux. Wilbur Schramm (1988) argues that cave paintings represent the earliest in a line of communicative practice innovations that culminate in the modern mass media, based on physical evidence—buttocks prints in the dust of the cave floor, undisturbed over the millennia—that the ancient pictures were exhibited to an audience, possibly of initiates. At this remove, we cannot really know the purpose of the paintings, but early commentators argued that they exhibit the exercise of hunting magic. In other words, by representing their prey, and by manipulating the images in certain ways, these early artist-priests sought to gain control over a vital and largely unpredictable resource. Later interpretations have focused on the social functions—such as the development and maintenance of power relations—of such artistic activities and the secrecy that evidently surrounded them.

Levi-Strauss has commented on part of this basic process in his discussion of the relationship between art and science. He argues that artistic representation is essentially a reduction, physical and/or otherwise, of an object, and "this quantitative transposition extends and diversifies our power over the homologue of the thing, and by means of it the latter can be grasped, assessed, and apprehended at a glance" (Levi-Strauss 1966: 23). At the same time, the representations are not just "projections or passive homologues of the object; they constitute a real experiment with it" (Levi-Strauss 1966: 24). But the real power of this process comes into play when the effect of the homologue goes beyond our understanding of the object and results in a modification of the object itself. Alfred Gell (1998) discusses the traditional recognition of the power that a representation can exert on its object in the practice of volt sorcery, a form of magic in which harm to an image is thought to result in harm to the object. In *Mimesis and Alterity* (1993), Michael Taussig observes that the underlying idea of a copy having a causal effect on the thing it represents is a ubiquitous, although unstated, feature of contemporary life.

These observations apply *a fortiori* when the object of representation is social rather than natural. For example, the representation may be a legal brief and the object a conflict among social entities. Similarly, a social scientific paper may describe and analyze a structural problem in society, or a news story may report a political or economic event. In each of these cases, the secondary medium is the system of categories and logic that pertains respectively to law, science, or journalism. The medium used may or may not be physically different from that of the object. For example, a news story may be about physical violence, in which case the medium of expression changes from physical to verbal. If the story is about a speech deploring (or inciting) violence, however, the expressive medium, language, is the same. But in each case the conceptual medium—categories of thought and analysis—may be different, and if this is so the representation is by no means a passive homologue. It necessarily constitutes not just a thought experiment with the situation, but a highly invasive one because it implies that readers will act in accord with the representation. This is exactly the point that Walter Lippmann, one of the greatest American journalists and philosophers of mass news media, makes in his analysis of the power of the "pictures in our heads" created by the news media (Lippmann 1922). Lippmann addressed the power of government propaganda, and its threats to the integrity of journalism in the context of World War I, when the American public's knowledge of and opinions about the events of the European war were formed—and *acted upon*—on the basis of newspaper representations.

The artist representing nature may have virtually no direct influence over the object itself. Despite the intentions of the artist-magicians of Altamira and Lasceaux, their work had no immediate, direct impact on the behavior of the animals they hunted. On the other hand, however, their paintings, with the ceremonies and belief structures that attended their production, may very well have had a major impact on the perceived relationships and patterns of action of the members of the community—both among themselves and toward the animals. Such actions would then have a very real impact on the animals and their continued availability.

Stories in *The Nation* or opinion pieces in the *Wall Street Journal*, similar to cave paintings, serve to orient and coordinate understandings as well as potential actions among their respective tribes of readers. But the news story, legal brief, or social scientific theory—despite elaborate institutionalized protestations to the contrary, which may themselves be looked at as aspects of the necessary embedding rituals or ceremonial structures of each—do in fact transform the objects they represent. Functionally, this restructuring impact on the object of representation and the constellation of ongoing relationships surrounding it is precisely what is demanded of control communication. By analogy to natural science, control communication systems—embodied as law, social science, philosophy, religion, mass media news, or other institutional form—are the technologies, high and low, of social life. Unlike natural science technologies, however, they cloak themselves in naturalism and necessity, hiding the methodology of their effects.

A communication theory of news media, therefore, requires an account of the obscured causal relationships that enable control communication to bring about changes in structural communication. Here again, law, as a clear-cut, explicit example of control communication, can serve to illustrate the workings of the broader type. In law, one can observe two well worked out dimensions of order that impose themselves upon, and replicate themselves within, the object to which law is applied. One dimension is that of substance. The categories and principles of legal discourse are a medium within which real life conflicts can be represented, just as a painter uses pigments and stylistic conventions to depict a concrete object. Like the painting, the legal analysis is at once an existential reduction and simplification of the concrete complexity and at the same time, a conceptual enlargement through generalization. The legal categories provide a pre-existing mold into which the conflict is pressed, redefining it and making it amenable to resolution through the operation of legal reasoning. As it evolves in real life, a conflict case is highly amorphous, ambiguous, and hard to handle, and it is the selection of a forum of resolution that shapes it one-way or the other (Felsteiner et al. 1980–81). The control communication system that is employed rewrites the history of the conflict, and more importantly, it specifies a future for the pattern of interaction that defines the conflicted relationship. Newspaper studies (e.g., Henry and Tator 2002) have employed critical discourse analysis (Fairclough 1995) to discover the implicit conflict categories in the text of news stories, but in this book I want to move off the page and look at the ways conflict is conceptualized in the broader news community. That is, the question is not only how the news story reflects the discourses underlying the production of the narrative, but also how the story points out the dynamic mix of conflict discourse systems in the audience dimension of the news community. A news story, then, points to the past—the event reported—but at the same time to the future—the reception of the report in its audience.

The other dimension of order inherent in control communication systems is that of form. For example, in law, the *way* participants communicate about conflict is highly controlled by the rules of procedure. My argument here is that just as the substantive conceptual categories of the control communication system impose themselves on structural communication, the procedural order of the former is also replicated within the "repaired" structural communication patterns that are the output of the conflict management routine. This process of replication calls to mind Parsons's genetic metaphor in which communication is thought of as the DNA of social order (1968). DNA is a set of instructions, a mode of communication that governs the production of physical structures and the regulation of their system interactions. Businesspersons in a contract dispute can go to a legal setting to reach a new understanding, but law recreates and restructures their relationship in its own legalistic image. It cannot, in its severe rationalism, reconstitute the positive affective dimensions of the association that may have been lost, and other, less formal conflict discourse systems must attend to that work.

Of course, procedure or form is important in all such systems, not only in law. Religion is another type of institutionalized control communication system that illustrates the workings of formal as well as substantive ordering as it influences its adherents' patterns of interaction. At the level of doctrine, rules are stated and categories of analysis are insisted upon. But the forms of worship are also part of the picture. The nature of the relationship between priest and congregation, deity and human, member and outsider, and so on, are dramatized by the forms of worship, and these relationships constitute archetypes or templates for the construction and repair of social interaction patterns. Within the Christian religion, for example, the Reformation may have been as important for its changes in styles of worship and organizational management as for changes in doctrine in altering the impact of the church on the lives of adherents. Greenhouse (1986) provides ethnographic evidence, for example, of how Protestants in a southern town make use of religious forms in interpersonal and community level conflict management. In line with the strongly egalitarian organization of their church, and in the consequent absence of authority relationships as a resource in dispute settlement, the Baptists of "Hopewell," Georgia, deny the possibility of overt disputing within their ranks and rely on subtle, very indirect allusions embedded in ordinary conversation as a vehicle of in-group social control. Greenhouse argues that "Baptists' remedies are verbal: narratives and gossip, joking, dueling with scripture, and prayer" (1986: 25).

The law is extremely effective in resolving specific cases of conflict. The central dimension of social ordering in law is settling the dispute between A and B, the particular parties to the legal action, who may be individual people, giant corporations, or even branches of the government. In another dimension, however, the law's sphere of social ordering is general because the ruling in the specific case casts a huge shadow in the larger social context. Although the facts of its cases come from the full spectrum of social life, and its categories and rules ultimately derive from social experience, law has carved out a strong position of autonomy, with very specific categories, values, logic, and forms of rhetoric, which are maintained and perpetuated by rigorous training and hierarchical discipline. The law can handle cases that involve economics, religion, medicine, agriculture, and so on, but it has its own tightly structured forums and powerful sanctions to enforce its decisions. Other highly organized discourse systems in society, like medicine, social science disciplines, religious sects, and so on, have powerful control communication capacity as well, because they have well developed categories, logics, knowledge, and rhetorics of their own in which conflicts can be represented and manipulated. What they lack, as compared to law, are dedicated adjudicatory forums and powers of enforcement beyond their own discursive ranks.

In some ways, the news media would appear to be almost the mirror image of these systems. News provides a procedural framework for public conflicts, or the public dimensions of conflicts that encompass both public and private levels, without being able to deal effectively with the individual case. Procedurally, the news media are well-developed, with ways of processing disputes on almost any topic, but substantively they appear to be empty. In its own rationalizing self-descriptions—statements of its text ideology—the US press boasts of its neutrality in this regard. If one were to accept the characterization of the news media as objective, one might be tempted to argue that news cannot be a control communication system after all because it is totally parasitic substantively on other systems. News stories may describe and explain a conflict such as the AIDS epidemic in terms of economics, law, religion, medicine, or any other developed form of discourse, but journalism does not have its own unique categories of analysis and representation. It is clear that a news story casting a conflict in economic or legal terms is not economics or law per se. The formal characteristics of the medium mark it firmly as news. Rather than a direct representation of conflict, it is a representation of a representation of a conflict. The implications of this *second order* mode of substantive ordering are related analytically to Barthes' (1968; 1972) conceptualization of higher orders of signification in semiotic theory, including ultimately the "mythic" dimensions of basic identity work (see Peterson 2003).

The AIDS epidemic in the United States illustrates some of these points. In its scope and complexity, the AIDS epidemic is a major societal conflict. I use the term conflict rather than problem because, from the perspective of control communication, it represents a complex series of linked subconflicts, each defined by specific issues and types of parties. One of the tasks of control communication theory is the development of a typology or natural history of large-scale conflicts as systematic disturbances in structural communication.

In the case of the AIDS conflict, the underlying clash is not social, but natural. Even here there are two distinct perspectives to be considered. At the personal level it is a conflict between person and pathogen, while at the group level it appears as a conflict between organized society and an aspect of the environment. Each level suggests different institutional actors, conceptualizations, strategies, and control communication systems. It is perhaps stretching the communication paradigm a bit far in this case to construe the illness as an unacceptable form of communication between human and virus, but in a footnote concerning the need to rethink the associations and actors involved in social movements, Bruno Latour mentions AIDS activism, arguing that the analyst needs to consider how "deeply innovative it was for patients to make politics out of retroviruses" and that it is "just this type of innovation that requires completely new definitions of the social" (2005: 23). From a Latourian social assemblage perspective, the association between the virus and the patient is clearly of central importance, and a conflict discourse analysis should recognize it as well. Medicine in the primary sense of therapy may or may not be usefully conceptualized as physical, interactional *communication* about a problem, but, as an organized social activity, medical science clearly has both the highly structured substantive order and the equally stringent formal order—the "how" of the medical scientific method of discovery and reporting—characteristic of a control communication system. Beyond this initial level, however, the conflict quickly takes on a more conventionally recognized social character.

At the level of individual against individual, for example, one finds a variety of AIDS torts, including knowing or negligent transmission. Conflict between individual and corporation could include cases of workers who do not agree with a company's policies about hiring or retaining people with AIDS. Parents of AIDS afflicted children may be in conflict with local school authorities, or it might be the parents of the nonafflicted children who are in disagreement with school policy. Government agencies might also find themselves in conflict with one another over AIDS, as when the National Institutes of Health (NIH), for example, might want a larger budget for research than Congress is willing to provide. Obviously, this is not an exhaustive but only an illustrative list of structurally distinct types of interlinked conflicts that make up the total societal problem. Not only the types included, but the quantitative distribution of actual instances of subconflicts with such categories distinguish distinct varieties of societal conflict, all of which the news media try to encompass.

If the greater AIDS conflict is seen as a composite of linked subconflicts differentiated along lines of parties and issues, it is clear that within the whole a variety of distinct forms of conflict management will be invoked by the social actors involved. From the point of view of control communication, these forms include the distinct media of conceptualization and logic within terms of which the conflicts can be represented. Law expresses a conflict in terms of individual rights and duties, while economics frames it as a question of the production and expenditure of wealth on the aggregate level. Medicine, politics, and religion each have their own way of re-configuring the concrete problem, and each of these systems also provides distinct types of possible answers or resolutions to the conflicts submitted to them.

Control communication systems consist of more than concepts and rules of logic, however. They also have institutionalized forums with established procedural practices that answer practical questions such as how conflicts may be submitted to them. Do the parties have to consent to the use of the system, for example, as in mediation? Or, as in adjudication, can jurisdiction be asserted without such consent? Does the system work—that is, produce a change in structural communication in society—only if the parties are subjectively persuaded by the logic of the system, or can physical or psychological sanctions be used to enforce the results? The answers will be different for each control communication system. The news media have their own distinctive answers to these procedural questions.

Cross Referencing among Control Discourses

A thorough analysis of interaction among control communication systems in specific societal context might indicate that substantive cross-referencing is a general characteristic rather than an exception pertaining to news alone. In law, for example, which is a prime example of a control communication system, the discourse of economics can have an important influence (e.g., Posner 1972), as it did under the Reagan administration in the United States legal system (Bilmes 1985; Bilmes and Woodbury 1991). Similarly, the tenets of individual rights that form part of the discourse of liberal political philosophy have also strongly influenced the law (Dworkin 1985), and the argument can be made for an open recognition of the role of ideology in law as a step on the path toward a mechanism of radical social change within the democratic tradition (Unger 1986).

It would appear that no control communication system operates independently, in isolation from the others. Many, if not all, seem to need—just as news does—the reinforcement of others to achieve the force, defined in terms of reflective cognition as well as habitual practice, necessary for social ordering. From the perspective of the individual, the interweaving and cross-referencing reinforcement among the multiplicity of discourses that constitute total social reality lend solid authority to each of them. In creating representations of social conflict, the news borrows from the substantive ordering of other systems—law, social science, medicine, and so on—to create its own second-order set of analytical categories and logical principles. In producing changes in the everyday life of society, news operates not only directly—in the sense of influencing individual decisions and courses of action of readers—but also indirectly, again in concert with other control systems, by influencing the outcomes of legislative and judicial processes.

While the substantive dimension of news—the content and the frameworks of analysis and evaluation that are used to portray the content—is important in gauging its ordering impact in society, it is essential to consider the formal dimension as well. The formal order is made up of the characteristics that do not vary with content, such as the dependence on the visual and the time constraints of television news, formulaic techniques of storytelling (chapter 3), and so on. Formal ordering may influence the organizational characteristics of groups who make strategic use of the news media in conflict management. Reporting the urban disturbance of the 1980 Miami riots, for example, the local and national news media not only reported what happened—arson, looting, and murder—but urgently addressed the question of what it *meant.* In a real sense the riot was treated as a message to be interpreted (Arno 1985). Who sent it, and to whom? As the news media searched for spokespersons—sociologists, police officials, politicians, and economists—to provide the answers and suggest appropriate replies to the riot as a statement—African American leaders converged on the scene. To the extent that segments of the African American community, local and national, were to participate in this mass mediated conflict dialog, they needed to organize hierarchically, with leaders selected for "star" qualities of media presence. This latter point emphasizes again that in studying news from the perspective of control communication, more than content and more than the agencies of production must be included. The readers, whether as individuals or as larger discursive assemblies, are an essential part of the news process, and their characteristics, taken together with the other two factors mentioned—substance and procedure—ultimately determine the social impact.

CHAPTER 3

Two Theories of News

*The Civic Model and
the Conflict Discourse System Model*

Journalism, as mentioned in the first chapter, is sometimes seen as an evil act. Harsh criticism of the mass news media—lambasting them for negativity, bias, and superficiality, to name just a few of the major charges—seems to be a permanent fixture of political speechmaking in the United States, and opinions expressed in private conversations often follow the same lines. Even journalists themselves join the refrain at times. For example, John Tierney, in a 2005 op-ed piece for the *New York Times,* argues that the press should no longer aggressively cover—that is, with gruesome pictures and details—the suicide bombings by insurgents in Iraq during the US occupation. After the first few examples, he argues, it is not news. Speaking regretfully of his own suicide bombing reporting in Iraq, he declares that he and other reporters came to realize that "there was no larger lesson except that some insurgents were willing and able to kill civilians, which was not news" (Tierney 2005). Tierney goes on to explain that relentless and sensational coverage of such everyday bombing in Iraq creates a "distorted picture of life for Iraqis." He praises former New York Mayor Giuliani's decision to stop the NYPD from providing details of daily crime to reporters in time for their deadlines, a practice Tierney links to the daily reporting of suicide bombings in Iraq by observing that "just as New Yorkers came to be guided by crime statistics instead of the mayhem on the evening news, people might begin to believe the statistics showing that their odds of being killed by a terrorist are miniscule in Iraq or anywhere else." The day after Tierney's op-ed essay appeared, the *Times* online edition ran a story by John F. Burns and Terrence Neilan with the headline, "At Least 79 are Killed in New Round of Attacks in Iraq." The lead paragraph and dateline read "BAGHDAD, Iraq, May 11—Insurgents struck in northern and central Iraq today in a series of bloody bombing attacks that killed at least 79 people in three cities, and wounded at least 120 others, according to figures provided by police and hospital officials. The attacks appeared to signify an intensification of attempts by Sunni Arab militants to disrupt Iraq's newly formed Shiite majority government" (Burns and Neilan 2005). The counterargument to Tierney's, then, is that the "larger lesson" of the coverage is not about the personal safety of the readers, but about American foreign policy and its consequences—moral and practical.

This chapter is intended as a contribution to the vigorous, if largely one-sided, debate about news media negativity in the US. As I argued in the introduction, the most obvious fact about news is that news is always and only about conflict. It always has been, it always will be, and there is no point denying or decrying the negative, alarming, conflict-focused nature of news. This is not to say that the news media can do no wrong, of course. They can, and they should be held to high standards of performance. For example, it is clear that the huge problems associated with the accelerating concentration of media ownership, as well as media ownership by giant conglomerate corporations, seriously limit the performance of the news media and make them dysfunctional (McChesney 1999). But we have to know what they do before we can evaluate how well they do it.

If a negative side of news media performance is their preoccupation with conflict and alarm, a potential positive side is their role in conflict management. This essential function is sometimes missed, or at least underappreciated, in public debate about news because the news media never accomplish it alone but only in concert with a great variety of other social and cultural institutions. The news media's role is an essential but somehow despised one, and other institutions get the credit for its achievements in the public mind. For example, the positive gains of the American civil rights movement are rightly associated with law, politics, church and volunteer organizations, but each of these institutions operates effectively only in context of the others and also—in a very important way—in conjunction with the news media (Arno 1985). News is the loud, obnoxious personal injury lawyer whom everybody, including at times his or her own client, hates, but who is essential to the ultimate balance of justice. While the role of the press in public conflict management is implicit in American law and political philosophy, especially as enshrined in the first amendment guarantee of press freedom, the nature of the role that the press plays is often only incompletely recognized, leading to confusion about when the news media are doing their job in society and when they are not.

Any participant in conflict has to know who he or she is—and the values, rights, and duties associated with being that person—before knowing how to recognize a conflict issue or take a position on it. Identity, then, is the first step in conflict management, and news plays a crucial role in the formation of personal and group identity in society. We news reader/viewers are not merely passive targets, however, and the media's major role in identity formation is not to tell us who we are, but to offer material that we can construe as *confirmation*—proof of the objective validity—of our own evolving ideas about who "we" are, who "they" are, and what is happening in the world with regard to our interests.

That this basic first step should generally be left out in the classic formulation of the role of the press in the "marketplace of ideas" version of public conflict management is not surprising. Not to know who one is can be thought of almost as a form of craziness in a way of life that celebrates rationality in civil society. Labeling something as craziness, however, is not to deny that it exists, but simply to reject it and refuse to talk about it. US Americans of the eighteenth and nineteenth centuries must have had just as unsettled a sense of social identities as they do today, if not more so, but US political philosophy could not afford to recognize that fluidity. Perhaps it was so much of a problem that it had to be countered by what we told ourselves—in laws and textbook social theory—about our institutions. Today, however, we can no longer afford to ignore that basic first step—identity—in conflict management. The dynamics of formation and fragmentation of personal and group identity have been thrust into public consciousness by new technologies and new economic and political realities in America. Multiculturalism and the infinite regress of subcultures are not new, but our perception of them is new, and new theories have to be constructed to deal with them (Arno 2002).

The Civic or Rational Consensus News Scenario

The Civic model is what I would call a commonsense US view of news, which I am by no means rejecting. In fact, it remains my own personal ideal standard for what news ought to be, and it continues to be a vital part of the ongoing policy debates about how the news media do and should operate. In the most primitive, archetypal version of this scenario, an *event*, E, happens that is relevant to person X. Person Y observes that event, perhaps investigating to learn more about it, and then tells the story of the event to X. Person Y's *story* or report, then, is *news* to X. One might imagine this kind of interaction as like those taking place in one of the villages, Tilling or Riseholme, invented by E.F. Benson in his novels about Lucia and Miss Mapp. The inhabitants go out shopping each morning as a pretext for bumping into one another and starting conversations that begin "Any news?" The response to a story or observation about ongoing social conflict in the village thus elicited is "No!," which translates as, "Tell me the rest." Projecting this little interpersonal activity to the level of mass communication, the practice becomes institutionalized in such a way that Y becomes a newsgathering and disseminating organization, rather than just a person, and X becomes the mass audience, but despite these changes in scale, the logic of the process remains the same. The potential substance of the news is the body of all events that are reportable as news (capable of eliciting the "No!"), and the actual substance of the news is the body of stories that are in fact selected for reporting. In the real life city, far from Benson's fictional villages, thousands of reader/viewers open the morning newspaper or turn on the television news with the implicit question, "Any news?" They may receive an account of a drug-related shootout in the local high school. The average response among the audience, openly expressed in some way or not, may be something like "Shocking! Scary! This can't go on." Ultimately, the response may be some attempt, at personal or political levels, to take corrective or evasive action: take the kids out of the public school system or vote for political candidates who promise to get tough on drugs. News, then, in the Civic scenario is understood as the work product of Y, which is a newspaper, for example, or a television news show. This scenario poses a number of questions for analysis and critical research. For example, how are the actual stories selected from the universe of possible events? Are the events accurately and fairly portrayed in the stories? What is the impact of the news reporting, positive and negative, on society and the individual?

These are all good questions, but in order to evaluate mass media news as a group level institution, one needs to identify the single most fundamental, legitimate purpose that it serves for the community involved, whether that community is local, national, or international in scope. "To allow newspapers to make a profit" is obviously not specific enough as a purpose, from the group's point of view. It is certainly legitimate in US society, but it misses the unique function of news. The same is true of the societal coordination function, formulated, perhaps, as "to focus and guide public opinion." To some extent the news media do inevitably serve this valuable and necessary purpose, but when it shades into propaganda and manipulation, it becomes definitely illegitimate. Instead, I think, the key function of the news media in the context of the Civic scenario is, as Harold Lasswell puts it, "surveillance of the environment" (Lasswell 1948). The environment here is both internal and external to the group, and the purpose of the surveillance is to provide information about problems and potential troubles and to disseminate that information to the group in way that promotes *rational solutions*. In other words, the mass media news is an institutionalized form of communication about public conflict. As such, it is one among many other similarly focused but quite diverse institutions whose potentially positive societal function—the effective performance of which can be shaped by critical evaluation and policymaking—is the management of public sphere conflict. Coupled with the US political ideal of the individual citizen as the ultimate decision maker, the Civic news scenario emphasizes the function of providing full and accurate information so that each individual can act appropriately—personally and politically—in dealing with current problems. The Jogger Rape story (discussed in chapter 4) was a huge story in New York City in 1989, and it illustrates at one level the Civic model. On April 21, two days after the incident, the *New York Times* reported the attack on Page B1 with a story headed "Youths Rape and Beat Central Park Jogger" and a large picture (Wolff 1989). The story continued on page B3, and another story—one that recognizes the surveillance and personal threat management function of news—is printed on the same page, "Park Safety: Advice From Runner" (Hays 1989). That story includes a large map of the park jogging paths showing exactly where the vicious assault took place. The sites of three "other attacks" that had been reported are also indicated. Clearly, this map and story would help joggers decide where or whether to jog in Central Park. Although critics of the press may argue that coverage of sensational crimes has the negative, anti-social effect of frightening people who are not really in danger, the civic model is based on the idea that individuals need all the information possible about issues of public concern such as law and order, and each reader can make up his or her own mind about the individual or group action that is appropriate.

The Conflict Discourse Systems News Scenario

This second view is consistent in many ways with the Civic model, but it places different emphasis on certain parts of the process, some of which are merely implicit in the Civic scenario. For example, it starts with C, a community of people who are at least potentially in communication with one another. We still have persons X and Y and event E, just as in the first scenario, but here we take explicitly into account the obvious requirement that these people have to be socially linked in some way before the news report can happen. The event has to make sense to both parties, which implies a common understanding, and each has to be motivated—Y has to have some reason to make the report, and X a reason to listen. In other words, they, and the other members of the community, share not only a basic means of communication, but also a degree of common experience and knowledge, as well as general values.

The community in this modern scenario, however, is not homogenous. In fact, it contains many distinct subcategories of people, and they are continually in conflict with one another, within and across category and subgroup lines. It is only realistic to recognize that all communities have both consensus and conflict dimensions, and social theories purporting to describe a given community have to make a choice: they can emphasize conflict, they can emphasize consensus, or they can ignore the issue. The Civic scenario more or less ignores the issue and assumes consensus about basic values by default, but the Conflict Discourse scenario is a conflict-oriented model, which is particularly appropriate in talking about news. The very fact that there is an enduring community, however fractious, means that the community has developed institutions for dealing with conflicts and keeping them within manageable bounds. It is these institutions, which are organized ways of talking about and rationalizing conflict in the group (Arno 2002), that I argue are the most basic and essential elements of mass media news as a social process. They are the conflict discourse systems, and for convenience I will refer to them here as CDS.

The recognition of the multiplicity and variety of CDS—what they are, how they work, how they interact with one another, and so on—is at the heart of the Conflict Discourse news scenario as distinguished from the Civic Consensus model. A particular CDS exists in the group as a set of social roles, the reciprocal definitions of which govern how people in those roles will interact with one another, and it also specifies a body of knowledge, a hierarchy of values, and ways of reasoning shared by the individuals who embrace the CDS and in that sense are members of it. Every conflict discourse system grows out of a way of life, total or partial, and its specific job is to regulate and maintain that way of life.

The legal system, as I argue in chapter 4, is one of the most explicit, universal, and powerful conflict discourse systems in American society. Its scope is broad, although not unlimited. By and large, it governs the public sphere rather than the nooks and crannies of the intimate social world. It has a hierarchy of values and rules—from the broadest constitutional statements to the finest and most specific of regulations and laws. It has a specific vocabulary and strictly enforced rules of procedure, as well as clear-cut lines of authority. It also has an intricate set of overlapping identities from the general concept of the legal person to the myriad specific reciprocal identities of landlord and tenant, master and servant, agent and principal, bailee and bailor, and so on. This archetypal CDS, law, is related to episodes of social conflict in this way: it identifies the event in terms of its own categories of analysis, it provides a way of talking and reasoning about the situation, it clarifies the identities of the participants and their respective rights and duties, it exerts authority to resolve the conflict or dispute, and sets out a blueprint for future conduct. In this description I say *it*—law as a CDS—"identifies," "provides," "clarifies," and "exerts authority." Obviously, what I mean is that people do this, but they are the people who take their identities, authority, and justification from the legal system, such as lawyer, judge, plaintiff, bailee, and so on. They are created as role players by the system itself.

As massive and complex as the legal system may be, it represents only a minor part of the conflict discourse system scene in any society. The others may not be so sharply defined and invested with legitimate power to compel compliance as law, but they make up the bulk of people's talk about, and action with regard to, social conflicts, and they have tremendous power to govern society. A specific moral or religious system—for example, born-again, fundamentalist Christianity—may identify and address social problems and conflicts that the law does not recognize, and it may also provide an alternate approach to conflicts that the law claims as within its own province. Like law, it provides a system of categories, values, and identities, as well as a hierarchy of authority and for dealing with conflicts. The two may reinforce one another at some points and be at odds at others. And both exist in an ecology of conflict management systems encompassing a great variety of other, different types. For example, economics and other social sciences—although they are not normally total ways of life in themselves to the extent that a religious system might be—can constitute fairly distinct and powerful conflict discourse systems in their own rights. They—embodied as people who adhere to them and express them in their talk—recognize and define problems according to their own categories of analysis, provide ways of reasoning and judgment of alternative solutions, and propose paths of action. Thus, a United States senator, in a televised hearing on the then ongoing (1993) Waco standoff between the Koresh cult and the FBI, could comment that the operation was very expensive—citing a dollar figure per day of standoff—and warn that the US taxpayer would not endure such an expense for long. This way of talking, and of ultimately acting, with regard to conflicts is not an absolute alternative to the various other systems—legal, moral, medical, and so on—so much as a strand interwoven in the fabric of societal discussion of conflicts. The persistence of the economic frame in conflict discourse is illustrated by the remarks of Senator George Voinovich, quoted in a June 2007 *New York Times* article. Referring to the ongoing war in Iraq, Senator Voinovich said "my heart has been heavy for a long time. We're talking $620 billion. We're talking over 3500 people killed" (Zeleny 2007). Attorney General Janet Reno, who gave the go-ahead to federal agents to introduce tear gas into the Koresh cult fortress and force a culmination of the conflict, was particularly concerned with the welfare of the many children in the compound and asked specifically about the health effects of the tear gas on children. Her questions reflected a heightened sense of concern for the impact of the standoff and cult doctrines generally on the welfare of the children of the cult. For Attorney General Reno, child abuse was an important part of the situation—a part that strongly suggested a course of action. *Anti-child Abuse,* then is a CDS nested within more encompassing conflict discourse systems such as law and family values, and as such it can serve as a rhetorical resource—as when Reno used it to explain her decision—and it also no doubt played a role in her actual decision making.

In the Conflict Discourse System news scenario, the community can be conceptualized as host to a teeming variety of CDS, some well entrenched and powerful, and others tentative, ill defined, and ephemeral. They are continually coming into existence and dying off—as are the ways of life they serve. Some refer to more or less imaginary ways of life—something its adherents wish for, perhaps, or see in the future, such as utopias—while others are attached to a widely shared and explicitly developed social reality. The Koresh cult, just mentioned, was an extreme example of a system of beliefs, values, identities, and so on that its adherents translated into a total way of life. As such, it offered a coherent conflict discourse system relied upon by its members in their battle with the rest of the world. On the other side of the barricade, the FBI agents—and millions of readers and viewers of mass media news—understood and acted upon their own understanding of the conflict in a completely different way. For the vast majority of them, law was a major instrument of consensus, coordinating their understandings and actions.

The government case against Timothy McVeigh in his 1997 murder trial for the Oklahoma Federal Building bombing, however, revealed yet another important CDS—that of the survivalist anti-government militia movement—with its own reading of the Koresh standoff story. Of course, individuals such as McVeigh are responsible for their actions—"the discourse made me do it" is not a moral or legal defense—but it is at least clear that the militia discourse system was heavily implicated in both the inspiration and the practical details of McVeigh's crime. It is also clear that survivalist, anti-government militia *discourse* went on trial with McVeigh and suffered a setback in credibility—which is a CDS's lifeblood. No doubt this blow to the larger "evil government" discourse weakened to some extent the reach of Jim Traficant's appeal discussed in chapter 4. Some commentators have argued that, similarly, the 9/11 terrorist attack on the World Trade Center and the Pentagon in 2001 gave terrorism a bad name. It is at least interesting that the IRA in Northern Ireland and the Tamil Tigers in Sri Lanka became temporarily more tractable and amenable to peace talks in the wake of 9/11. The appeal of survivalist militias in the US seems to have abated as well, as the "war on terror" has repositioned anti-government resistance.

Not all confrontations among CDS are so extreme, but each CDS is at odds with certain others and defines itself in opposition to them. Some form firm alliances among themselves and, although distinct, agree to treat one another as complementary. Altogether, they are a lively and powerful, although invisible, company of entities in the community, just as essential at their own imaginary level of existence as the flesh and blood people of the community themselves.

Because a CDS need not refer to an actual, exclusive way of life existing in the community, its own mode of existence need not be continuous. It can flicker to life and become intermittently observable of peoples' actions and conversations about conflict. In conversational settings—especially if the topic is an alarming news event—a CDS can spread from one person to another, who might carry it to another conversation later on. For example, soon after the 1996 TWA plane crash (Kleinfield 1996)—an incident in which TWA flight 800 inexplicably crashed soon after take off into the ocean off of Long Island, New York, killing 230 people and sparking a flurry of speculation about whether an anti-aircraft missile might have been the cause—I had lunch, as usual, with a number of frequently flying colleagues in the campus cafeteria at the University of Hawai'i. As soon as we sat down, the crash became the topic of an animated discussion, based on information drawn entirely from the news media accounts. This situation was a classic example of people interacting on the basis of "pictures their heads," to use Lippmann's phrase, that had been created entirely by the mass media. None of us had any direct knowledge of the event. Various interwoven threads of conversation—jointly produced by speakers in the group, agreeing, disagreeing, or extending what others said—interpreted the events and drew conclusions based on theories of international relations, terrorism, government regulation and economics, the technologies of crime and detection, psychology, and other distinct ways of framing and discussing the event.

To me, this kind of spontaneous discussion, multiplied by millions, is the heart of the mass media news process. Talk about news events, organized by coherent but multiple theories of history, identity, and action, is comprehensively interlinked with mass news media content, and neither can be understood separately. It is in settings of this kind, as well as in the content of the news report in the media, that a particular CDS can be observed in action. If people quit referring to it—whether it be feminism, multiculturalism, science, economics, or law—and quit using it to organize their discussions about conflict issues, it simply dies. If more and more people take it up, however, it becomes correspondingly more vigorous and powerful. People in the community move from one CDS to another over time or according to the situation, and one person can participate in a number of them at once. The common feature of all of these systems is that they are focused upon conflict. Each one categorizes—in talk—events and situations in a way that fits the set of conflicts that it recognizes. All other kinds of conflicts are invisible to it, and once it has defined the conflict, it provides a way of talking about, analyzing, and managing that conflict. I think of a community as host to a parliament of conflict discourses. Those that have the most powerful support in the lives and talk of the members of the community form the government, in the sense of actually controlling social institutions and practices at the civic level. But there are many opposition discourses that wax and wane, and sometimes even the largest CDS needs to form coalitions with others to govern social life in the community.

News, in the Conflict Discourse scenario, is defined as something that happens within the multiplex of constantly changing communication circuits constituted by the CDSs of the community. In an objective sense, news is partly definable, as in the Civic model, as the work product of the news medium—that is, as a body of alarming reports intended for the mass audience. But the Conflict Discourse scenario goes beyond this definition to insist that news must be news *to* someone. Editors and reporters produce stories that they hope and predict will be news to many people in their audiences, but that does not mean that it *is* news. Being news to someone is something that happens within the frameworks of meaning and identity created by conflict discourse systems, and the news media provide the raw materials that a CDS needs to display itself in people's thoughts and actions. To extend the metaphor of the CDS as an active being, one could say that the news media provide a feeding trough to which the CDS swarm to compete for nourishment. They have to get people talking about conflicts in the vocabulary, categories, values, and identities they prescribe, or they will waste away and die.

Yes, they are imaginary. They are like Tinkerbell, who lives or dies according to how many people clap and how loud they clap, but they are also very real and very powerful in social life. The Chicago gorilla pit story, which achieved tremendous play in the news media in August of 1996, provides a good example of how the Conflict Discourse model of news applies to much that one reads or views in the news media. It is a good example of the CDS model precisely because it is such a weak example of news from the Civic scenario perspective. Briefly, what happened—event E in my formalistic scheme—was that a little boy fell from a railing fence eighteen feet onto the concrete floor of the gorilla pit at the Chicago zoo, and he was rescued by a female gorilla who, displaying what one can hardly describe as other than intelligence and compassion, carried the unconscious boy to the door of the exhibit area through which human keepers could reclaim him and give him immediate medical attention. This event became a very big story, but was it news? In a perceptive essay, syndicated columnist Rekha Basu characterizes it as "just one of those simple feel-good stories that restores your faith in nature, and [that] for a delicious moment was devoid of any conceivable partisan political context" (Basu 1996). Basu goes on to criticize Rush Limbaugh, the conservative talk radio host, for violating the political innocence of the story in his ranting denunciation of the enormous press play the story received. According to Basu, Limbaugh saw the media attention as evidence of liberal efforts to use the story to advance animal rights and the theory of evolution, both anathemas to the far right. Basu concludes that, deplorably, "in the misanthropic mystery of talk radio, every incident can be reduced to a game of liberal or conservative one-upmanship, every angle a check on the political scoreboard" (Basu 1996).

From the perspective of the Civic news scenario, the gorilla pit report is indeed just a feel-good story. It is not news, in the sense of a hard news story—such as a report of the crash of a commuter airline plane—because it is not, on the face of it, an alarming report about some immediate danger to the interests of the civic community. On the other hand, one cannot deny that it is still a big story—not just an *ordinary* feel-good story. There is something about it that captures people's attention and gets them to talk about it. To a great extent, I think, Limbaugh was right about what was going on. Readers and journalists with a politically moderate perspective could not see it; it just felt good to them, and that was enough. But Limbaugh, from his highly critical, marginal position, correctly observed that the gorilla pit story is about an existential conflict of identity. The questions it raises are among the most fundamental to human identity: what is a human being, and how is the human person related to nature and to nonhuman animals? Put this way, the issue seems to be philosophical or academic in character—hardly likely to stir up reactions of threat or alarm or to provoke public controversy. Only a moment's reflection is needed, however, to see how immediately this question underlies some of the bitterest current political and public conflicts: abortion, stem cell research, environmental regulation, teaching creationism (intelligent design) in schools, animal rights in medical research settings, and others that continue to arise. In a real sense, the question of identity is generating these issues, rather than the other way around.

Basu links the gorilla story to a powerful mythic theme in popular culture: the nurturance of a human child by animals. She cites the Disney animated world in which animals are human-like and sometimes nurturant toward humans, as in the Disney movie version of *The Jungle Book*. One might also cite the mice in Disney's *Cinderella,* and so on. The gorilla pit story gives this classic Tarzan theme an interesting, thought provoking twist because it was reported that the gorilla herself had been raised by humans, which presumably predisposed her to identify with humans and take care of the little boy. But there is also a very big difference between stories of Tarzan and others nurtured by animals—as known to us from books and bad movies—and the report of the little boy who fell into the gorilla pit of the Chicago zoo. The difference is fundamentally that between news and fiction. News creates an aura of factuality that myths need in order to ground themselves in our sense of real life, as opposed to pure fantasy. This is the sense in which I argue that the news media are feeding troughs for conflict discourse systems. Factual reality, paradoxically, is essential to the nourishment of myth because it confirms to the believer the reality of a specific system of ideas, values, and identity. But facts and real events are profoundly ambiguous; they can be interpreted any number of ways by competing systems of meaning and identity.

Limbaugh was right to observe that the gorilla pit story could be used to strengthen the environmentalists' basic system of values and identity by illustrating the psychic unity of animalkind and the idea of the human person as part of nature. But the most interesting example of how a CDS feeds on the news is provided by Limbaugh himself, who interprets the news coverage as factual confirmation of a system of values and identities that divides people into two clear-cut, opposed identities: the independent, freedom loving, Godfearing conservative on the one hand, and the liberal, tree-hugging, Governmentfearing, bleeding hearts who use the media to control and manipulate society, on the other.

The CDS news scenario does not contradict the Civic model, but it expands it in several ways. It widens the focus of study and analysis of the news media to include not only the production and circulation of stories in the media, but also the interpretation and discussion of those stories in the community. In other words, news is not just the published work product of the journalist, it is also the work product of the readers who talk about the story on the their cell phones, at work, at the dinner table, Internet chatrooms, and so on. The unit of analysis of this extended process, however, is not the individual, but the coherent, shared systems of values, identities, and implied ways of life that shape that extramedia part of the process and give it its energy.

The CDS perspective also widens the ascribed function of the news, and it provides alternate criteria for evaluating media performance. In the Civic scenario, news serves to alert the rational, autonomous citizen decision maker to civic problems that need attention. The same function is recognized in the CDS model, but it recognizes a further, equally fundamental function of news, namely the formation of personal and group identity in the context of conflict management. The two are related because one cannot recognize and know what to do about a civic problem unless one knows who one is and what interests one has to protect. A conflict discourse system does exactly that; it provides a way of talking about and solving problems because it provides a set of interrelated identities. Rush Limbaugh devotees see themselves and others in terms of their shared discourse system, and news items provide the grounding in reality that turns the implied way of life of their CDS into an actual way of life for them.

Structure and Agent, Discourse and Subject

Posing the problem of understanding news in terms of these contrasting models—the Civic versus the Conflict Discourse scenario—raises perennial issues associated with structure and agency in social analysis. Why am I insisting on the complicated idea of a mass of writhing, imaginary discourse systems as my study population rather than simple flesh and blood people? And would not it be more straightforward to just say that people talk about the news and employ a variety of arguments to make sense of it? This is the usual standard of rhetorical analysis. And it would seem more straight forward because of our culturally ingrained habits of thought that tend to cast the individual in the active role. But at the same time, it is an awkward and indirect way to talk about the dynamics of a social process that is beyond the control, or often even the complete comprehension, of the individual.

Individual persons are generally thought of as agents or actors, and social institutions and routines are seen as the structures within which people jointly establish the shared meanings that enable them to pursue social lives. Individual people, then, are actors, and structure is what they enact. As actors, people have intentions, goals, and meanings, which establish them as agents—the source points of social process and change. I think this perspective is inherently appealing because it flatters us. It makes the individual seem powerful and in charge, and it reinforces the strong streak of Romanticism in Western culture. At the same time, of course, we are constantly made aware by everyday events that the individual is far from being all powerful and is not even close to being completely in charge of his or her life in society. Rousseau laments that "man is born free but is everywhere in chains," and the constraints we all face are not simply those of other, stronger individuals' wills but, more profoundly, the binding rules of society that constitute social structure. Even Caesar Augustus was subject to the laws of language, and language is only one among the complex of rule systems that even the most powerful individual must obey in order to exercise his or her vaunted agency. This challenge to the ultimate supremacy of the individual is resolved, however, from the perspective of an individual centered theory of agency, by the view that structure, although powerful, is passive. The individual agent is still the hero of the scenario, and structure is reduced to an obstacle to be overcome and a tool to be used.

For example, in the Civic model of news, the individual decision maker is the star of the show, the driving force in the marketplace of ideas, and that marketplace constitutes the structure of the news process by providing a rationale for its institutions and practices. The Conflict Discourse model, however, places much more emphasis on the structure, even to the point of assigning it a type of agency—that is, a sense of being the effective origin of purposeful action—that is normally reserved to the person. Despite the resistance to this kind of view offered by commonsense, which insists that only the individual can form intentions and act on them, its usefulness in understanding social phenomena is shown by the current popularity of academic analysis based on the poststructuralist idea of discourse, largely identified with the writings of Michel Foucault. For present purposes, the basic insights of poststructuralism are: 1) that the individual is created as a social and even psychological being by a way of life; 2) that the way of life is constituted, embodied, and maintained by a system of communication; and, 3) that there are more than one such systems, and they cannot be measured against one another to determine that one is better, truer, more realistic, and so on, than any other. From this perspective, the human being is not born "free," in Rousseau's sense, at the moment of his or her biological birth. Socially, the new biological entity is already, even well before birth, enmeshed in a system of externally assigned identities and expectations. And psychologically, as a conscious agent who has intentions, goals, and a sense of self, the biological person is not yet born at all at the moment of physical parturition, but enters into another, longer period of gestation—a social and psychological pregnancy that comes to fruition only when the biological entity has grasped and internalized the shared reality of the group, anchoring his or her own personal identity at a definite position within it. That position within a shared reality provides subjectivity to the person, creating him or her as a subject in relation to the discourse.

Once the reproduction of social agents is liberated from the biological process, it becomes obvious that the psychological equivalent of reincarnation presents almost endless possibilities of rebirths, perhaps celebrated most patently in contemporary American society by self-styled born again Christians (Luhrmann 2004). Other subjects may not choose to call themselves "born again"—feminists, environmentalists, economists, and so on—but they represent the same kind of agent reproduction process in society. The social world's constantly emerging, constantly self-reinventing, communication systems can reach a point of self-consciousness, with fairly clear-cut boundaries of inclusion and exclusion, or they may remain too diffuse to achieve named recognition in society. In full operation, they provide their bearers—or those whom they bear, to continue the birth metaphor—with a sense of identity internally and in relation to others, stocks of knowledge and methods for creating more knowledge, and values that guide and motivate action. Each one is what Wittgenstein called a form of life, in the sense of a way of living in society. But can one go further and consider them social life forms, corporate entities that tap the psychic energies and consciousness of individuals as they interact with one another?

A major barrier to this reconceptualization of the problem is the lack of a widely recognized archetype. In the familiar scenario that credits the individual agent as the author of social actions, one can fall back on one's own individual everyday experience of having goals and trying to get things done. What is needed is an alternate scenario—something we all see and experience everyday—in which structure itself is also an active agent in the social process. In *Consciousness Explained* (1991), Daniel C. Dennett elaborates on Richard Dawkins's notion of the *meme* as an incorporeal entity that reproduces itself by restructuring the human mind. The meme is a replicating unit—just as is the gene—and like the DNA molecule, it can develop variability, it can make copies of itself, and it is controlled in its reproduction by its fitness to its environment (Dawkins 1989). But memes are ideas. They are not just basic ideas like "red," "cold," "round," and so on, but "the sort of complex ideas that form themselves into distinct memorable units—such as ideas of: wheel, wearing clothes, vendetta ... deconstructionism" (Dennett 1991: 201). From this perspective, the conflict discourse systems I have been talking about are ecologies of memes—distinct mental environments in which the included ideas relate to, and take their own specific identities from, one another.

Meme ecology is an alternate archetypal idea or scenario of social explanation that complements the standard, commonsense notion of the human agent acting to bring about social reality. True, the meme is parasitic; it can only develop and reproduce in the human mind, and for this reason it seems in the abstract rather repellent, if not dangerous. The material equivalent that comes to mind might be something such as a communicable virus. And there is nothing about a virus that is understandable in human terms except that, although without the barest trace of consciousness or conscious intent, it is hell bent to reproduce itself and has incredibly ingenious strategies to attain that goal. But putting a pleasant, even noble face on the meme requires only listing some of the ideas that constitute the highest achievements of human culture, such as honor, justice, and beauty. This exercise, however, immediately suggests a major weakness of meme analysis. Ideas like honor, justice, and beauty are so completely restructured by cultural context as to become unrecognizable from one context to the next. How can an isolated idea or concept be a unit of analysis if it is so malleable?

Dawkins's idea of the meme, of course, is itself a meme, and by looking at its course of replication and evolution in academic discourse, some salutary lessons are offered about the vulnerability of the meme. With regard to weighing the respective influences of biological *genes* and cultural *memes* on human consciousness, Dennett cautions that, "we would be foolish to 'side with' our genes—that is to commit the most egregious error of pop sociobiology" (1991: 207). As Dennett's comment suggests, the particular meme that might be identified as "sociobiology" (here again, however, it is not clear whether this complex idea is a meme in itself or an integrated collection of memes) has had a less than smooth career in the social scientific community. Sociobiology was effectively articulated in the early 1970s by biologists E.O. Wilson and Robert Trivers and anthropologist Irven DeVore at Harvard, and it was well received as an exciting perspective on the undeniable biological constraints and influences on social behavior in all animals, including humans. When it entered the discourse of naïve behaviorist pop psychology, however, sociobiology mutated and became anathema to many cultural anthropologists who saw it as an absurd reduction of the most intricate cultural practices to specious, post hoc accounts of physical evolution and natural selection.

Unfortunately, it seems that the meme of the meme could suffer a fate similar to that of the meme of sociobiology. Matt Tomlinson (2004) offers a trenchant criticism of an emergent "memetics" (Blackmore 1999) in his analysis of the persistence in mass news media circulation—and the parallel lack of circulation in village level discourse—of a phrase, "failed businessman," in reference to George Speight, leader of the 2000 *coup d' ètat* in Fiji. From its independence in 1970, Fiji, a former British colony, appeared to be a model of biracial political harmony, accommodating the interests of its indigenous Fijian citizens and those of Indo-Fijian citizens, who, constituting a slight majority of the total population, were descendants of nineteenth century migrants who came to Fiji from India as indentured laborers. In 1987, however, Fiji and the entire Pacific Islands regional community were shocked by a military takeover of the government. The first 1987 *coup* was led by an army colonel, Sitiveni Rabuka, with avowed purpose of restoring and perpetuating political control of the country by indigenous Fijians. Rabuka relinquished control to a new civilian government, only to seize power again in a continuing dispute over constitutional guarantees of indigenous control. Rabuka, who ultimately became the elected civilian Prime Minister of Fiji, went on to become a well-known figure in the region. In 2000, after parliamentary elections had resulted in an Indo-Fijian's becoming Prime Minister, yet another *coup d'ètat* was attempted, this time led by George Speight. Obviously, this was a big news story in Fiji and in the region. For regional and world news media and their readers, the idea of a military coup in Fiji immediately connected with the previous stories, but who in the world was this George Speight? Early on in the reporting, a source described Speight as a failed businessman, and the phrase stuck tenaciously. Virtually every time Speight was mentioned in news stories, it was as "failed businessman George Speight." As an anthropologist engaged in fieldwork, Tomlinson also had access to discussions of the coup among Fijians at the village level, and he observed that the phrase "failed businessman" or its equivalent in Fijian did not catch on among Fijian discussants. Tomlinson's question, which is very close to the general topic I am addressing, is how an idea or phrase that enters mass media communication circuits develops a seeming life of its own, being picked up and repeated widely. And at the same time, how is it that the same phrase fails to take hold in another, highly interested community of discourse? Can meme analysis account for this pattern?

Tomlinson cites Susan Blackmore as perhaps the most accessible and systematic exponent of memetics and he quotes her own take on news: "Certain kinds of news spread more effectively than others. These are the things people get to hear about and want to pass on again. As a result, people talk more" (Blackmore 1999: 85). Tomlinson goes on to point out the circular nature of this analysis: "The chain of reasoning goes round and round: memes circulate because the things that circulate are memes" (2004: 189). Tomlinson continues his critique by noting the failure of memetics to specify, except in the circular way just noted, a unit of analysis—how do we know exactly what constitutes a meme? But the core problem with memetics, from which its methodological problems stem, as Tomlinson shows, is its failure to account for human agency. Turning away from memetics as a way of explaining the situation—although he agrees that the notion of the meme is a useful metaphor to the extent that it focuses attention of the circulation of cultural products in various settings—Tomlinson explains his own observations about the circulation of the "failed businessman" phrase in terms of an ethnographically grounded analysis of the ways that people comment on their culture, a form of talk that Greg Urban (2001) calls *metaculture*. Memetics fails because "human desire and agency must remain factors, not for ideological reasons, but for the simple fact that interests are not reducible solely to imitation, and imitation is the core of the memetic universe" (Tomlinson 2004: 195). To simply deny that human agency exists—to say that memes are in command of our consciousness and actions—is to replicate in the dimension of culture what Dennett called the "most egregious error of pop sociobiology." That is to say, sociobiology overreaches itself, in its pop version, by reducing culture to biology, and memetics overreaches by reducing culture to the play of self-replicating ideas, negating human feeling and motivation.

In the following chapter, I will further explore the problem of agency in the circulation of news, attempting to steer a course between the Scylla and Charybdis of pop sociobiology and pop memetics. To put the problem in larger context, it is worth noting the recurrent turbulence associated with the agency issue in Western intellectual history. The idea of human agency arises naturally from everyday experience, probably without the need for explicit theory. But nonhuman agency, imputed to natural order and events, is inherently troubling, and represents a threat to a person's sense of control. Agency attributed to the gods represents an ancient and enduring solution, but when the God hypothesis is stripped away, as in modern systems of thought such as science, agency reemerges as a troubling issue. Goethe, quoted in Will and Ariel Durant's account of eighteenth century European social thought (1958), commented on the dramatic quality of chemistry and physics in which apparently dead, senseless material is seen to form itself into distinct entities that are violently attracted and repelled by one another, to attack, destroy, and regenerate—all without consciousness or intent. Jerome Buckley, in *The Triumph of Time* (1966), writes about the Victorians' literary response to the modern shake-up of traditional ideas of order and agency, quoting the painter and novelist Wyndham Lewis who, in *Time and Western Man* (1957), commented on the destabilizing, disorienting effects of modern science in which "chairs and tables, mountains and stars, are animated into a magnetic restlessness, and exist on the same vital terms as man. They are as it were, the lowest grade, most sluggish of animals. All is alive; and, in that sense, all is mental" (1966: 5). In more recent, but equally stirring terms, Bruno Latour argues for the recognition of the social activity of objects, and he notes that in social theory,

> As if a damning curse had been cast unto things, they remain asleep like the servants of some enchanted castle. Yet, as soon as they are freed from the spell they start shuddering, stretching, and muttering. They begin to swarm in all directions, shaking the other human actors, waking them of their dogmatic sleep. (Latour 2005: 73)

Meme formations, clustered into coherent conflict discourse systems, offer a similar spectacle in the nonmaterial realm, and in chapter 5 I will present a model of the process whereby they clothe themselves with material presence through participation in the news process and absorb psychic energy, consciousness, and intent through their parasitic relationships with individual minds.

My suggested approach to the agent/structure debate in the context of news is to recognize that any theory of the agent or subject is already structural. Once you start to describe and explain the subjective, you are reducing it to the objective, and the best one can do to get even a glimpse or an intuition of the agent is to provide articulated theories of psychological process on one side and social process on the other, capturing the human agent in the untheorized space—a space that is neither social nor psychological, but perhaps the raw material of both— between them. Dualisms such as spirit and matter are often the basis of philosophical systems, but surely there is always something between the two, which, as William James might say, is their integration in direct human experience. Myazaki (2004), whose work I discussed in the first chapter, suggests what he calls a methodological solution to this puzzle in social theory.

Two Paths of Discourse Theory

The Conflict Discourse System approach draws on some of the key insights of recent mass communication research—most basically the fundamental idea that the mass media, and news in particular, exerts a powerful impact on society because of its interaction with dynamic aspects of culture and identity formation. The idea of semi-autonomous discourse formations that feed on reported conflicts derives largely from the theories of discourse that have shaken up entrenched functional-ist social theory in the last thirty or so years. Discourse theory in news analysis can be seen as splitting into two distinct paths. One path, largely associated with French language philosophy, concerns itself mainly with the text of discourse and picks out the "tropes," which are dominant ideas—perhaps memes in Dawkins's sense—and shows how they control the options for understanding and action of producers and consumers of news text by excluding or discrediting alternative tropes (e.g., Gal-tung and Vincent 2004). This text-based path of discourse theory has been particularly influential in literary criticism and the humanities. The other path, which is more or less Anglo-American, takes an inter-active turn, and is more amenable to ethnographic, empirical forms of social inquiry. The ideas of both Wittgenstein and J.L. Austin are fundamental in this line of discourse theory—the basis of my *news act* model presented in chapter 4—because they stress the communication dimensions of discourse rather than the text dimensions. As I argued in the previous chapter, the key insight from discourse theory in general is that truth and values—central to news reporting—are plural, contested, and continually being constructed.

The only real difficulty with fitting the Conflict Discourse System model of news into the empirical tradition of social science research is, as I have argued earlier, the counterintuitive sharing of agency—the capacity for purposeful action—between the human subject and the nonmaterial entities of discourse. But the idea is actually a very old one, and the Platonic notion of Truth, certainly both nonmaterial and very powerful, is part of the classic justification for the marketplace of ideas. Truth, it was said, would always triumph over error, making Truth sound very much like an actor in the news reporting process. The difference is that we now know that truth is not only plural, but parasitic, drawing its capacity for action from the human minds it restructures. Agency, then, is best thought of not as located in an actor but as a function of the relationship between and among entities, material and nonmaterial, involved in what Latour (e.g., 2005) calls the assembling of the social.

CHAPTER 4

The News Act

News Analysis and Semiotic Theory

News Books and the Pleasure of Metaphor

Books about the news are generally about what is wrong with the news. They warn readers that there is something very seriously wrong and perhaps even dangerous about the way the news media operate, and they often find a remarkably ready and willing readership. Apparently it is easy to persuade the reading, talking public that there is a connection between a variety of social problems and the media. In an influential, best-selling example, *Breaking the News: How the Media Undermine American Democracy,* James Fallows (1997) reports that the news media are degrading the political economy of the country. If this is true—or even if it might be true—it is clearly an issue that is worth writing and reading about. Fallows states the problem—that the country's political system is in bad shape and getting worse all of the time—which many of us, although for almost as many different reasons, recognize as at least arguable. Certainly today, a decade after the book's publication, it still rings true. The next premise held by Fallows is that the news media are contributing to this, big time. Yes, again, we have suspected as much. Now comes the explanation, the theory, which is the pleasurable part— the reason we buy, read, and talk about the book. Just as in fiction, the reader's pleasure in the nonfiction, social commentary domain is related to the experience of metaphor (Arno 1993: 125–148). Every good social theory works like a metaphor (Lopez 2003), linking two things or two series of things—simple objects or complex processes—that are not usually thought about together. The degree to which the reader is interested in both legs of the metaphor measures the potential impact and effectiveness of the metaphor, and, once the two are linked, what he or she knows about the one gives the reader insight into the other.

Fallows brings together the *media* and the *self*—two complex topics of great interest to the American public—revealing the dynamics of the news media situation in terms of personal motivations and institutional reward structures. Fallows's analysis also provides a narrative framework with which the reader can understand and evaluate what is going on in the problem area and place it in historical perspective. According to this proposed way of looking at the situation, journalists—responding to industry sticks and carrots and newsroom socialization—are seeking the big, sensational story, and many have abandoned the sense of integrity and propriety that once guided the great journalists—the Walter Lippmanns, and others—of a former era.

Theories about alarming situations are especially pleasurable, in the Freudian sense of pleasure as the reduction of tension, because they convert raw anxiety into rational puzzle solving, which implies that there is a solution to be reached. This is psychic comfort food. An actual solution to the problem would remove it as a problem, of course, but the contemplation of a solution—which is more like what a book in this area is going to provide—is at least reassuring. The bigger and more anxiety producing the problem, the greater the potential for pleasure in the analysis and solution, as long as there is some kind of plausible connection between the two. This is why a book that suggests something only slightly wrong with journalism does not have the readership potential of a book that postulates, plausibly, imminent political collapse. This is also why a book suggesting that there is nothing wrong with journalism would have almost no readership potential at all.

Fallows's proposed solution, which flows nicely from his problem statement and analysis, is that we develop a new kind of responsible, community conscious journalism. This suggestion is not really new—the paradigm controversy about the "social responsibility model," analyzed in the 1956 classic, *Four Theories of the Press* (Seibert et al. 1956), for example, was widely discussed in its day, but that does not actually matter now. It is new to a lot of readers, the situation is different now, and it can lead to some journalistic experiments. There have been many such attempts at civic journalism, and they have sometimes succeeded brilliantly within their scope—such as providing access to information about city government activities on open access cable channels. Although they have been valuable to those who have participated as journalists and news consumers, I think it is very safe to predict that all of these experiments will fail to solve the problems that provoked them. They will not reform the major institutions and practices of the mass news media.

They will fail because they are not based on a theory of news that goes deeply enough into its fundamental nature. In fact, in much of the abundant critical news media commentary—in books, newspaper columns, speeches, and talk shows, and authored by journalists, politicians, and academics—the theory and its object are at the same level; they are the same thing in an important way. News media critics report what is wrong with the news media, giving little attention to what is good and functionally useful about them, and one of their principle complaints is that the news media focus on what is wrong with society, ignoring what is good and positive. Fallows criticizes journalism for excessive coverage of political insiders and their positioning moves rather than the substantive issues they are dealing with, and in doing so, he in turn focuses on journalism insiders and their positioning moves within the industry. This characteristic hypocrisy of news media criticism—doing exactly what it says it is against—is inevitable to the extent that both the criticism and its object are alarming reports. And the characteristic futility of such criticism is inevitable because the alarming report is a basic speech act type, an elemental building block of culture that no amount of adjusting ethics codes and reward systems can alter. Like the human beings who engage in them, news acts have a persistent underlying nature that cannot be ignored. Improvements can be made, but they must be made with an awareness of the essential character of news.

The Myth of Negativity

As I have argued in the introduction, the conflict focus of news is neither good nor bad, it is definitional. Having a conflict focus is simply not a problem for news as a fundamental, functionally distinct form of societal communication. Because of its conflict focus, news is inherently upsetting and disruptive, but on the positive side, as I suggested in the previous chapter and will argue in more detail in the following chapters, it is also the first step in dealing constructively with the problems it reports. No reform of journalistic practices can make news entirely educational or productive of social solidarity and pro-social enthusiasm. If you make news educational, it becomes, to that extent, education; if you make it pro-social, it becomes moral socialization, and so on, and it may or may not retain much of its functional identity as news. A certain amount of confusion in news media criticism derives from implicitly defining news as the content of what are labeled news media. The idea that "good" news—stories about what is going well and that have the effect of civic boosterism and moral cheerleading—can be mixed with "bad" news to mitigate its negative, demoralizing effects, is a confusion of categories. If bad news is news about conflict, then there is only bad news, and the proposal to mix in good news is really a suggestion that news media add education and moral development functions to their offerings, along with existing advertising and entertainment functions. Clearly, at a civic level, it is highly desirable to link news to education and moral discourse so that the social and personal response to the problems posed by news can be as constructive and rational as possible. By the same token, there is little functional value in linking news to entertainment or consumerism, but as long as there is any news left in the news media content, it is going to be negative. The desired linkage between news, education, morality, and so on, need not be achieved within the format of a mass media news product, however. Maybe news should be talked about more in schools and churches, where there is some existing motivation for education and moral development—motivation largely absent in newspaper reading. If public radio and television could effectively liberate themselves from corporate and government influence, they would provide an excellent composite source of news and education. To a considerable degree, they already do. The exciting potential of the Internet for linking these functions, including responsible and critical blogging, remains a work in progress (Posner 2005, but see Shafer 2005). Geert Lovink (2008), in *Zero Comments: Blogging and Critical Internet Culture,* suggests a general theory of blogging—exploring its philosophical, psychological, political, and literary roots—that rejects the simplistic view of blogging as an alternative or counter form of journalism that challenges the mainstream news media. Blogging is primarily an opinion genre, like op-ed writing, and lacks independent sources of reportage. When blogging is combined with dot org Internet sites devoted to political data collection, such as maplight.org, for example, which digs out and presents information linking Congressional voting patterns to corporate political contributions, a more complete form of Internet journalism might evolve.

The News Act

I like the term *news act* because it can be read two ways, drawing on two almost opposite meanings of the word "act." On the one hand, it implies that the news is just an act, a pretense, which poses the important question of its relation to truth. In the other meaning, the act is something real and factual—something actually done, in contrast to mere talk or contemplation. In this latter sense the term *news act* relates news to J.L. Austin's idea of the speech act, which is crucial to the development of an interactional path of discourse studies mentioned in the previous chapter. The term speech act challenges one to recognize that speech cannot simply be contrasted with action, as common sense would have it, because talk *is* an act, and under certain circumstances it can have very powerful social and material consequences. Austin's book, *How to Do Things with Words* (1962), was the beginning of a fruitful discussion in the philosophy of language, and philosophers following Austin's lead have identified a number of specific kinds of speech acts. A key insight at the base of the discussion is that an important dimension of language is completely ignored when language is considered only as an abstract system, which is a tendency in linguistics. This crucial lost dimension was even neglected, at the time Austin wrote, by philosophers of language, who concentrated on trying to clarify the capacity of language to represent facts in the real world. They did so by looking very carefully at the *proposition*—that is, the type of statement that asserts a fact that can be shown to be either true or false in the real world. The questions that no one was asking were the very questions, however, that make the most difference in interpreting the meaning of language that one encounters in real life. Who is saying this? To whom is he or she talking? What is the context? And what is the purpose of the speech? Austin's particular concern was with the kinds of speech acts that in a very central sense constitute the performance of an action—so that instead of readily evoking the question "is it true or false," one is more likely to ask "did it work or not?"

Rather than deal with these questions on a case by case basis, as we do in everyday life, Austin looked at the problem in general terms and observed that—as an act—speech has at least three distinct kinds of force or impact in the world. All three are united in the speech act as a whole, but they can be abstracted analytically to explain how different kinds of utterances work in communication. One of these aspects is the physical articulation of a meaningful utterance, that is, producing a unit of language that makes sense grammatically and semantically. Austin called this *locutionary* force, and he more or less dismissed it from consideration, going on to the two other, more salient kinds of force associated with speech as an act. The *illocutionary* force of something that is said is its point or purpose, but Austin did not equate this purpose with the speaker's private intent. Rather, the illocutionary point of a verbal utterance is what the competent listener, who understands how language is used in the community, would justifiably consider it to be. Obviously, one of the ways a speaker can lie or be manipulative is to conceal his or her own private intent or motivation for a speech act, which is possible precisely because the illocutionary force and the private intent of an utterance are not rigidly linked. The third distinct type of impact or force of the speech act is the influence it has on the thinking and feeling of the hearer. Austin calls this the *perlocutionary,* and unlike the illocutionary force, it is determined by a private, individual state of mind. For example, the illocutionary point of a particular utterance may be to warn the hearer about something. Everyone who hears it may easily recognize it as a warning, and let us even say that the speaker in this case is not being tricky but honestly intends it as a warning. For example, at the mass communication level, the government warning on cigarette packages is clearly intended and understood as a warning to smokers. But even so, the resulting perlocutionary effect for a particular hearer might not be the expected one at all. It could be boredom or amusement, perhaps, rather than fear, depending on the knowledge and attitude of the particular hearer. Of course, by and large, the two types of force *do* coordinate—the warning does produce fear or at least alertness as its actual effect in most cases. If this were not true, the communication system would not be reliable because when one asked a question, gave a command, or stated a fact one could never be sure that the average hearer would react appropriately. A major part of being able to use language in a group is being able to accurately calculate—given the identity of the speaker, that of the audience, the social and physical setting, and so on—the conventionally understood illocutionary intent and its presumed perlocutionary effect.

Speech act analysis, with its catalog of illocutionary types—questions, warnings, promises, and so on—normally presupposes a situation of interpersonal communication, but can it apply to mass media communication as well? No one would object, surely, to calling a situation in which an audience listens, views, or reads mass mediated news a communication *event.* The term speech act might raise some resistance because it seems to imply an actor rather than an event focus, but Austin's perspective, at the crucial illocutionary level, is much more group than individual oriented. The illocutionary speech act is actually a communication event enacted by individuals at the interpersonal level, but given its nonpsychological, community perspective, it can also be thought as being enacted by more abstract social entities at the mass communication level as well. A number of expansions of the concepts are necessary, but they do not seem to invalidate the analysis. For example, we are no longer dealing with just face-to-face talk, so the locutionary act—that is, the production of articulate language—would have to include printing, broadcasting sounds and images, and all of the technological facts involved in fixing and transmitting the text or image as a physical task. The concept of the *speaker* or *source* of the message has to be radically enlarged also to encompass the individual and corporate entities that are part of publishing, editing, writing, and performing that express a conventionally understood "intent." And what are the categories of purpose or intent, the equivalents of illocutionary speech act types, in the mass media? To begin with, they might be embodied in an entire show, performance, segment, or article—something much longer and more complex than the usual speech act examples based on interpersonal utterances. For example, one easily distinguishes between a political speech, a televised State Department briefing, a television or print advertisement, a written Supreme Court decision, and so on. Each can be thought of as having a distinct point associated with a broadly defined conventional expectation of impact. The distinct perlocutionary effects are ultimately individual, but in the mass media situation they can also be seen as categorical or sociological, and the average or predominant effect in a group. Thus an ad may have the effect of increasing my individual desire to have a particular product, but, being a mass communication event, it can be thought of producing that sort of effect on "the consumer" as a statistical element within a market segment. The mass perlocutionary effect, like the individual one, is not a sure thing but remains to be determined by what actually happens. Do sales of the advertised razor blade go up? Does the election result go one way or the other after a barrage of political ads?

In most academic writing the term *speech act* is equated with the illocutionary act. Anthropologists, for example, are often interested in the performative aspect of speech—that is, what speaking certain words accomplishes in social life. Different types of illocutionary acts, such as a warning, a question, a factual report, and so on, could be introduced in each case by the implicit declaration, "I hereby ...," as in "I hearby warn you, question you, or inform you." How the hearer takes the communication does not alter the fact that a warning, a question, or a report has been accomplished, although it does bear on whether or not it has been successful. The conventional, in fact virtually universal definition of news in academic studies is illocutionary or performative in this sense. The TV news anchor or the print journalist can be thought of as prefacing his or her work with "I hereby report news." But I am rejecting this definition precisely because it stops the analysis right at the text, leaving unexamined the most important dimensions of the news process. The journalist can say "I hereby report ...," but he or she cannot say "What I am saying is hereby news to you." News is not a perlocutionary *act* in Habermas's sense of dishonest manipulation of the hearer, but my argument is that it is defined by a specific kind of perlocutionary *force*, alarm, that attaches—or not—to a speech act.

News, then, is a unique kind of speech act. There is a very strong and distinct sense in which giving and receiving news is a particular type of communication act at the interpersonal level, and the mass media version depends on the same psychological motivation that drives the interpersonal archetype. The only reason we have news in the mass media is because—and to the degree that—the individual wants to hear about conflicts that potentially affect his or her interests. Investigating the character of news as an interpersonal speech act means looking carefully at the identities of the speaker and the hearer, the context of their interaction, and the conventional expectations in the community that govern intent—that is, why the news is being told—and the effect on the listener. Examining the *news act*, the mass media version of the interpersonal news speech act, requires a somewhat different approach but the basic questions are the same. Most important, news at individual or mass level is about conflict, the expected reaction is one of alarm, concern, or in some cases a sense of relief at a bullet having been dodged.

When I explained my definition of news as an alarming report—concerning a threat to the hearer's interests—to a skeptical colleague, he argued for a nonpsychological definition of news as anything that is *reportable*. In the tradition of ethnomethodology, the reportable is anything that a person could tell a story about to someone else. It would have to be nontrivial and not too boring to report, but it could certainly include good as well as bad events. My colleague suggested, "Cure for Cancer," as a *good news* headline, but to me this is an easy one. Any story about cancer, even a cure, which indeed is a good thing, is only news because cancer itself is so scary. The cure (good) story draws its news value from the threat (bad) that it concerns. A cure for a rare disease that the reader has never heard of is also good news to a slight degree, but it is not *big* news. "Then how about 'Man Walks on Moon'?" my friend suggested. I admit this gave me pause. What threat was evoked in this huge news story of the 1970s? Later, thinking about it in context of the times, I realized that "Man Walks on Moon" was really "American Walks on Moon," and it was very much a story about the Cold War—which was a major, scary threat in those days. An earlier story, "Soviets Launch Sputnik," was good news as well, scientifically, but it was really major news to Americans of the time because of the link to US/SU competition and the always looming possibility of nuclear mass destruction.

A Triangular Doorway to the News Act

Of course, denying that the conflict focus of news is a problem to be fixed is not to say that there is or can be nothing wrong with newspapers, television news, or other ways of creating and disseminating news

reports. Robert McChesney's powerful critiques of corporate influence and concentration of ownership, for example, and many earlier
critiques of reporters' journalistic practices in newsgathering provide
ample evidence that many things about news production and dissemination need urgently to be fixed. Even if a preoccupation with conflict
is taken as given, as I propose, important problems inevitably remain
in the dimensions of truth, communication, and pragmatic meaning,
three areas of concern that are inextricable in practice but analytically
separable. One way to picture the relationships among these basic problems at the level of mass communication is to conceptualize journalism
as the play of interrelationships among three elements—event, story,
and reader. This trinitarian move, displaying a complex problem in the
form of a triangle of selected analytical elements, is in some sense arbi-
trary—any number of other "elements" might have been abstracted and
postulated as basic—and must be judged finally in terms of its usefulness in thinking one's way into and out of the problem. Why should the
proposed triangle be any more likely to guide discussion toward enlightened action than, say, a pentagon formed by adding culture and technology as elements? The more elements one can delineate, one might
think, the closer the theoretical model to the reality and therefore the
more useful. But theoretical usefulness, or the lack thereof, is not neces-

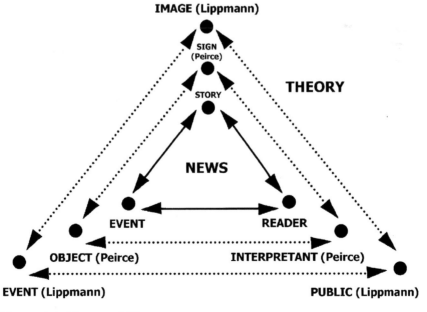

Figure 4.1 News and Theory

sarily dependent on an objective correspondence between the problem itself and the picture one draws of it (Arno 2005). It is much more to the point to examine the previous, related uses that have been made of such triangle shaped analyses in discussions of other social problems.

A diagram like my proposed triangle is not so much a picture of the object of analysis, then, as a doorway between two areas of thought and experience. Its form suggests an opening upon a commonsense view of the institution of mass media news in one direction, by naming and suggesting linkages among some key identities, events, and products that we experience as consumers of news—event, story and reader—but just as importantly its form also suggests an opening upon a body of writing and thinking about social problems. For example, it clearly evokes Walter Lippmann's (1922) classic "pictures in our heads" discussion of news media as linked to public opinion through a triangle of relationships among the event, the image of the event created by the news media, and the incorporation of the image into the mind and thinking of the public. The crucial observation that Lippmann's diagram of the problem brings out is that although the image and the opinion it shapes may be imaginary, the readers' socially coordinated actions, like the events they are impelled to act in relation to, are part of concrete reality and have real flesh and blood consequences. The other famous analytical triangle I want to allude to is C.S. Peirce's definition of the sign. For Peirce, the sign is not a dualist relation between signifier and signified—that is, a concept and an arbitrarily selected sound bound to it by convention within a language community—as later suggested by the great Swiss linguist and founder of structural linguistics, Ferdinand de Saussure. Rather, Peirce saw the sign as one element of a triangular figure formed by the sign itself, the object it stands for, and the interpretant, which is the resulting sign evoked in the mind of the person addressed by the sign. In other words, Peirce's sign stands *for* something, and *to* someone. Representation does not exist outside this triad, just as, for my purposes, the news story does not exist outside the news triad.

Both Peirce and Lippmann are exponents of pragmatism, the very American, muscular school of philosophy that concerns itself with the practical consequences of abstract ideas and denies that ideas and meanings have any autonomous existence on their own. Pragmatism arose in the late nineteenth and early twentieth centuries as an alternative to the dominant idealism of German philosophy, which celebrated the transcendent realm of the spirit and seemed to dismiss the material, flesh and blood and steel and concrete world of social and physical action so salient to the America of that era. Neither Peirce nor Lippmann ultimately denies the dualist split between mind—personal or collective—

and an external physical reality, but they insist on revaluation of the two categories, giving practical consequences their due dignity in analysis.

Peirce argues that we cannot *know* directly an external objective reality because knowledge and thinking consists of relations among ideas, which are mental representations, signs, and not real objects. This implies that the truth of ideas, words, concepts, stories, descriptions, and so on, cannot be established by comparing them to or measuring them against reality in the sense of comparing a picture with the 'real thing' of which it is a picture (Rorty 1991). If we cannot know anything other than pictures, we can only compare one picture against another picture. But Peirce, unlike Rorty, is concerned with salvaging natural science as something distinct from, say, literary criticism. He insists that we can *experience* objective reality directly and therefore can test ideas against that experience. The test is not a comparison, however, it is a test of usefulness. Some ideas prove to be useful as a guide to action, while others are useless or even dangerous. Useful ideas are "hard concepts," epitomized for Peirce by the ideas of experimental science, a category that Peirce values above the glib, untestable ideas and words that have no stable, practical meaning (Peirce 1955).

Lippmann brings Peircean pragmatism to bear on the problems of journalism. Writing about public opinion and the mass media-created images of reality that shape public opinion, he admits that they are radically disconnected from the concrete reality of the events they refer to, but he also insists that the *actions* they inspire reestablish a connection with real events. Media accounts, imaginary and disconnected from events as they are, may send a country's war industry into overdrive and support political decisions to send troops overseas. The stories are imaginary, but the weapons produced and the destruction they can cause when deployed are real. Media accounts and public opinion are socially constructed, then, but they do not become socially constructed reality for the pragmatist until the public acts upon them. Lippmann was writing about World War I, but the application to the US war against Iraq, initiated in 2003, is uncannily powerful.

News as Social Construction: Social Construction as News

Remarkably, arguments about the social construction of certain kinds of reality and the possibility of forming of hard, experience-tested concepts not only *describe* the processes that constitute news as a communication act, they can actually *be* news. In May 1996, the *New York Times* ran a boxed front page story about an academic hoax that demonstrates how charged with conflict such seemingly arcane issues have become in contemporary American society (Scott 1996). Alan Sokal, a mischievous NYU physics professor, fed up with what he saw as the arrogant, pretentious nonsense of postmodern social analysis, decided to play a very mean trick on the editors of *Social Text*, a leading journal in the field of cultural studies. In the phrase of Stanley Fish, a major victim of the joke who wrote an op-ed rebuttal a few days later, Professor Sokal carried off the hoax because he "pretended to be himself" (Fish 1996). That is, he submitted a paper purportedly written by a highly reputable scientist—himself—that demonstrated a convergence between postmodern social theory and the latest ideas in theoretical physics, culminating in the claim that both areas of scholarship agree that it is highly questionable whether we, or anything, actually exist(s). The pretending involved not the identity of the author, but his intent. This is a great example, at the mass communication level, of the split between private intent and illocutionary force in speech act theory. The article was submitted as if it were serious academic work, but it was actually intended as a parody of cultural studies scholarship, designed to show that the highest authorities in that field cannot distinguish between serious work and nonsense. The serious point of the attack, explained by Sokal in another published article and in an interview with the *New York Times*, was that cultural studies "denies the existence of objective realities," and that this kind of sloppy thinking is dangerous because it undermines "the prospect for progressive social critique" (Scott 1996: A22). One could argue that what the episode actually demonstrates is not that the field of cultural studies denies that there is a real world—which its exponents say is not the case—but rather that it demonstrates the validity of one of its almost equally disturbing conclusions, namely that Professor Sokal himself, in the context of the publication and subsequent flap, is a figment of discourse and not an autonomous subject, as he probably thinks of himself. In other words, the identity of a "physics professor at a good university" is not a part of the natural world, but is definitely socially constructed and socially invested with authority in academic activities. And it was that identity—not the ideas in the paper he submitted to the journal—that insured his being published. If he had pretended to be a graduate student or an assistant professor of English at an obscure community college, instead of asserting his "real" identity, it is unlikely he ever would have been published in the journal. The editors of *Social Text* should not be embarrassed by this event, which confirms an important point about discursive identity and authority, and the extent to which they are embarrassed is a measure of the extent to which they are pretending to be "social scientists," enjoying the illicit—because of poaching on the reputation of hard science—socially constructed prestige they themselves are enthusiastically deconstructing.

But what is the *news* value of this story, and why should it have been on the front page of the *New York Times?* The answer, of course, is its relevance to conflict. The reporter frames it by saying that "[i]n a way, this is one more skirmish in the culture wars, the battles over multiculturalism and college curriculums ..." (Scott 1996: A1). This framing connects the story immediately with a whole body of threats to economic security and cultural identity perceived by many Americans as caused by a loss of the power formerly vested in standard, nonhyphenated, nonimmigrant, middle class folks. This is news for the same reason Republican presidential aspirant Pat Buchannan saw these same concerns as hot issues in his 1995–96 primary campaign. Of course, the Sokal hoax is also a funny story, a retelling of the emperor's new clothes fable, which is a theme with enduring appeal. Graduate students and professors of English whose work has been rejected by *Social Text* must find it particularly amusing, and the initial story, when read together with Stanley Fish's op-ed rebuttal and a number of letters to the editor, is educational as well. One letter writer comments that "Mr. Fish has made a scholarly contribution to a complex and abstruse field, provoked by Mr. Sokal's prank" (Kreitzer 1996), for example. But the fact remains that it is the conflict element that makes it news. The entertainment and educational values, while undoubtedly necessary to the editor's decision to run the story, are in no way sufficient. As Lippmann's analysis makes clear, it is the reentry into the world of action that makes a story and the opinions and attitudes it shapes worth worrying about. And the different functions of the story determine the specific kinds of actions it engenders. As entertainment, the Sokal story may be retold as a joke among academics, and as education it may used to illustrate points about the sociology of knowledge (e.g., see Flyvbjerg 2001), but as *news* it becomes part of the "culture wars" it reports on, perhaps to some degree ultimately influencing important, contested social policies such as affirmative action. If the story had become news in 2005 instead of 1996, it would have found fresh legs as news for a certain segment of the readership because of its link to *relativism*, declared by the newly elected Pope Benedict to be a major threat to religion.

Truth in News

The theoretical news triangle underlying the argument of this chapter is a way of framing, as I have suggested, three problems that present themselves in the practice of news: *truth, communication,* and *practical meaning.* Within the triangle, truth can be defined as a judgment about the relation between the event and the story, and I believe this is pretty close to the common sense definition of truth adopted when most readers talk about accuracy in journalism. Judgments about the story/event relation are part of the news act and are governed by its rules. Readers of news are concerned with truth, and they make judgments about it—that is the nature of news. The space enclosed by the triangle, when mapped onto the practice of news production and consumption, is not simply empty geometric space, but it is the social interaction space, invested with dimensions of identity and power, within which the news act is accomplished, and in which the conventions and expectations of the news act are played out. This element of journalistic truth, then, is the judgment of the reader in the role of a consumer of news who demands truth in the news act—but who may well be cynical and suspicious at times and credulous at others—and for whom truth means a substantial correspondence between the event and the report. This internal perspective on truth in news is subjective and necessarily varies with the position of the particular reader. In fact, when the reader makes a truth judgment by comparing the story to the event, he or she is equating "event" with a conjectural "direct first hand account," not with some metaphysical event-in-itself of absolute reality, independent of any observation. What the reader wants to know is this: if I had observed and dug into this event myself would I have come up with the same story? If "yes," the story is true, and if "no" it is false or misleading.

On the other hand, the critic or analyst of the news media—and this role is played by journalists and editors as well as by social theorists, politicians, and at times the usually nonreflective ordinary reader him or herself—is outside the news triangle and therefore can offer an "objective" evaluation of the truth relation between story and event. But the critic/analyst is caught up in a *criticism triangle* that is itself framed within the conventions, roles, and objectives of media criticism—as contrasted with those of the population reading or watching the news directly. Obviously, a person can go from one role to the other almost instantaneously. Even a Mr. Fallows, or Lippmann, or Boorstin, driving home after a hard day at the office writing about the philosophy of journalism might turn on the car radio to hear what went on in politics or the stock market that day. As critic, one can only offer a *relatively* objective evaluation of truth in the news act, and there can never be any absolute objectivity because, conceptually, the evaluator would have no place to stand. Every critical author or speaker is locked into a textual triangle with his or her reader governed by the conventions of, for example,

Marxism, orthodox social science, religious fundamentalism, language philosophy, postmodernism, or some other platform of criticism, and each critic can provide only a version of "objective" truth in the news from that point of view.

This is a convoluted definition of truth in news, requiring some perspectival gear shifting, but it deserves the effort because truth is the fundamental issue and avenue of news criticism, and truth in communication is a complex problem. Old-fashioned common sense notions of truth and representation have yielded in contemporary academic thinking, as indicated by the Sokal/Fish exchange, to subtle but hotly debated arguments of language philosophy, and news needs to be examined in light of such arguments.

Communication in News

The other sides of the news triangle demand consideration as well. If truth is the problem associated with the story-event leg of the triangle, the problem raised by the story-reader leg can be labeled communication. This label, of course, could be used in a broad sense to include virtually all of the other issues. Truth and meaning, for example, exist, from the interactionist point of view that I adopt in this book, only in context of communication. But in a narrow, analytical sense, there are distinct communication issues of intelligibility and access that are as essential in the construction of the news triangle as those implied by the truth of the story or the practical significance (meaning) of the event to the reader/viewer. For example, consider the reader who is confronting the story of the Sokal hoax. Undoubtedly, there were some *New York Times* readers for whom the question of the truth-value of the story was never reached because the story itself was immediately unintelligible. Literacy, verbal or visual, is not enough, obviously. The reader must also have enough background knowledge so that the story makes a connection with what he or she already knows or the news triangle will never come into existence. Clearly, this fact is a major constraint on the writer and editor, who must make sure, above all, that communication is established. Stories may have to be written "down" or stretched in various ways to make the essential contact with the reader's knowledge, but here again, knowledge is not enough—the reader must be motivated by some kind of salience that evokes his or her interest. In general, this kind of salience is probably akin to that associated with memory. Specific memories, like more abstract bodies of knowledge, can be salient because of association with an intense experience or, temporarily, because of mere recency. One might remember what one was doing the day of the John Kennedy assassination (or, for younger readers, the 9/11 attack), and one might also remember clearly, for a different reason and only temporarily, what happened yesterday. This is why mass media news stories, even at the risk of distortion in the truth dimension and purely for reasons of establishing communication with the reader, are often written so as to link up with big stories from the past—Viet Nam, Watergate, Pearl Harbor, and so on—or to recent but soon-to-fade stories about a spectacular plane crash or a Washington political maneuver, for example. Recent stories, like big, benchmark stories, create avenues of lowered resistance to communication, and this accounts partially for the way clusters of similar stories tend to occur within and across media. Very strong stories, however, do not need to be linked to other recent stories because they tap primal sources of salience on their own. For example, the 1996 crash of a ValuJet plane into a Florida swamp, although by now perhaps largely forgotten as a news event itself, had an inherently powerful communication dimension in part because of the horror of the setting. The dark, sucking mud, like the icy depths in the Titanic disaster, energizes the story-reader leg of the news triangle (Bragg 1996; Navarro 1996).

Practical Meaning in News

The event-reader leg of the analytical triangle is where the rhetoric meets the road in the news act. It is this dimension that distinguishes the news act from other kinds of communication events. Here, it acquires its essential character as an alarming report, and that character derives from the coming together of two dimensions that I have mentioned earlier: the conflict focus and the potential for concrete, pragmatic action. To constitute a news act, the issue involved must stand to the reader in a threatening posture. The event reported may have either positive or negative relation to the issue—for example, the event might be the outbreak of a deadly new virus, or it might be the discovery of a cure for that virus—but the underlying issue must pose a threat. Here again, as in the judgment of accuracy in news, the determination lies with the reader and varies with his or her position. It is not an objective determination, and the threat may be weak or strong, immediate or remote, and it may threaten any number of different kinds of interests of the reader.

The alarm that the news report produces in the reader, as its perlocutionary effect in Austin's terms, varies from one person to the next, but mass media news is expected to have such an effect on most of its audience, and over the long run that expectation determines the conventional, illocutionary force—the understood point or purpose of news. What newspaper editors and television news producers present is what they have learned from experience will have the news effect on a large number of people. But the fundamental decoupling of the conventional purpose from the actual impact at the case-by-case level presents interesting problems for the institution of journalism because in the short run the direction of influence may run the other way. That is, merely presenting some item as if it were news may have the effect of eliciting a reaction of alarm even though it would not have done so in another illocutionary context. In a way, this structural leeway between the actual and the statistical provides the possibility for another form of lying, parallel to the lie noted earlier that is made possible by the disconnect between private and public intent. The inherent, structural remedy for both is the same; the liar must eventually be exposed by real events. The media to some extent train their audiences to react to certain kinds of stories as news, but the extent to which they can do this is limited by real experience. In the end, it is the reader/viewer's total cultural environment that determines what can be news and what cannot. This is precisely because the event-reader leg of the news act triangle exists in the real world, and the two interact with one another sooner or later.

A very important limitation on the news media's ability to manipulate the news act so as to create news out of something else, then, derives from the potential recoupling of the news with concrete reality that takes place when the reader acts with reference to the event that has been reported. Here again there are two cycles involved, long and short in time span. In the short run, the news reports may spur readers to inappropriate action with seeming impunity because of remoteness, delay, and causal complexity in the reader-event linkage. A false news report could spur a financial panic or an ethnic riot, for example. In the long run, however, the functional effectiveness of the news media in alerting people to salient problems is tested against the balance of nonmedia reality. Two stories I have mentioned earlier, the Sokal hoax and the ValuJet crash, illustrate the great range of complex connections between events, conflict issues, and public action spurred by news reports. The intended, illocutionary level conflict issue raised by the Sokal story is, according to the reporter, the "culture wars" in the context of multiculturalism in the United States. The connection between the event—the publication of the phony article—and the larger conflict issue is one that requires a certain amount of reflection to grasp. The specific link between the reader and the conflict dimension of the event is also quite vague in both directions in this instance. Many readers would be unsure what multiculturalism means for them—that is, it is unclear exactly how it threatens them or protects them against another threat—and they would be equally unsure what they could do in their own lives to support or attack it. Clearly, this story made it to the front page on the strength of its communication dimension, in spite of its vagueness in the dimensions of truth and practical meaning. Although it is interesting and intelligible to relatively few readers, those particular readers who grasp its concepts represent an elite segment of the readership to whom the editors want to cater. Also, for those readers, the narrative aspects—the humor in the emperor's new clothes situation, for example—are so strong that it overcomes the weaknesses in the other dimensions of the triangle.

The ValuJet story is entirely different in the meaning or event-reader dimension. Here, the reader immediately perceives a very strong, two-way causal connection between the event and him or herself. Realistically or not—and objective realism is not the issue within the news act triangle—the reader who sometimes rides airplanes identifies immediately and strongly with the passengers in the crash. The threat—against life itself—is so strong that it largely overrides the counterbalancing calculation of likelihood. The reader is also able to take immediate steps to protect him or herself—cancel those ValuJet reservations and rebook on an expensive line. In this story, there is little ambiguity in the truth dimension because there is so little interpretive distance between the conflict issue that emerges from the story—air safety—and the event. The connection is obvious, and the reader's position almost coincides with the reporter's. The communication dimension is virtually transparent as well. The range of readers who can read and understand the story and the strength of their motivation to read it are maximal because almost everyone responds immediately to *air crash* as a dramatic genre. Richard Vincent and Denis K. Davis (1989) provide a literary critique of air crash stories in television news, noting the powerful dramatic structure of the reporting.

Attack of the Megatropes

Before exploring further the theoretical perspective I am adopting, I want to point out that this conflict-centered, functionalist view, drawing on pragmatist ideas of truth and action as well as the communication focus of speech act theory, can be used in constructing and filling out a grade card for the news. Of course, all media criticism provides criteria for judging performance, but in news act analysis as presented so far, the reader/viewer does not escape responsibility, and the bogus issue of "negativity" is avoided. The news act triangle provides three dimensions of comparative assessment for individual stories, separating judgments of truth, meaning, and communication, so that profiles of editorial policy can be demonstrated among news media organizations. Some may tend to tread the paths of lowest resistance in communication, running stories that have an attractive narrative angle but trivial, nonfunctional news value. In television, the excessive pursuit of visual excitement at the expense of the truth and practical meaning dimensions of journalism illustrates this problem, but print media are also prone to it.

For example, what can one say about the extraordinary "Tyke the Elephant" story that ran on and on for weeks on the front pages of the *Honolulu Advertiser* in 1994? Tyke was a circus elephant who broke loose from her chains, killed one of her handlers, and injured others before escaping to the streets of downtown Honolulu, where she damaged a number of parked cars before being shot to death by city policemen with shotguns and high-power rifles (Nakaso 1994). What I have called the communication aspect of this story—that is, the accessibility and attraction of the story for the reader, abstracted from its truth and meaning dimensions—is tremendous. Even without photos or television footage, the visual imagery of the story is striking. An enraged elephant running down a city street at rush hour smashing cars joins the surrealism of a King Kong or Godzilla fantasy with the horrifying reality of the animal's and the trainer's deaths. One certainly cannot quarrel with the local news media for playing this event as a big story. Any violent death in public poses the news act function of an alarming report. Unexpected and bizarre public violence legitimately elicits alarm, and reader/viewers can be expected to demand immediate, accurate accounts in the news media. After the initial shock, however, it seems obvious that the conflict issue anchoring the meaning or reader/event aspect of the news act is not public safety in the most immediate sense. No participants in the news act can reasonably interpret an elephant attack as an enduring threat that requires public attention in an urban environment. Realistic and important issues with a more abstract connection to the event are raised, of course. One is the competence of the city police in handling the emergency, and another is the set of deep psychological and moral conflicts involved in the animal rights movement (Hoover 2004). But at the level of journalistic practice, these issues seem to be providing legitimation for an apparent milking of the communication dimension—the bizarre image of the rogue elephant on a city street dying in a blaze of police gunfire—by both reader and the media, who have by mutual consent enthusiastically perverted what I described in chapter 3 as the civic function of the news act—its functional relation to rational public policy discussion.

But I feel there is much more to be said about Tyke the Elephant and the collision of her story with community consciousness in Hawai'i. The simple civic grade card I have prepared with the news theory presented so far is not adequate, and more theory—theory that goes deeper into cultural and psychological dimensions of the problem, introduced in chapter 5, needs to be explored. As suggested in the Conflict Discourse Systems scenario outlined in chapter 2, recent currents in social theory have indicated several specific points at which a theory of mass media news can be loosened up enough to go beyond the functional, civic grade card kind of evaluation, and one such point concerns the rejection of grand theory as a goal in social inquiry.

Michel Foucault, Jean-Francois Lyotard, and other poststructuralist thinkers have moved from the recognition that ways of talking and thinking in a group involve a necessary merger of language and power to the logical implication that *theories* are inherently political in nature. Theories, as expounded and used by people, set up categories that sort themselves out, in the arena of social action, into one kind of person telling another what to do. They are all about authority. If this idea is accepted, the struggle among theories appears to be as inevitable the struggle for wealth and power in society, and the idea of grand theory takes on sinister connotations. Grand theory, no longer the holy grail of social analysis, is now seen as a totalitarian, imperialist form of talk and thought that actually translates into political and economic domination. The idea of rejecting grand theory, then, along with the identification of particular theories with specific forms of social life rather than as just intellectual options, constitutes a declaration of communicative independence for every kind of formerly illegitimate social analysis that has recommended itself to a marginal social group or category.

But it is quite clear that poststructuralist attacks on dominating theories have in no way created the marginal groups and ways of thinking that they bring into the theoretical range. Systems of belief and action that are nonscientific, nonmodernist, nonrational, and so on, have always been and continue to be well represented in the United States, as elsewhere. Religion and the arts are sanctuaries of legitimized, conventionally accepted expressions of such ways of thinking and acting, and they are accepted by the dominant modernist rationalism as long as they stay in their place. But even though rational, scientific modernism is the official way of talking about most secular problems in the United States, it is probably a thin veneer over a vast reservoir of "unrealistic" or even magical thinking and analysis, and an understanding of the news act must take that fact into account.

For example, the June 1996 news stories about Hillary Clinton's "conversations" with Eleanor Roosevelt and Mahatma Gandhi overtly posed the significance of the revelation of such activities as damage to her reputation among voters. Almost a decade later, in 2005, the now Senator Clinton could joke about her conversations with Eleanor in a fundraising speech (Healy 2005), but in 1996, the media framed the issue in another way. The path of lowered communicative resistance between story and reader/viewer chosen by most media outlets followed the narrative slipstream created by the numerous "damage to Hillary's reputation" stories that had recently flowed from the congressional hearings about the Whitewater scandal. But the media's apparent premise about the event-reader or meaning dimension—namely, that having conversations with dead people is considered weird and frightening—was probably quite wrong. The issue died quickly in part because a great many more readers than editors were aware of or may have agreed at some level with positions more or less like that of Sister Teresa Ann Coronas, Convent of St. Theresa, who wrote the following letter to the editors of the *Honolulu Advertiser:*

> Don't fault Mrs. Clinton for having mind exercises with Eleanor. Whenever I see the searingly beautiful sunsets here on the island, I talk to my dear sister who left her cancer and this world a few months ago. I ask her where she is in the beauty before me.
>
> I ask permission from the plumeria or puakenikeni trees before plucking their fragrant blossoms.
>
> Oh yes, I speak to God, to Our Lady, and to the saints and angels throughout the day. Before starting my car, I ask my Guardian Angel to guide and protect me.
>
> I am unabashedly normal. So, let's leave our first lady alone. Freedom of speech also means freedom to do with our minds what we will. (Coronas 1996)

This is an unusually bold and confident statement, and it is one written under color of religious authority. Perhaps not many people would express themselves so definitely, but it does represent a way of thinking that is tucked away in the corners of many otherwise rational minds, and many US news consumers are fairly often—depending on the topic and circumstances—somewhere between this kind of thinking and the purely scientific, modernist rejection of such ideas. One of the virtues of a postmodern recognition of the de facto multiplicity of nonstandard, grassroots theory is precisely that it allows a more realistic analysis of social institutions such as journalism. Of course, the news act can still be analyzed, and media performance graded, on the basis of the politically and legally dominant concept of the marketplace of ideas that is the basis of the first amendment freedom of speech. This wonderfully powerful and politically successful concept, the basis of the Civic news scenario explored in chapter 3, assumes an autonomous, rational citizen decision maker who recognizes and embraces the best and truest among the ideas put forward for public consideration. But clearly there is more than this going on in the news media as we know them, and postmodern thinking about the problem expands the theoretical scope of analysis to include a marketplace in which the role of consumer is not always played by the autonomous, rational, realistic dimension of the person that is nurtured and given authority in our culture by the triumph of the Enlightenment.

Starting at the social actor, in this case a member of a news community, the analyst seeking a structural basis for generalization can go in either of two directions. One path plunges more deeply into the person, beneath the social actor surface to the *structure*—that is, the general, shared pattern—of the mind and body. In this direction lie structural analyses of human cognition, psychodynamics, and deep universal structures of language and communication. The other path, however, moves outward from the social actor in the direction of society and the external (to the body) physical world. Here, one finds materialist forms of structuralism, both critical (Marxism) and noncritical (liberalism), which see the unrelenting necessities of the economic mode of production and the market as determining the possibilities of human agency in the news process. The "unseen hand" of the market or, alternatively, the Marxian laws of history that govern that hand reduce the scope of human action so much that the human agent is in danger of disappearing from the analysis—or at least of becoming something that is dragged in and tacked on in an unconvincing way. But structuralisms that are external to the actor can also, if they have a cultural or ideological rather than materialist inflection, take linguistics as an inspiration, and in such cases "discourse," as in the conflict discourse system scenario of news, takes the place of the unseen hand. The CDS news model is not wedded to a fixed theory of the news consumer, such as "rational decision maker," but takes the position suggested in the introduction that every actor in a conflict space is best described in terms of the bundle of interests—rights and duties vis-á-vis others—prescribed by the conflict discourse system adhered to in specific news act interactions by that actor. In the following chapter, I contrast the formalized way the law leaves open the definition of identity in conflict communication with the more wide-open process of the news media. The rights and duties that constitute the native Hawaiian conflict actor are explored in the series of current "Kalipi rights" cases reported by the Supreme Court of Hawai'i, while the analysis of an extended C-SPAN interview with former Congressman Jim Traficant looks at identify formation talk in context of a polymorphous but powerful anti-government discourse. In chapter 6, a series of *Honolulu Advertiser* stories about a highway construction site accident illustrates the way news text reaches out to overlapping, situationally valorized conflict identities in the broad context of the Hawaiian sovereignty movement.

CHAPTER 5

News and Law as Conflict Communication Systems

Where landlords have obtained or may hereafter obtain allodial titles
to their lands, the people on each of their lands shall not be deprived
of the right to take firewood, house-timber, aho cord, thatch or ki leaf
on the land on which they live, for their own private use, but they shall
not have the right to take such articles to sell for profit. The people shall
also have a right to drinking water, and roads shall be free to all, on
lands granted in fee simple; provided that this shall not be applicable to
wells and water courses, which individuals have made for their own use.
—Hawai'i Revised Statues § 7-1 (1985)

I'm 'on put the hay where the goats can reach it on that house floor.
—Jim Traficant

Communication about conflict is a constant and widespread activity,
taking place in virtually every social setting. It can be found in all cultures, at every level of social interaction from the collective and global
to the intimate, and across activity domains such as business, politics,
religion, and, at a more general level, identity construction. And yet
despite the tremendous variation among the many ways that it finds
expression—ways that are influenced by cultural convention, technology, and institutional constraints in each setting—it provides a workably
clear-cut conceptual focus, being both relatively easy to identify in its
many forms and also highly significant in our lives because of the vital
issues it touches. Communication about conflict is obvious—one sees
and participates in it everyday—but it is also fascinatingly complex. Its
two component elements, communication and conflict, are arguably
the most powerful and basic elements of social life, and each has evoked
a rich body of theoretical and empirical literature.

The goal, or in some cases the unanticipated consequence, of such practices is not only to limit conflict, but also to reach an understanding. "Understanding" in this situation includes both "an understanding" in the sense of a pact or deal that serves to diminish overt conflict and also something more—a mutual recognition of the opposed positions. As Jürgen Habermas puts it, "the goal of coming to an understanding [*Verständigung*] is to bring about an agreement [*Einverständnis*] that terminates in the intersubjective mutuality of reciprocal understanding, shared knowledge, mutual trust, and accord with one another" (1979: 3). The analysis of news presented so far, however, presents a somewhat less optimistic view of the possible outcomes. In terms of the conflict discourse dynamics within a news community, the only kind of understanding that can be reached is one in which tenuous coalitions are established among many competing, would-be hegemonic systems of identity and interpretation. For the individual news consumer, an understanding reached by competing conflict discourse systems could mean that two distinct perspectives, such as a green, environmental discourse and a discourse of indigenous rights, for example, both make sense and reinforce one another in the news consumer's interpretation of a single news event.

The competing interpretations often clash rather than harmonize, however, and reaching an understanding *across* conflict discourses—rather than within them—is a very uncertain enterprise. Conflict communication is involved in the creation and exacerbation of conflict, therefore, as often as in conflict management. The same message may serve many different functions depending on the settings and participants that frame it. For example, in a *New York Times* story headed "Imam at German Mosque Preached Hate to 9/11 Pilots," the imam, identified as Mr. Fazazi, is reported to have said "Christians and Jews should have their throats slit," and he "called on followers to 'fight the Americans as long as they are keeping Muslims in prison'" (Frantz and Butler 16 July 2002). The quoted statements were recorded on videotaped sermons produced by the imam and seized by the Hamburg state police in a raid on a bookstore near the mosque, according to the story. The major point of the story is that Mr. Fazazi used his sermons to stir up conflict by inciting his listeners—among whom, as the report speculates, may have been Mohamed Atta, the 9/11 suicide pilot—to violence. The videotapes of the sermons presumably were intended by Mr. Fazazi to bring his message to a wider audience. Confiscated by the police, however, the same tapes were no longer exclusively instruments of incitement, but now became evidence to be used in a criminal investigation and perhaps ultimately in court proceedings. Quoted in the news article, the same statements again assume yet a different institutional relation to conflict, given the change in audience and forum. *New York Times* readers in the US are made aware of the conflict situation and its dangers—vividly brought home by the quoted words—enabling them, theoretically (in the Civic model of the press), to take realistic steps, or to support appropriate policies, to avoid or mitigate it. In other words, the statements are now part of institutionalized practices that could serve to mitigate or avoid a dangerous threat. Both law and news media serve overt conflict management purposes in society, but unintended consequences must be considered as well. There is probably not even one reader of news or viewer of legal proceedings who is completely "ideal" in the sense of being totally rational and oriented to the civic virtues championed by the law and the press in democratic society. The fact that the quoted statements target Christians and Jews—categories that include many of the readers—and the fact that Mr. Fazazi was identified as an imam speaking at a mosque to a congregation that included Arabs, means that some degree of incitement to religious and ethnic conflict may still adhere to the words, despite the new context. The words are watered down now in their impact, being quoted rather than directly addressed to the audience, and they convey the inverse of the original targeting because Arabs are now the target. Clearly, concepts of framing (Goffman 1974) and context are essential to understanding the layers of meaning involved in even the most straight forward-seeming examples of communication about conflict.

To take another example, in May 2005, *Newsweek* magazine ran a piece that included the assertion, based on information from an unnamed government official, that US interrogators had flushed a Koran down a toilet in order to demoralize prisoners at the Guantànamo Bay prison camp. The assertion, which defies the constraints of normal plumbing and was a relatively small detail in the story, was intended as a contribution to a continuing debate about prisoner abuse by US soldiers. As such, it raised questions about the political and moral blame that might attach to high pentagon and administration officials. Within a week, however, the news story was linked to anti-American riots in Afghanistan and Pakistan in which 17 people were killed. Leaping from its original context, the story had become an inflammatory incitement to violence—given extreme cultural sensitivity to charges of defilement of the Koran—in the pre-existing turmoil of Central Asian politics. On the rebound, the story, now freighted with deadly consequences, returned to the arena of US media politics. The original, still unnamed source having by this point begun to waiver on the truth of the original allegation, *Newsweek* apologized and retracted the story, opening itself to criticism by government spokespersons, who portrayed the episode as an example of irresponsible, "bad" news. The president's press secretary suggested that *Newsweek* help to "repair the damage [to] our image," possibly by "pointing out what the policies and practices of the United States military are when it comes to the handling of the holy Koran" (Stout 2005).

As I argued in chapter 2, the civic model of the press lends itself to interpretation of journalism as an instrument of conflict management, allowing citizen/decision makers who share values, stocks of knowledge, and social identities to reach agreement about public conflict issues. But when news crosses conflict discourse boundaries, as it inevitably does, how can it operate to broker an understanding among divergent ways of reading the *reality* offered by news? It can do this—within limits, of course—by allowing the various forms of discourse that have reached a level of self-consciousness among their adherents to encounter one another in the news text. Thus, in the jogger rape case discussed in chapter 6, reporters interviewed authorities in many different conflict discourses, allowing them to expound on their specific interpretations.

The classic critical studies of US journalism that have examined the issue of bias in news—resulting from reporters' tactics and practices as well as from undisclosed conflicts of interest traceable to media ownership and general commercialism—have been concerned with identifying the host or dominant discourses of the media. For example, *New York Times* stories may allow feminist perspectives to be presented to a degree—and a specific reporter may well be a feminist—but the *New York Times* itself is not a feminist paper. Feminist views do not have the same weight in the *Times* that they would in a feminist publication. The general question, then, is how a conflict management institution rooted in and growing out of a dominating discourse can effectively recognize competing interpretations of conflict and social reality. In modern society, as Weber recognized, law has taken on this task. Situations in which competing ways of life, fundamentally different in material and cultural modes of production, confront one another in law offer comparative insight into the way the mass news media handle the problem.

Law as the Paradigm of Modern Conflict Discourse Systems

The archetypal example of institutionalized communication about conflict in a modern society is law. Of course, legal systems are a very late development in human history and hardly represent the most basic form of conflict-focused communication. Less formal but still organized communication about conflict in one form or another is no doubt as old as human culture itself. But the very artificiality of law—its self-consciously constructed nature—brings into sharp focus some of the basic features of conflict communication that may not be obvious in more natural, less rigidly structured situations. For example, one of the most clear-cut features of law is its system nature. As a system, law is bounded. Some institutions and social processes are clearly part of the system, and some are not, which means that law can be set off conceptually from other parts of social life. Systems are internally organized as well as being bounded, and those institutions and practices that fall within it are related to one another in a way that makes the whole conceptually and functionally coherent. Of course, the delineated system boundaries do not mean that law and other, extra-legal, activities are unrelated. For example, judges and lawyers trying a case are doing law, while a group of people running a department store is not, but the whole point of law is that it can be applied to other activities beyond its own boundaries. Virtually all actions that might take place at the store—including negative activities such as fraud, employment discrimination, health and safety standards, and so on—can be called legally into question.

The idea that law is applied to activities outside itself raises a very fundamental point about the role of communication in law and other systems of conflict management. From an idealist point of view—which the law itself must adopt for practical reasons—violation of, or conformance to, law is inherent in the act itself, whether anyone raises the question of legality or not. Otherwise, one could perhaps say that a murder takes place only when someone raises a question about the legal status of a killing. From the idealist point of view, then, the law, as a set of rules, has its own transcendental form of existence, being present everywhere (only within its jurisdiction!) and all of the time. From the discursive practice point of view, however, law or any other form of institutionalized communication about conflict comes into existence when people enact or perform it in interaction. In this sense, law itself is a set of discursive practices rather than a body of doctrine. Of course, the reality of one's experience suggests that law really is pervasively present even when not talked about. For one thing, it can be present in people's minds when they act, or in the minds of witnesses to the act. Another way law may be present without being talked about is in the routine practices that it shapes—even when the actors are not aware of the legal rules. But here again one can argue that law exists in such cases only as a potential explanation, which is itself a form of communication. For example, an accountant may report expenses a certain way because that is the standard practice, but an explanation of why the practice is adopted may include—among many other functional or logical reasons—legal requirements. The accountant may or may not actually know the legal rules behind the practice, but nevertheless he or she can be held responsible for violations. This creates the apparent effect of transcendental existence for the rule, but in the end it boils down to something that the rule enforcer might *say* about constructive knowledge.

Abstract features such as the system nature so obvious in law are also found in other, less formally organized examples of communication about conflict, including mass media news. In another example, gossip has been identified as a form of social control (e.g., Brenneis 1984; Brison 1992), and in certain settings it can have a well-defined system nature. Studying social control in a Fijian village in the 1970s, I found that talking about one another's conduct was a very important way of managing conflict (Arno 1993). Members of the community did not consider their activities in this regard to be gossip, *kakase*, but rather an appropriate and proper—and quite enjoyable—social duty, a way of enforcing public standards of conduct. Looking at such talk as a system, that is, as having interrelated elements and a coherent boundedness that allowed it to be applied to other forms of social action distinct from itself, led me to general observations about the possible organizational range of conflict discourse systems.

For one thing, the Fijian system of conflict talk was well integrated into existing social institutions such as the kinship system, the church, and the chiefly system, drawing upon them for rules of procedure—how and to whom one can talk—as well as substantive standards of evaluation. Far from being a stand-alone system, this way of managing conflict was more like one among many parallel but distinct dimensions of political, economic, and sentimental practices (see Arno 2005) in the village. Modern news media, looked at from this perspective, have a similar openness to all manner of social control institutions. Although Fijian community members felt that it was proper to discuss wrongdoing or malfeasance of all kinds—given always that the etiquette of kin relations was scrupulously observed—they did not see the total process as a distinct institutional entity. Nevertheless, the pieces all fit together into a highly effective way of managing conflicts in the village, and the emergent system had interesting properties. For one thing, the process was distributed in time and space—people talked in small groups at various times and places—so that public confrontation was strictly controlled. Drawing on authority relations and sanctions at the private, family level, the system could effectively deal with public, village-wide concerns even in the absence of centralized civil authority (Arno 1980). Many of these observations apply very well to the mass news media as conflict management systems—the news process is dispersed throughout the community in time and space, and many different systems of values and authority are drawn upon.

When a general, comparative perspective on communication about conflict is adopted, insights can flow in both directions. Not only can one learn about informal systems from analogies with the formal, but one can also develop productive questions about formal legal systems based on what can be observed about conflict talk in other areas of life. For over fifty years, sociologists and anthropologists have looked at the formal institution of law in context of other systems of social control, with more and more emphasis in recent years on communication or talk. Anthony Amsterdam and Jerome Bruner (2000) closely examine the narrative and rhetorical techniques of legal language and link appellate decisions to cultural dimensions of reader interpretation. Conley and O'Barr (e.g., Conley and O'Barr 1998; 1990) have produced books and articles in which they have linked courtroom interaction to ways people talk in ordinary life. In one study (Conley and O'Barr 1990), they observed claimants and judges interacting in small claims courts and delineated two distinct ways of telling conflict stories—that is, of presenting cases. One, centered on social relationships, is appropriate to everyday interaction and the other, focused on rules, is required by courts. In a more in-depth ethnographic study, Merry (1990) looked at how conflict was talked about among working class residents in everyday settings and also in the courtroom in a New England town, tracing the intricate interactions among styles of conflict talk. Merry's analysis also shows how three very broad but distinct forms of US conflict discourse, therapy, morality, and legality—ways of framing and talking about conflict that are embedded in popular culture—are present in the court talk at which she looked. In another US study, Philips (1998) looked at the overlap between law and political ideology—two putatively distinct discourses—in the way judges talked in courtroom proceedings. One thing these studies make clear is that although many ways of talking about conflict may be present together in a particular setting, they are never on equal footing. There can be a definite home court advantage shaping the hierarchy among discourses, so that therapy, for example, has a different weight and spin in a clinic as opposed to a courtroom. Studies that examine the dynamic interrelationships among conflict discourses in relation to specific issues and in specific institutional settings raise important questions of power and justice. For example, in the small claims courts described by Conley and O'Barr, the ordinary citizen, frequently a first time user of the court who tells his or her story in terms of good faith and trust, often loses to the court-wise department store representative who talks instead about contracts and written records (Conley and O'Barr 1990). In such studies, power and justice are not abstractions, but are concretely defined in the reality of peoples' lives.

Conflict Discourse Systems in Colonial Situations

When the power gaps among conflict discourse systems—reflecting similar gaps between the ways of life that the discourses grow out of—are very wide, disparities of power and justice can be dramatic. For example, Diana Eades (1995), studying Aboriginal English in Australian court cases, brings precise sociolinguistic analysis to bear on episodes of acute injustice that occur when two ways of talking—and two ways of life—collide in the courtroom. Empirical studies of communication about conflict like Eades's are based on interaction at the level of people talking—in courtrooms and on street corners—but they imply a much larger perspective. This is because ways of talking, taken to include contexts of situation, are forms of life, as Wittgenstein (1953) said about language games in general, and the confrontation of Aboriginal English and Standard Australian English in the courtroom that Eades describes is a token of the larger confrontation between the two cultural systems involved. Another excellent large scale example is provided by Sally Merry in *Colonizing Hawai'i: The Cultural Power of Law* (2000), a book in which she uses court records, archival material, and newspaper accounts from the time of the Hawaiian Monarchy onward to describe a century-long segment of the still continuing confrontation between US and Hawaiian cultures. Basing her analysis in part on lower court records from the Monarchial era written in Hawaiian and English by magistrates in the town of Hilo, Merry documents in the legal texts themselves the classic power squeeze of the iron triad of Pacific colonialism: the missionaries, the administrators, and the commercial interests. Often at odds among themselves, these forces have nevertheless relentlessly opposed and reformulated the object at the center of the triangle, Hawaiian culture. Although accounts of the transformation of Hawaiian culture and society can be, and have been, written from historical, political, and economic perspectives, Merry's account has particular power precisely because it focuses on systems of law, including religious and secular, foreign and indigenous systems, and the evolving patterns of hierarchy and dominance among them. In the conflict centered approach to news media I am advocating, the study of discourse struggles within the news community are of key importance, and they can often be documented in news settings as well in nonnews settings, such as law.

Studies of law and other systems of communication about conflict, such as the missionaries' articulation of Christianity and the indigenous Hawaiian system of kapu, can get very close to the precise mechanism of cultural transformation as it takes place in real life interaction. For example, Merry shows how the New England version of Anglo-American law adopted by the Kingdom of Hawai'i, and as reinforced by ambient missionary rhetoric, imposed dramatic changes in the intimate family and sexual lives of traditional Hawaiians who were brought into court. Obviously, the intimate sphere of rural Hawaiian life was by no means unregulated before the imported systems of law and religion were introduced. Ethnographic accounts such as Handy and Pukui's, *The Polynesian Family System in Ka'u, Hawai'i* (1972), depict a powerful traditional system of values, social identities, and rules of interaction that could be brought to bear on individual behavior in the community. What the court records that Merry examines show is the violent overthrow of the traditional system—violent in the sense of the legitimate state violence of legal punishment, fines, and imprisonment—when the two collide in specific court cases. Merry uses the phrase "the criminalization of everyday life" in talking about the process, and she draws on a literature concerning the similar role of law in breaking up traditional rural life in Europe during the early stages of modernization.

Looking at the transformation of family life and sexuality in Hawai'i from the perspective of communication about conflict—as a complex contest of distinct discourse systems played out not abstractly, but in specific social interactions—one can see that defeat in one setting, such as a courtroom, does not mean the complete collapse of an entrenched opposing system. Most of life, after all, takes place outside of the courtroom—and away from the policeman's gaze—and clearly many aspects of Hawaiian culture survived their confrontation with New England law and religion and continue to evolve on their own terms. In many cases, a conflict discourse system growing out of traditional Hawaiian family life, although opposed or unrecognized in specific aspects by law and commerce, may have found reinforcement in missionary Christian discourse, strengthening the resistance of traditional practices to being obliterated or radically altered. Such capacity for alliance formation among opposed conflict discourses is an important part of communication about conflict in society, as I argued in my discussion of conflict discourse systems in the news process (chapter 3). In an empirical manifestation of this kind of conflict discourse alliance, one can observe the integration of Christianity and tradition in many Pacific Island societies (White 1991; Engelke and Tomlinson 2006).

Obviously at this point I am extending the idea of a conflict discourse system beyond its most obvious application, law. It is easy to see law as a semi-autonomous, highly institutionalized way of talking about conflict that can be applied, with very real consequences for people's behavior, to conflict situations. But in my analysis, to achieve a broader approach to communication about conflict, I define a conflict discourse system as any coherent, regularized way of talking about conflict that grows out of and recursively modifies a way of life or a set of social practices. Such systems are defined only in operation and in relation to an object, such as a social practice, on which they are operating. There cannot be a set list of such conflict discourses independent of how they are being used. The defining pattern of use is as follows: the conflict discourse system identifies the target conflict within its own set of categories, it provides conceptual and procedural resources that allow the identified conflict to be analyzed and evaluated, and it produces a solution with some degree of sanction bite in the parties' lives (Arno 1985). Conflict discourse systems are institutionalized to the degree that they have established, recognized forums, ways of proceeding, and role positions that define who can speak with authority. What I mean by saying that the definition is situational and relational is this: one cannot simply say that law, for example, is only a conflict discourse system. It depends entirely on how it is being employed in the specific situation. In a courtroom, during the trial of a legal anthropologist accused of educational malfeasance, law is a conflict discourse system. But suppose the forum shifts to an anthropology of law conference in which a professor is reading a paper critical of how the law operates in society. Now law is the set of social practices being operated on, and legal anthropology is the conflict discourse system, complete with all of the criteria mentioned—categories of analysis and evaluation, forums, figures of authority, and even, although perhaps to a minor degree, some influence on behavior.

Returning to the problem posed by Merry about the transformation of the intimate sphere of Hawaiian family life, one can see that the very idea of traditional family life implies a conflict discourse system that grows out of that life as it is lived. In everyday life, people invoke tradition in conflict situations—situations in which people are at odds with one another over rights, duties, identities, values, meanings, and so on—as a way of understanding, talking about, and resolving the conflict. Although a shared vision of the ancient past may be invoked, it is the present moment in the culture that provides the forum, the authority accorded certain speakers, and the contextual meaning of the words and concepts. By the same token, the world of commerce and money or the local church organization are also capable of being evoked in corresponding, distinct conflict discourse systems. Although the discourses of conflict may come together in opposition to or support of one another, the setting and the definition of the situation is critical in determining their relative weights.

For example, the conflict might have something to do with the shared use of property or wealth, and a discussion of it might take place—either actually or virtually (that is, the conversation may evoke a context that is not physically present)—in a banker's office, a pastor's study, a family council, or a law court. The banker or the judge might allude to family values, and the preacher might bring up economic necessities, but the effective force of each form of discourse, and the nature of their interrelationships will vary as the conflict moves from one setting to another. An important corollary point from the communication about conflict perspective is that a conflict cannot be said to be "really" about anything outside of a specific context of its discussion. The parties, their emotions, and the physical events of the situation, as well as the lack of social consensus, are very real, but the play of conflict discourses can shape them into complex formations of interlinked conflicts. That is to say, people can experience the total conflict as having legal, moral, medical, and other elements.

Studying conflicts in society, therefore, requires a text of some kind locating it in a defining framework. Records of face-to-face interaction can provide an excellent view of the dynamics of conflict discourses in action, but other kinds of texts, as long as they are located within an institutionalized conflict communication system, can be read as specifying an expected reader and as anticipating specific responses (Amsterdam and Bruner 2000; Silverstein and Urban 1996). Appellate decisions in legal cases, for example, can document crucial struggles of alliance, accommodation, and conflict among conflict discourses and the social worlds they help to shape.

Kalipi Rights in Hawai'i: An Alliance of Conflict Discourses

The evolution of Kalipi rights in Hawaiian jurisprudence is an excellent example of how radically opposed ways of life can try to reach accommodation through alliances among their characteristic conflict discourse systems. The Kalipi case, *Kalipi v. Hawaiian Trust Co,* 66 HAW 1 (1982), is about—and here one can clearly say what a conflict is about because it has been defined by the legal setting—one of the most important issues of the Hawai'i sovereignty movement (see Osorio 2003 and Silva 2003).

That fundamental issue is the accommodation between the traditional Hawaiian system of property rights and those of the modern capitalist economy, which of course are staunchly supported by law. The facts of the case are stated in the opinion, and here again the law provides an excellent example of a general property of conflict discourse systems, namely the way that "facts" are created—selected and shaped—by the discourse system itself. That is to say, the facts are created as "legal facts" of the case, not as actual events. There are uncounted potential facts related to the actual events that make up Mr. Kalipi's story, but the only ones relevant to the Kalipi case are those chosen and formulated in the opinion. According to the text of the opinion, Mr. Kalipi, a native Hawaiian, was prevented from collecting certain plants and natural materials—as his family had been doing for years—on land owned by, among others, the Hawaiian Trust Company. The owners were using the land as a cattle range, and Mr. Kalipi's entering and collecting did not interfere with that use. Mr. Kalipi owned a house lot in the particular *ahupua'a*—a large land division established by traditional Hawaiian land tenure practice—that also included the land owned by Hawaiian Trust Company and the others in the suit. At the time he attempted to collect plant materials on the land, Mr. Kalipi and his family were not living on his house lot in the ahupua'a in question. Although many Hawai'i residents are not aware of it—and very few indeed were aware of it before the decision in the Kalipi case—all land in Hawai'i, even in urban and suburban areas, is divided into named, traditional ahupua'a.

The landowners who stopped Mr. Kalipi from collecting plant materials on their land argued that it was private property and that they therefore had the right to exclude people from trespassing on it. On the other hand, Mr. Kalipi argued that as a native Hawaiian, he had the right, established by traditional culture and protected by the constitution and laws of the state of Hawai'i, to collect materials for traditional uses within his own ahupua'a. The Hawai'i state constitution, containing the guarantee of rights relied on by Mr. Kalipi, was reenacted and clarified at the Hawai'i State Constitutional Convention in 1978, a time at which the revitalization of native Hawaiian culture was being intensely debated on many social fronts. That decade saw a dramatic upsurge of interest in the knowledge and practice of Hawaiian language, music, and dance, and there were also demonstrations aimed at redeeming indigenous Hawaiian land rights. For example, in 1978, Hawaiians briefly occupied and shut down the Hilo airport, which is constructed on land held in trust for native Hawaiians, to protest inadequate compensation for its use. Fifty-one people, out of a much larger group of protesters, were arrested (Clark 1978).

The specific rights in question in the Kalipi case, however, had already been protected in 1851 by laws of the Kingdom of Hawai'i, which were subsequently continued and reenacted in the current code of state laws. Here are the texts of the laws—which had been largely ignored for many years— the Kalipi case brought back to life:

> The State reaffirms and shall protect all rights, customarily and traditionally exercised for subsistence, cultural, and religious purposes and possessed by ahupua'a tenants who are descendants of native Hawaiians who inhabited the Hawaiian Islands prior to 1778, subject to the right of the State to regulate such rights.
> —Hawai'i Constitution article XII, § 7 (1978)

> Where landlords have obtained or may hereafter obtain allodial titles to their lands, the people on each of their lands shall not be deprived of the right to take firewood, house-timber, aho cord, thatch or ki leaf on the land on which they live, for their own private use, but they shall not have the right to take such articles to sell for profit. The people shall also have a right to drinking water, and roads shall be free to all, on lands granted in fee simple; provided that this shall not be applicable to wells and water courses, which individuals have made for their own use.
> —Hawai'i Revised Statues § 7-1 (1985)

These texts can be used to make a general point about the way rules are used in conflict communication. Rules, like words in general, cannot really be said to have *a* meaning except in specific contexts of use. Of course, when stated in general terms—as, for example, words in a dictionary or rules compiled in a code—they have tremendous amounts of potential meaning. These sets of potential meanings are collections of possible specific meanings that will be defined by the social situations, including authority and power relations, in which they are ultimately employed. Having been ignored in legal settings for years, the laws just quoted could almost have been considered meaningless for courts and lawyers. Among social activists passionately engaged in the renaissance of Hawaiian culture during the 1970s, however, these legal texts were far from being ignored and had a set of powerful meanings—powerful in the sense of having an influence on what people do and how they understand their actions.

From an abstract, communication perspective, then, two powerful conflict discourse systems, law on the one hand and Hawaiian political activism on the other, were potentially linked by the law texts at the time that Mr. Kalipi attempted to collect culturally meaningful materials on his neighbors' land. A social or political movement can generate an organized conflict discourse system to the extent that it is used by its participants to define problems in social life, analyze them, and offer solutions that specify future actions or understandings of the past. Although they may be more fluid in organization than a formal system like law, social movements foster systems of interrelated personal identities that define authority sufficient to make statements of definition, proscription and prescription by particular people—leaders of the movement or respected figures—effective in critical situations. When emerging spokespersons for the movement were discussing the legal texts, as, for example, during the debates on Native Hawaiian rights that were part of the 1978 Hawai'i State Constitutional Convention, they employed them as supporting elements within the compass of their own critique of the political situation in Hawai'i.

At the end of this chapter, I will return to the role of the mass news media in providing a forum in which conflict discourse systems that are out of power—that is, marginal to the politics of the community—can display their ideas and their leaders in a way that can lead to power sharing with the establishment in political and legal institutions. In this regard, it is instructive that two critics of established power and advocates of native Hawaiian and *local* cultural issues, John Waihe'e and Benjamin Cayetano, who both gained attention in the press coverage of the 1978 State Constitutional Convention (the "Con Con" in press coverage), went on to become governors of the state. Governor Waihe'e, who in 1978 was a 32 year-old lawyer and who had stated that he had no intention of running for office, was able to advance Hawaiian issues in the Con Con by rhetorically blending them with a broader, composite discourse of local identity, sloganized by exponents at the time as "palaka power." An *Advertiser* profile of Waihe'e at the conclusion of the Con Con highlighted his skill in political alliance building. Reporter Sandra Oshiro writes that according to Waihe'e, "the Con Con was to be one arena in a continuing struggle for institutional power between 'locals' and 'newcomers.'" "The power between the two is now somewhat balanced," Waihe'e said. But what he calls "people with mainland-oriented attitudes" were people reaching for "tools" that would help swing the balance of political control away from the local-born and raised (Oshiro 1978). By constructing this narrative framework, which is a marshalling of conflict discourses, Waihe'e was able to invest virtually all of the issues being considered—from abolishing the legal doctrine of adverse possession to a proposal for legislative *initiative*—with dramatic energy. Oshiro reports that Waihe'e's reading of the Con Con represented "a palatable philosophy and, as one delegate put it, a vision that Waihe'e successfully 'sold' to those delegates who went to the convention with no real mission or sense of purpose" (Oshiro 1978). Waihe'e's political momentum was propelled by an alliance of convenience between *local, Indigenous Hawaiian,* and *labor* discourses. Indigenous Hawaiian discourse—Hawaiian values, knowledge, and social identities—gained major purchase in state political power through the Con Con-proposed establishment of the Office of Hawaiian Affairs, dedicated to addressing the political and social injustices flowing from the illegal overthrow of the Hawai'i Monarchy in 1893.

In office, given the necessities of alliance formation, Governors Cayetano and Waihe'e were far from radical, but their Con Con performances helped propel them into office, and the bare fact of their having been elected advanced the baseline credibility of, among other discourses represented in that "local" alliance, resurgent Hawaiian culture. Less dramatic but arguably quite effective advancements of native Hawaiian discourse also grew out of the Con Con, including the adoption of Hawaiian diacritical marks—indicators of long vowels and glottal stops—for official usage. A marble and bronze entry marker for the campus of the University of Hawai'i at Mānoa erected in the 1990s, for example, had to be corrected at considerable expense because it failed to display these marks. After the 1978 Con Con, the Hawaiian language became an official state language for the first time since the overthrow of the monarchy.

In the Kalipi decision, as in the Con Con, one sees law and Hawaiian indigeneity, coming together again. The Con Con was a political and legislative arena, but in Kalipi, the legal system served as the host discourse. The decision in this landmark case was written by Chief Justice Richardson, who is himself of native Hawaiian ancestry and who could therefore be seen as speaking with authority for both systems. But the format of an appellate decision—the legal language, categories, and reasoning—marks it as definitively legal rather than political discourse. Judge Richardson brilliantly and persuasively incorporates the traditionalist Hawaiian perspective into the law in his explanation of the cultural logic of the pre-contact Hawaiian economy and land tenure system. Describing the traditional way of life in Hawaii, the judge explains that the rights protected by the law were necessary in a subsistence economy in which each household needed access to various resources unevenly distributed throughout the ecological zones of the islands. The decision makes it clear that in a important sense, the colonial transformation of Hawaiian culture can be viewed as a confrontation between two very different economies, the local, traditional subsistence economy versus international capitalism, and that each kind of economy had a specific, key property concept (Arno 2002; 2005). Thus, in the concrete setting of the Kalipi case, the landowners, as presented in the decision, argued vigorously that private property, with its rights of exclusive use, is at the very heart of a capitalism system, which in turn is the basis of modern technology and democracy. On the other side, the traditionalist argument is that without the kind of common property rights necessary to its physical expression as a viable way of life, Hawaiian culture would be severely compromised. For example, in order to build and maintain a traditional house, families need timbers and thatch, which are available only in certain locations on the island. One solution might be to establish a market for such materials, so that a family could buy them from owners of the land where they grow, but this would represent a radical transformation—at worst, a kind of simulation or Disneyfication of Hawaiian traditional culture. After all, it is the *social relations* of economic production that are critical to a way of life, not the material resources in and of themselves. In the text of the decision, these two visions of life, apparently incompatible, are being portrayed, and the question for the judge is how, or whether, the two can coexist.

The holding of the Kalipi case, that is, the shortest and most direct answer to the legal question posed by the conflict, is that Mr. Kalipi loses. He was not entitled to enter the lands and collect the materials he needed, and the reason, according to Judge Richardson's decision, is that the law applies to "tenants" of the ahupua'a, which means that the person actually must be residing there. Merely owning a house lot in the traditional land division, as Mr. Kalipi did, is not enough. But the narrow holding is by no means the most important part of this case. The discussion of the law, and the location within it of the traditional Hawaiian way of framing and reasoning about the conflict issues, is by far more important than the mere result because the discussion establishes the willingness of the court to take the rights—that have come to be called Kalipi rights—seriously. The enforceable result of the case—the precise holding—is clearly essential in legal discourse because it distinguishes the decision from mere philosophical discussion; it provides the teeth of the discourse. But the extended discussion in the decision provides the scope for extensive changes in community life. As I argue in chapter 7, it is the policy talk dimension—present in journalism as well as law—of the rule utterance that locates it within the projected social universe of its application.

The Kalipi decision, and its role in the continuing accommodation between indigenous and global ways of life, provides an excellent example of another general point that can be made about the dynamics of conflict discourse systems. This point is that specific cases do not

stand alone, but are linked together as the encompassing conflict discourse system develops or unfolds. In Anglo-American law, this process
is absolutely central to the system, and the basic legal principle of *stare
decisis,* following the precedent of previous cases, provides a clear paradigm for exploring less formal systems. For example, the Kalipi case was
followed in 1992 by the *Pele Defense Fund* case (73 HAW 578), in which
Kalipi rights were expanded. In Pele Defense Fund, native Hawaiians
again wished to enter undeveloped land for cultural purposes and, like
Mr. Kalipi, they did not reside in the ahupua'a to which they needed
access. They did show, however, that ancient custom in the area had
traditionally allowed nonresidents to gather materials in this particular
ahupua'a. They argued that under these circumstances, they did have
the right to enter the land, and the court agreed with them, thus further
fleshing out the scope of Kalipi rights and reinforcing the alliance between modern Hawaiian state law and traditionalist conflict discourse.

An even more striking development in this evolving alliance of conflict discourse systems took place in 1995 with the PASH case. PASH is
Public Access Shoreline Hawaii v. Hawai'i County Planning Commission (79
HAW 425), a case in which an extremely sensitive dimension of Kalipi
rights—their potential application to developed land—is addressed.
In the original case, Judge Richardson directly confronted what is undoubtedly the scariest aspect of Kalipi rights for nonnative residents of
Hawai'i, the idea that native Hawaiians could enter residential or commercial property at will to collect cultural materials. In the bicultural
social world envisioned by the policy discussion in the Kalipi decision,
could a native Hawaiian enter another person's yard without permission
to take fruit or culturally useful leaves? Or to take an absurd leap, could
he or she forage through another person's refrigerator? Richardson
clearly stated that attempts to exercise the rights on developed lands
would cause endless interpersonal conflict and therefore could not be
the intent of the law. In the Kalipi fact situation, the land in question
was an undeveloped cow pasture, and any disturbance created by collecting plant materials would have been minimal. In the PASH case, the
land was also undeveloped, but the crucial fact was that the owners were
in the process of developing it—they wanted to build a hotel and resort
complex on the site and were applying for the appropriate land use per-
mits. PASH (Public Access Shoreline Hawai'i), a political action group
concerned about problems of overdevelopment, and whose membership included a native Hawaiian resident, asked the planning commission for a contested case hearing.

Rather than the usual kind of open hearing in which the public is
allowed to express opinions and concerns informally, a contested case

hearing requires formal testimony to be taken and recorded for use on appeal. In requesting such a hearing, PASH told the planning commission that they would present testimony that the hotel development could interfere with native Hawaiian rights. Specifically, they were prepared to show that their native Hawaiian member's family had traditionally used a saltwater pond on the property to collect brine shrimp to use for bait in catching small shoreline fish, which would in turn be used as bait for open water fishing. The planning commissioners, however, refused to hold the contested hearing because they did not agree that any legally protected native Hawaiian rights were at stake. They apparently agreed with developers that such rights, even if they might exist in the undeveloped land, could not be used to *prevent* development. After a full discussion of the cultural and legal issues, the Hawai'i Supreme Court ordered the planning commission to recognize and protect the cultural rights that PASH asserted. Just as in the original Kalipi case, the narrow holding of this case—an order to the commission to formally admit the appropriate testimony—is far less significant than the impact of the court's policy discussion of the law in relation to indigenous culture and the implied vision of the two forms of political economy coexisting in a bicultural way of life. It is not at all clear where the law will go from here, and what the effects will be on everyday life in Hawai'i, but the coming together of the two conflict discourse systems has obviously invigorated both.

The Expulsion of Jim Traficant: The Discourse of Anti-Government Paranoia

Although I have been discussing legal cases and the impact of legal discourse on Hawaiian culture as an example, my main concern in this book is not law specifically but a more general, abstract model of public communication about conflict that applies as well to other, more ambiguous forms of conflict discourse, particularly mass media news reporting. For example, the importance of cases in law suggests the question of whether there might be analogous units in other systems. Donald Brenneis (2008), in an elegant discussion of the ways theory and method operate in a broad range of legal and academic settings, shows that cases represent an important crosscutting medium of analysis and persuasion. In the conflict discourse system model of mass media news, for example, news stories are used as logical game pieces that are marshaled, much like cases in legal argument, to carry out the conflict discourse functions of the system. These functions are, briefly, to set up a coherent platform of critique applicable to events in social life, to frame disputes and conflicts within its own categories and logic, and to offer a program of action to deal with the conflict. Within each conflict discourse system, adherents develop a common understanding of the significance of specific news events and cite them to explain their analysis of a current situation. For example, *Ruby Ridge, Waco,* and the *JFK Assassination* are units in the discursive and logical apparatus of a particular, loosely organized but quite powerful system of understanding and talking about public events in US society.

Ruby Ridge refers to an incident that took place in 1992. According to James Bovard, writing in the *Wall Street Journal,* "the 1992 confrontation between federal agents and the Randy Weaver family in Ruby Ridge, Idaho, has become one of the most controversial and widely discussed examples of the abuse of federal power" (1995: A14). In the event, federal law enforcement agents, initially as surreptitious, unannounced trespassers—one of whom was killed in a shootout—and later as snipers laying military-style siege to the Weaver family's house under blatantly illegal rules of engagement from FBI authorities, killed Mr. Weaver's son and his wife. Mrs. Weaver was shot in the head and killed by an FBI sniper as she stood behind a closed door, holding an infant in her arms. Anti-government websites often mention that the federal agents shot and killed the Weaver dog as well. A subsequent Justice Department report recommended criminal prosecution of certain federal agents, and a 1995 Senate investigation strongly criticized the government (Bovard 1995).

Waco, of course, refers to a controversial and widely discussed example of paramilitary law enforcement that went spectacularly wrong. On 19 April 1993, after a siege of over fifty days and seemingly endless frustrating negotiations between a religious cult leader, David Koresh, and a small army of federal agents led by the FBI, the government forces initiated an assault on the cult's fortified stronghold, which burst into flames. The remains of 75 people, including those of 25 children under the age of 15, were recovered from the burnt-out compound. As for the assassination of President Kennedy in 1963, it may seem a strange item to include in a litany of complaints about government abuse, but among the incredible assemblage of conspiracy narratives that have accumulated around the event are some that point the finger at government agencies and officials.

One can argue that a list of news stories, as cases in conflict analysis, can be interpreted so many different ways—absent the kind of accepted crosscutting principles provided by a formal system like law—that any sense of coherence or logic is dissipated in the uncontrolled, noninteractive settings of mass media. The coherence, however, is provided by the audience—not the total audience, but the scattered segment of the audience who are party to the particular discourse system. This segment waxes and wanes—people are recruited to a particular conflict discourse and away from it continually, but some such conflict systems show remarkable persistence over time. The idea of broadcast conflict talk connecting with a ready audience segment was expressed in a colorful phrase by former Congressman Jim Traficant in a televised hearing before a subcommittee of the house ethics committee on 18 July 2002. Mr. Traficant had already been convicted on ten felony counts, including bribery, corruption, and racketeering, in federal court, and would later be sentenced to eight years in prison. The question for the house ethics committee was whether or not to recommend to the full House of Representatives that Mr. Traficant be expelled from the body for violating its ethical rules. In the following exchange, Mr. Traficant had been told by the chair of the hearing that the full committee had found against him on nine of the ten counts alleging violations of congressional ethics. Mr. Traficant asked why they had not found him guilty on the tenth count:

(Overlapping talk indicated by aligned brackets; **T** is Mr. Traficant, **C** is the Chairman)

C: ... Mr. Traficant, it will be in the report, and we will have the sanctions hearing at two o'clock this [afternoon ...

T: [Mr. Chairman I request you go light ...

C: well, you'll get [that opportunity ...

T: [I request that you be fair ... and ... ah ... Do I have to be there?

C: You do not have to be there. [you have the opportunity ...

T: [frankly I don't think I'm going to be there, and I'm gonna ask for an extended period of time on the house floor, beyond the house rules, to make my statement to the American people. And I know Mr. Walker is definitely afraid of that, but I'm 'on put the hay where the goats can reach it on that house floor. (*Hearing of the House Ethics Subcommittee, 7/18/02 (from a C-SPAN video archive on the web)*)

Putting "the hay where the goats can reach it" is an interesting metaphor for using the mass media—in this case nationally televised (via C-SPAN) proceedings of the House of Representatives—to reach a well-defined segment of the audience in order to portray a conflict event in a way that makes particular sense to them. They have to reach it—get the point of it—individually, but the speaker feels sure that he knows whom he is talking to and what they will make of it.

In his political career, former Representative Traficant cultivated a clownish public persona, regularly giving one-minute speeches on the floor on absurd topics, ending with "Beam me up!," or to convey special emphasis, "Beam me up, Scotty!" By the end of July 2002, however, he was in serious trouble, facing a long prison sentence and expulsion from the house. During the time of his investigation by the House Ethics Committee, he tirelessly courted opportunities to appear on television and present his version of the events. Despite his chaotic, rambling, and sometimes vulgar style—which seemed well calculated to, and in fact did, attract media attention—he maintained a clear focus on presenting his interpretation of the case, an interpretation carefully framed in terms of a conflict perspective centered on anti-government sentiment and a paranoid conspiracy theory of public events. This body of sentiment is a good example of the kind of conflict discourse system described in chapter 3, and a quick look at Mr. Traficant's statements on television can provide an example of how such a discourse system is evoked in mass media talk. The beauty of a call-in format in political programming is that it can provide some idea of the listener response that can only be conjectured in noninteractive settings. A C-SPAN interview show, *Washington Journal,* which aired on Sunday, 14 July 2002, featured Mr. Traficant and allowed him to respond to callers whose calls had been sorted by the producers according to geographical origin and party affiliation. The opening of the show demonstrates something of Mr. Traficant's eccentric style of interview participation seeming to demonstrate his intent to break away from the conventional format in order to take control of the event and bending it to his own perspectives and purposes:

(**M** is the moderator, **T** is Traficant. Overlaps shown by aligned brackets)

M: Thanks for joining us this morning …

T: Good to be here. Good to be anywhere, Peter.

M: You're [on our …

T: [You really have come up. You know C-SPAN … ah … was once just a reporter of facts and news that were relative to the hill. Now you branched out. Multimedia service. I look out this highrise and see the,

the Mall and the beautiful dome and, ah, you really got the digs here, Peter. You showin' me somethin'.

M: Well thanks for joining [us

T: [You're not in control. What do you want?

M: ... wanna know how you feel that the hearing went yesterday. (C-SPAN Washington Journal, 7/14/02)

At this point, Traficant becomes the cooperative guest, giving a re-signed, pessimistic assessment of his chances and then moving on to his version of the conflict in which he is engaged. He explains that,

> It's a hell of a situation that I'm in. I've been targeted for twenty years, the only American to ever defeat the Justice Department in a RICO case ... Justice Department pulled out all the stops, and quite frankly I think America is in fear of our government, and it's a very bad thing in America. My own assessment. I think that they're afraid of agencies like the IRS, the FBI, Justice Department, Treasury, that manifest great control. Even the judges appointed for lifetime terms are afraid of these agencies. (C-SPAN Washington Journal, 7/14/02)

RICO is the acronym for "racketeer influenced corrupt organization" legislation that was designed to elaborate conspiracy law in order to facilitate the federal investigation and prosecution of organized crime activities. In the following comments, Mr. Traficant interweaves his own story of targeting and government vendetta with references to news events that are highly significant to the listeners he hopes to reach. This is an example of citing previous news events as precedents or cases that ground the speaker's narrative in a very specific reality.

> I came to Washington not liking nor trusting our government. Never be-lieved the Kennedy ... you know ... bullshit, to be quite frankly, ah, hid-den away for seventy-five years. I don't believe what our government's told us about PanAm 103, Ruby ricko ...'r Waco, Ricky Ridge, ah Ruby Ridge. I did call Janet Reno a traitor. I believe she did in fact commit treason by not investigating that money that went from a Red Ar', Chinese general, from the army, to the Democrat National Committee, and without inves-tigation then investigating the love triangle between Monica and couple other sta', cabinet members I think was a fiasco. I think Janet Reno be-trayed America and someday we'll see a Chinese missile because of it. (C-SPAN Washington Journal, 7/14/02)

He concludes before the first call with a statement of his identity within the conflict situation. This identity work is a very important part of evoking a conflict discourse in order to frame a current event or issue.

> So I am one that has really been an outsider in, ah, Washington, maybe a bastard son, that don't trust the damn government quite frankly, and I think America should not fear their government. There's something inherently wrong here, and I'm prepared for the worst. Quite frankly, Scarlet, I don't give a damn, and I'm prepared to go from there. (C-SPAN Washington Journal, 7/14/02)

News events, like cases in a legal system, provide logical building blocks that allow argument and analysis to frame the particular conflict under discussion in terms of the vision of reality shared by adherents to the conflict discourse system. That is to say, the vision shared by those who understand their own lives and identities in terms of the world that the conflict discourse system grows out of and helps to construct. Aside from PanAm 103, Waco, Ruby Ridge, the JFK assassination, the Chinese political contributions, and the Monica Lewinsky affair, Traficant goes on to discuss other past news events such as the Demjanjuk case—in which an elderly man living in Cleveland was identified as "Ivan the Terrible," a notoriously sadistic Nazi concentration camp guard and was finally stripped of his US citizenship in February 2002—and the Salvati case, in which it appeared that the Boston-based FBI withheld exculpatory evidence in a murder trial and allowed Joseph Salvati to spend thirty years in prison before the evidence came to light. All of these cases, some only mentioned, others discussed in detail by Congressman Traficant, can be read together as confirmation that government agencies routinely lie to and abuse citizens. From this perspective, it seems plausible to argue that Traficant is a victim, not a criminal, and that he should not be punished.

Along with more specific stories, Traficant also makes use of broader media issues such as the alleged abuses of the IRS, which had been a focus of congressional action several years previously. In discussing his own case, which seemingly has little specifically to do with the IRS, Traficant says that,

> the IRS in the backroom can come and take your damn home, without a warrant, and I changed that law. They could abuse you and scare the hell out of you, and I changed that law. We can now sue them for a million dollars. (C-SPAN Washington Journal, 7/14/02)

Along with "fact" situations and cases, the conflict discourse system of anti-government paranoia also features a set of personalities, heroes and villains, who can be evoked to populate the social world that it draws upon and helps to construct. Every discourse needs to clothe itself in the flesh of real people, and Traficant's discussion of J. Edgar Hoover and a proposal to rename the FBI building gives an indication of some of the discourse's key historical figures—heroes and demons—and their evaluations. In a sense, each stands for some important tenet of the system. Proceeding from a discussion of FBI misconduct in the Salvati case, Traficant goes on to say:

> The mob paid off the FBI in Youngstown for years and covered it up just like they did in Boston. An' my God we had a FBI director by the name of Hoover testified before the Senate said there's no mafia in America. This is nothing but a fairy tale. And the truth of the matter is the Mafia had him in pictures of drag ... dressed as a woman, and compromised. J. Edgar Hoover. And I think Hoover's name should be taken off the damn FBI building. We should put Martin Luther King Jr.'s name on the thing, Robert Kennedy's name on it, Oliver North's on it. Put an American on it that's a patriot. (C-SPAN Washington Journal, 7/14/02)

No doubt some of Traficant's listeners, even those very passionately in accord with him on the basic issue of the government as evil, would not have included Martin Luther King Jr. on the list of patriots. A "patriot" in this system of talk is a hero whose words and actions are invested with authority. Those people whose own identities and views of the world are shaped by this general discourse can still disagree on the canonical list of patriots as well as on underlying subthemes such as racism and anti-Semitism, including or excluding such accounts of reality to various degrees. Traficant and one of the callers put it like this: "I am not an anti-semite, but ..." in this sequence:

(**T** is Traficant, **C** is a caller from Dallas)

T: I am not an anti-semite, but I have been accused of one. Because I brought John Demjanjuk home from Cleveland who was convicted of being Ivan the Terrible and sentenced to die in Cleveland. ... And I've been targeted. Number one out of five hundred and thirty-five by the powerful American-Israeli Public Affairs Committee. And quite frankly they own most of the newspapers, they own most of the TV stations and most of their ads come from there, and I am tired of it. I have nothing against the Jewish people, and I want 'em to get off my ass now.

...

C: ... And my last comment I wanted to say ... I'm not anti-semitic ... but the, this country is ran, truly as far as I'm concerned, it looks like the Israelis, uh the Jewish uh, uh lobby that they have on our government? They do control a lot. They control our media they control everything, and they have literally destroyed you, and I just want you to say, I just wanted to say to you: stan', continue to stand for something or you'll die for nothing. So you go ahead, and keep your head up, and you continue to speak out, and that's why people don't like you because you don't step in—you don't march to the tune, you step out. So you keep your head up OK? (C-SPAN Washington Journal, 7/14/02)

The social world being evoked by Traficant, though it may offer a different collection of bugbears for different adherents, is a scary world, and it takes brave individuals, true heroes, to respond to it. Traficant remarks:

I wanna say this to the American people ... In the old Soviet Union the KGB would come out and shoot Peter right behind the head. In America they'd just destroy you in a court and take away everything you have, and quite frankly this is from Jim Traficant to the IRS and the FBI: "Go to Hell! Now, shove your case up your subpoena, do what you gotta do with me. This one American don't give a damn and is not afraid of yah, period!" (C-SPAN Washington Journal, 7/14/02)

The John Wayne-like quality of this statement is probably not accidental. Institutions such as the United States Marines, as narratively enhanced by Hollywood war movies over the years, can also be invoked to connect this vision to the real world, corroborating it by linking it to real events like wars, and so on, and contrasting the evil and effete civil agencies with the rugged individualist military—a contrast which introduces a complicated and perhaps a bit nonsensical relation with hierarchy and obedience. In the interview, Traficant identifies himself, and the predicament he finds himself in, with the body of military/individualist values and sentiments thus evoked, referring first to one of his supporters, whom he likens to Clint Eastwood, and then to another, whose name I have deleted:

[referring to a person who agreed with him that the government's criminal case against him is ridiculous] ... I called him Clint Eastwood 'cause tells it like it is, he's a great patriot. And I want everybody to know that this little pin I'm wearing was given to me by a marine. You know, [ ] who works with me. And let me tell you a story. It really's the plight of America. We had a four day war, in Desert Storm, and people come home to great parades. [ ] was in a foxhole, in Viet Nam. His partner was blown up and killed. His, his right arm was basically shattered. Had a bullet wound in his right leg, and he laid in a rice paddy for four days. He didn't know if the Viet Cong were gonna find him or the marines, Thank God it was the marines. They never leave their dead—boy do I love the marines—and they never leave their wounded, and he gave me this the day before I come down here, a little bit of tear in his eye ... he's not that kind of guy. He's a great marine, and he gave me this and he said "you're in a hell of a fight." I'm not a marine, folks! I'm wearin' this for [ ] and he said, "I want you to wear this." An' you know he reminds me a little bit of Oliver North. (C-SPAN Washington Journal, 7/14/02)

Most of the statements quoted above were made in response to callers, whom the moderator identified by city and political party. The callers asked very few specific questions. Most expressed support for Traficant, accepting his version of the case against him—as a government vendetta spearheaded by the Justice Department because of his attacks on Janet Reno—and allowed him to elaborate further on the view of the world he shared with them. Here are some samples of viewer calls:

(**M** is the moderator, **C** the caller, and **T**, Traficant)

M: Jackson, Tennesee. Republican.

C: Yessir, Mr. Traficant, I watched yesterday, and I called ever' friend I had that was at home, to watch. I believe (laugh), especially with the Ethics Committee, that this is the pot calling the kettle black. I don't think you've done anything wrong, I think you're a hero, I think a lot of people that called in, I tried to call in yesterday and couldn't get in, believe the same way I do. And I think the people on the Ethics Committee and the people in Congress in general need to watch what they're sayin' and what they're doin'. Thank you.

T: Well, I appreciate that and I think members who support me can call their members of Congress and say "Hey, don't vote the guy out, give him a chance. We've got an appeal process."

...

M: Orwell Ohio, Good Morning.

C: Yes, I grew up in the Warren-Youngstown area. I think I understand it pretty well. And Congress needs to look the word ethical up in the dictionary. The Congress is not ethical. As a humble sixty-four year old grandmother, I do not trust the government. The government has no conscience, and the IRS is a Gestapo. And if Traficant goes to jail I think all the public should be in jail with him.

T: (laughs) thank you very much

…

M: Warren, Ohio, in the Seventeenth District, Good Morning.

C: Good morning. Good morning, Jim, God bless you.

T: Thank you

C: Now the America is just beginning to realize why we love you so much in this community, and why we sent you to Congress over and over again. Because you speak the truth to power, you're unafraid, you're coura-geous, and you're always in defending the people in this community right from the time you were sheriff and you wouldn't foreclose on the homes of laid-off steel workers. They can take a lot aways from you, but they can't take away the fact that you saved that man's life, Demjanjuk, and no other member of Congress I know can say that. That you have the love of this people, and I think you're gonna make more history. I think uh that you're gonna be re-elected as an independent no matter what they do to you because people know you here, Jim, and they love you, and I think it's not uh just that you're an American hero or patriot, I think that you're a prophet. I know that that's probably something that you'd may reject but don't forget after the crucifixion there's a resurrection. God bless you. (C-SPAN Washington Journal, 7/14/02)

To give Mr. Traficant the last word in this account of this televised performance, here is the way he summarized his position near the end of the show [the underlining indicates heavy stress]:

They have targeted me, and yes we have political prisoners in America, and I'm gonna make this statement. You are now being addressed by a political prisoner that will be serving in some jail. And you know what? I quite frankly, Scarlet, don't give a damn. Because I would rather go to jail, and even die in jail than admit to somethin' I di'n't do. And I had no intent to break the law. As they portrayed them, as they created a paper trail that was <u>unbelievable</u> … that … ah … I, I just can't believe that on a RICO case a man is convicted on hearsay. And da you believe that, the way they wanted me, that they had no wiretaps, they had no hidden mi-crophones, You know they had 'em. You watch television. Everything on 'em was probably helpful to Jim Traficant. (C-SPAN Washington Journal, 7/14/02)

Within a few weeks, Jim Traficant had been expelled from Congress for violating its ethics and sentenced to an eight-year prison term for his federal conviction on corruption and racketeering charges. Clearly, two powerful conflict discourse systems operated on the Traficant case, each construing the same events and actions in its own terms, as criminal or ethical violations respectively, and applied its own categories of logic and evaluation. Both of them, the legal system and the Congressional ethics procedures, were able to supply well-defined forums and procedures, endow the participants with the necessary distribution of authority, and come up with clear-cut judgments backed by sanctions. In his television appearances, however, Representative Traficant was clearly arguing his case—a third version of it, neither legal nor ethical—in another conceptual forum.

Weak and Strong Systems of Conflict Talk

What can one say about this third, much more ambiguous conflict discourse system? The most obvious approach, probably, would be to look at it as something completely different from the other two, as mere rhetoric, perhaps, with no definite structure or determinant outcome, no organized forum, and no legitimate authority figures. In the previous chapters, however, I argued that despite their highly ephemeral and polymorphous character—or perhaps partly because of it—ways of talking about conflict cases of this type actually constitute a very powerful class of conflict discourse systems.

Following the strategy that I discussed earlier in this chapter—taking law as the paradigmatic system and looking for parallels in less formalized conflict discourse systems—the crucial question of sanctions needs to be addressed. Law, and even congressional ethics hearings, can produce decisions that can be imposed against resistance—in other words, they are invested with power. With regard to ephemeral conflict systems of the kind represented by the anti-government discourse Congressman Traficant evoked in defending himself, however, the process is more indirect. Obviously, Traficant hoped that large numbers of "patriots," energized by his television performances, would call members of Congress, influencing their votes on expulsion. In other words, the sanction employed would be putting congresspersons in fear of losing their own seats through an erosion of voter support. Perhaps Traficant even hoped a sense of public arousal and indignation would guide the federal judge in his case toward a lighter prison sentence. These effects did not take place, but the point is that they might have. It was even remotely possible that Traficant could be reelected to Congress as an independent from his jail cell, as he has prophesied. These effects seem farfetched in the Traficant case, but this does not mean that a less intensely paranoid version of the anti-government conflict discourse is without any means of enforcing its conclusions.

On the contrary, in alliance with other discourse systems, and in many countries around the world, anti-government talk has energized highly successful right wing legislative programs of deregulation and privatization aimed at getting the government off the backs of the people and driving back the encroachments of the nanny state on individual freedom. Almost invariably in the talk that shapes such legislative action, government itself is depicted as corrupt, incompetent, arrogant, and dangerous. Eva Mackey identifies the participation of a "state v. people" discourse in the populist approach adopted by a conservative government in attempting to manage Canadian identity politics in the early 1990s (Mackey 1997). At about the same time in the United States, the right wing Republican "Contract with America," led by Newt Gingrich in the 1994 congressional elections, provided a dramatic, if temporary, example of the anti-government discourse's power to shape social events. According to a 1995 speech by Jeffrey Gayner, Senior Fellow of the Heritage Foundation, "[t]he Contract itself emerged publicly with the staging of the mass signing of the Contract on the steps of the U.S. Capitol by 367 candidates for office on September 27, 1994. On that day, all of these candidates publicly pledged: 'If we break this Contract, throw us out'" (Gayner 1995). Gayner describes the participation of right wing think tanks like the Heritage Foundation in formulating the text of the contract by previously writing and widely circulating policy papers documenting the failings of government so that, "[i]n this manner, an extensive philosophical groundwork formed the intellectual foundation for the Contract With America when it formally appeared in the fall of 1994. Sound ideas thus became anchored into concrete policy recommendations." The Contract itself then, "provided the mechanism to move from vague political rhetoric to creating a specific political program," according to Gayner. The introductory text of the Contract, followed by specific proposals, refers explicitly to a state of distrust between government and the people:

> As Republican Members of the House of Representatives and as citizens seeking to join that body we propose not just to change its policies, but even more important, to restore the bonds of trust between the people and their elected representatives.

That is why, in this era of official evasion and posturing, we offer instead a detailed agenda for national renewal, a written commitment with no fine print.

This year's election offers the chance, after four decades of one-party control, to bring to the House a new majority that will transform the way Congress works. That historic change would be the end of government that is too big, too intrusive, and too easy with the public's money. It can be the beginning of a Congress that respects the values and shares the faith of the American family.

Like Lincoln, our first Republican president, we intend to act "with firmness in the right, as God gives us to see the right." To restore accountability to Congress. To end its cycle of scandal and disgrace. To make us all proud again of the way free people govern themselves.

On the first day of the 104th Congress, the new Republican majority will immediately pass the following major reforms, aimed at restoring the faith and trust of the American people in their government: ... (REPUBLICAN CONTRACT WITH AMERICA, 1994)

While the Contract, envisioned by its supporters at the time as a revolutionary event in American government, eventually fizzled out, many of the sentiments apparent in the text's language—referring to [broken] trust, evasion, posturing, scandal, and disgrace, applied to a government that is too big, too intrusive, too "easy with the public's money," and which is opposed to God, right, and the values and faith of the American family—still endure, forming the commonsense view of political reality expressed by many in United States political talk.

In this dilute form, the anti-government discourse borrows its forums, sharing the common forum of the mass media with competing discourses, and it borrows its sanctioning powers also, attaching itself to elected officials. One way to look at this form of conflict discourse, as I said before, is to view it as "mere" rhetoric, which is being used instrumentally by powerful conservative business interests who hope to escape social obligations. From a communication about conflict perspective, however, what is happening is that, in a particular historical setting, two conflict discourse systems have formed an alliance in opposition to a third powerful system that portrays government as an instrument of social fairness and protection of communal interests. This is indeed a form of rhetorical analysis, but it takes a systems approach and recognizes the social organization of the rhetorical systems in relation to shared visions of social life. The conflict systems in play in the Contract example are unequal in power, but this is not because one is more "real" than the others. Each is real to the extent that its adherents use it in many diverse settings to explain—to themselves and others—their past, present, and future actions in the real world. Differences in power among them correspond to numbers of those adherents and the resources available to them.

In the broad arena of public life, a conflict talk system such as the evolving, situationally invoked anti-government discourse lacks the life and death power of law in American society, but in small isolated communities in which anti-government paranoia is so intense as to form the pervasive, commonsense view of the world, it can actually take on the mantle of ultimate sanction. Thus, among right wing militia and survivalist groups, such talk may be used to justify even the "collateral damage" of civilian deaths in a war against the government. The Timothy McVeigh case, although not as well documented with actual text—such as natural conversations among the people involved in planning and carrying out the bombing of the Oklahoma City Federal Building in 1995, for example—as a thorough discursive practice analysis would require, seems to demonstrate the incredible range of power that such discourse systems can exhibit from one situation to the next.

But can one say that the conflict discourse system is the same in the very different situations of its use? When the "humble sixty-four year old grandmother" called in to support Traficant by saying that the "IRS is a Gestapo," was she linked in some way to McVeigh's way of understanding the events at Waco in 1993? From an idealist perspective—the view that there is an independently existing, abstract anti-governmentism—the answer is no. But in terms of actual communication about conflict in specific settings—discursive practice—there is a connection. If the Warren, Ohio grandmother and Timothy McVeigh had had an opportunity to talk about Waco, Ruby Ridge, the IRS, and the ATF, I think they might well have jointly produced a rather well synchronized conversation about conflict. One hopes that she would have taken a completely different position from his on the bombing he carried out, but at least they would have understood each other up to a point. They could have debated the proposed action in common terms, each linking his or her arguments to a shared reality anchored in mass media news events. Despite the odds against their ever having spoken to one another personally, it is very likely that they were brought together as members of the mass media audience, viewing the same news events from similar perspectives. The mass media provide a scope for national or even global identity formation that is as pervasive, although voluntary in character, as the state's sovereign power to assign identities—citizen, husband, wife, minority, resident alien, and so on—through law.

The News Media, Mass Media Policy Talk, and the Parliament of Discourses

In this book, I am exploring the nature of the class of conflict discourse systems that, lacking their own dedicated public forums, display themselves in the mass media, finding articulation in news and policy programming. Lacking institutionalized roles—like judges and lawyers—that confer authority and legitimacy on their spokespersons, they create their own heroes through media exposure. Racist conflict discourse finds its George Wallace, and racial reconciliation finds its Martin Luther King. Anti-government talk creates, and then is shaped by, its Oliver North and Charlton Heston, while consumer protection defines itself and evolves under the discursive leadership of Ralph Nader.

Conflict talk systems at this level of organization also lack, as noted, the coercive power of state sovereignty to assign identities, with attendant rights and duties, to individuals. Instead, they must recruit people, again largely through media exposure, to voluntarily adopt the identities they offer. Media accounts of the life of Timothy McVeigh, for example, have mentioned his exposure to the survivalist movie *Red Dawn,* in which an evil (although in this case foreign) government is resisted by gun loving patriot heroes, and a BBC online profile reports that "an even stronger influence was *The Turner Diaries,* a racist, anti-Semitic novel which tells the story of a gun enthusiast who reacts against tighter gun laws and starts a revolution by packing a van with home made explosives and blowing up the FBI headquarters in Washington" (Walker 2001). Cult authors like Ayn Rand are credited with influencing campus political identities, while John Walker Lindh, "the American Taliban," who was captured by the US military during the invasion of Afghanistan, was reported to have drawn upon the movie *Malcom X* in finding his own unique sense of identity (Seelye 2002, CNN Website 2001). These are merely anecdotal examples, of course. Interview data or records of natural conversations would be necessary to corroborate them, but they indicate a way that film, novels, television fiction, and so on—not to mention a good liberal arts education!—can offer people identities and worldviews.

The progression from individual identity to conflict discourse system is not automatic. But if subjective identities can be translated into social relationships through the establishment of communication communities, sets of interrelated identities can become a lived reality for people. Reading Ayn Rand may offer a particular view of capitalism, and the economic and social identities that constitute it, but the Ayn Rand Institute interactive website (2005) and the local Young Republican club can allow those identities, interpretations of events, and so on, to become lived social reality. When a communication event centers on conflict analysis and management, any social reality, even if not a total way of life, but only a situationally focused one, can produce a conflict discourse system that draws upon its identities, categories, stocks of knowledge, values, and authority relationships. In the concluding chapters, the news media and venues of policy talk will be explored as the common public forum in which constantly evolving, growing and weakening conflict discourse systems contend in a process of defining and shaping civil society.

CHAPTER 6

News in
Extra-Textual Terrain

The precise problem I want to address here, as suggested in chapter 2 in relation to Miyazaki's *The Method of Hope,* is the fading out of individual agency in news theory. In *Missing Persons: A Critique of Personhood in the Social Sciences,* Mary Douglas and Steven Ney criticize the asocial, autonomous, and rationally calculating person—a fiction of classical economic theory—that has come to be accepted as common sense reality in US public discourse (Douglas and Ney 1998). For example, the marketplace of ideas, or Civic, model applies classical liberalism to the understanding of news, and it appears to place individual agents—playing the various roles necessary to the production and consumption of news—right in the center of things. If any kind of news theory held on to the individual, this should be it. On examination, the theoretical news consumer shopping the marketplace of ideas proves to be rational, consistent, diligent about seeking and debating ideas, and in the center of mainstream society and culture.

What is wrong with this picture? How many people does one actually know who fit this description all or even most of the time? As a political program, this conceptualization is excellent, but empirically, the empirical sounding theory has failed to capture the individual we know and experience in everyday life. The marketplace of ideas model is essential to the US political system, and it does explain a lot about the news. The way journalistic institutions and practices are organized—including genuine attempts by journalists to uphold objectivity and factuality as a goal—make sense from this perspective. The problem is that there is so much more to news as social process—aspects that the marketplace theory of classical liberalism can see only as dysfunctional. This kind of disapproving stance with respect to a large part of the activity being studied is bound to be limiting. One answer that has proved useful is

critical news theory, which rearranges the areas of function and dysfunc-
tion and which offers another kind of theoretical individual who is not a
ruggedly independent Jeffersonian decision maker, but instead is heavily constrained in thought and action by the political economy (Hardt
1992; Mosco 1996). Also, a poststructuralist theory, such as my proposed
conflict discourse systems model, which puts discourse at the center of
things, can readily dispense with the cardboard cutout character of the
marketplace individual in the civic news scenario—or the critical theory
journalist and reader/viewer as "workers"—as an artifact of modernist
discourse, but it offers nothing satisfying to replace it.

What is missing from all of these approaches is the very real sense of
the individual that we all know from experience. That individual is a
generalization and attribution to others of the *I* that is always left over
from any attempt to define the *me,* as William James put it. It is not—
and cannot be—in any theory, but it is always hovering over theory and
provides a restraining voice in checking theoretical excesses. This sense
of the individual agent exists in our everyday understanding not as a
theory, but as a leftover feeling—not quite an idea—that is shaped in a
negative sense by what it is not. The problem is how to keep this sense
of the individual nearby while theorizing, because it is useful, necessary
in fact, as a reality check. It can survive theory and retain its beneficial
effects on problem solving. Theory is always on the structure side of the
actor/structure dichotomy, in other words, and can never capture the
individual—this can be taken as inherent in the nature of generaliz-
ing—and the space between discontinuous bodies of social theory is the
only place the agent can still be. Georg Simmel comments that "causal
determination of, and purposive actions by, the individual appear as two
sides of the same coin" (1955: 141), and splitting the coin will always
result in the same two surfaces, multiplied. The individual who acts and
is acted upon, it seems, is not an object, but it is a relationship between
the two sides of the theoretical coin. The analogy in language theory is
to Saussure's identification of the sign not as an object in itself, but as a
relationship between the signified and the signifier, or the structuralist
interpretation of the phoneme not as a sound, but a complex bundle of
relationships among a set of sounds in a specific language.

A Proposed News Theory Stereogram

I would like to suggest that if the analyst juxtaposes *agent internal* and
agent external structural theories—the psychological and the social—the
untheorized social agent cannot so easily be ignored and in fact re-

emerges at the center of the model. A multidimensional, nontheorizable sense of the human actor—as reader, editor, and so on—pops out for the theory surfing analyst like the three dimensional image that emerges from a stereogram. It is not real, anymore than the 3-D image is real, but it is more realistic than either of the organized bodies of theoretic spots and dots that generate it.

The two sides of the theoretical stereogram I propose are a psychodynamic theory of the individual reader/viewer's cognitive and psychological involvement with conflict narrative on the one hand, and a theory of the shared social, intersubjective discourse aspects of such narratives, on the other. Figure 6.1 represents a picture of this idea in terms of two kinds of space through which a news report—which is always a conflict narrative, as I have argued—moves: psychological space and social space. As Henri Lefebvre (1991) explains, social space is never just an empty location, but is always infused with time and energy. When the metaphor of space is employed in describing mental activity the element of energy carries over.

Psychological space is the product of the individual mind and imbued with psychic energy. Psychic energy is nothing mysterious here—just mental excitement. Entering psychological space, the news story evokes anxiety and threat reactions. This stimulation in itself may be pleasur-

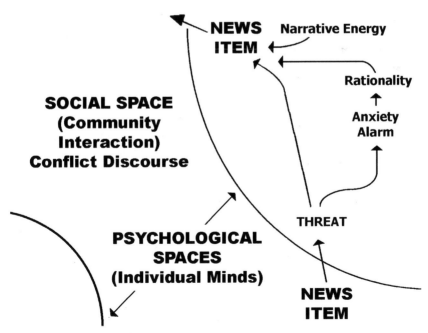

Figure 6.1 Energized News Spaces

able, if kept to tolerable levels, providing a desired spice of interest as it challenges the rational, problem solving aspect of the mind, the Freudian ego or secondary process. But just as the story acts on the mind, by stimulating it, it is also in turn acted upon, being invested with what one might call narrative energy, by which I mean that the individual is motivated to embellish, interpret, analyze, and, crucially, to talk about the story with others. A news story has "legs" in journalistic parlance to the extent that it absorbs narrative energy from its reader/viewers and is able to circulate in social space. A big story—one with major threat or conflict aspects—enters a communication community like a house afire, and it circulates widely and fast. It is able to do this, however, only by tapping the psychic energy of its hearers—who then become its tellers as well.

A news story cannot enter a communication community naked, however. In order to enter psychological spaces and interact with individual minds, giving alarm and receiving narrative energy, the story must be clothed in appropriate conventions of community discourse. At a threshold level, of course, it has to be in a language that is understood, if it is a story in words. And even pictures may be subject to certain conventions of communication, however widely shared or easily grasped they may be. At a more subtle, and therefore theoretically more important level, however, the story must be interpretable in terms of the specific value systems, theories of motivation, and social role scenarios that govern— or at least are recognized as potentially governing—communication within the community. It is at this level that a theory of discourse needs to be employed, and poststructuralism provides a good starting point because it recognizes that communication and power are inseparable. If a news story, such as the 1996 TWA aircrash, is cast in technological terms, the authority brought to bear—that is, the legitimate power to define what happened and determine what is to be done—is that of science and engineering. A powerful strand of the TWA aircrash coverage, especially right at the beginning of the extended coverage, concerned forensic testing to discover traces of explosives, the possible development of million dollar CAT scan machines to detect bombs in luggage, and so on. Along with other threads of the coverage, applied science provides a specific way of understanding, acting, and communicating with regard to the news event, and it reinforces—as it draws upon—the authority of scientists in our society. Seen in law and order terms, the same story implies a different hierarchy of authority in the process of defining the problem, determining facts, and deciding what to do. How the story is told has everything to do with who in society gets to exercise power with regard to the underlying conflict issue.

Theories of news discourse that look at the organization of language, knowledge, values, and communication among social roles as ways of life, as in British Cultural Studies approaches, have emphasized social control and have concerned themselves with domination. Typically, the poststructuralist discourse theorist has been concerned with the problem of how what he or she sees as a particularly problematic form of life such as capitalism or patriarchy, for example—identified as discourse in the socially extended sense of roles actually being played out and values enforced—can achieve and maintain dominance over more desired alternative ways of life in society. For the capitalist or the patriarchist, of course, such discourse dominance is not a problem, and the political impetus of the theory is muted. But clearly there is an empirical dimension as well, and discourse theory may be useful in exploring a variety of other kinds of problems encountered in describing and understanding the news act. For example, one might shift the emphasis of the analysis and try to account for the tendency toward a multiplicity of distinct discourses in news and look for types of interrelationships among them other than domination. At this point, agency becomes an issue because it is convenient to think and talk about forms of conflict discourse as if they were themselves some kind of rarefied, superorganic agents that shape news—selecting some aspects of events and ignoring others—in order to dominate or to seek alliances with one another in the process of extending their reach and influence. I as argued in chapter 4, this kind of talk strikes many people as at least highly implausible, and, in fact, it is actual nonsense if it pushes the idea of the real person completely off the theoretical page. But I think it is useful if counterbalanced by a psychological theory that explains how the individual is an essential part of the picture.

The Multiplicity of CDS and their Interactions

There is, as critical news theorists have noted, a tendency toward domination and attempted monopoly among conflict discourses in the news, but there is at least as strong a tendency toward diversity and complementarity (see Crawford and Hafsteinsson 1996). Such discourses are not created by or contained within the news media, but they are more like multiple conduits of narrative energy that weave in and among news items in the media, creating a sense of factual reality by relating different events to one another and giving them depth and dimensionality for the reader/viewer (Fig. 6.2).

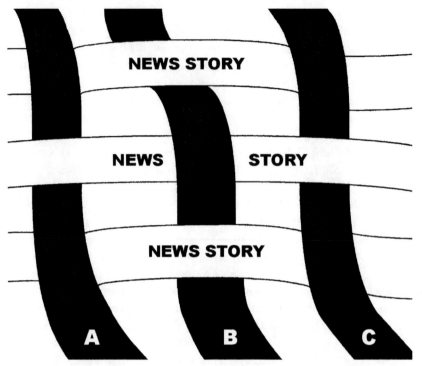

Figure 6.2 Conflict Discourses: A, B, C, etc., Weaving in and among News Stories

In chapter 4, I proposed a triad-based model of news that associated the relationship between reader and story with the fundamental issue of communication. From this perspective, it is clear that a vigorous conflict discourse system, packed with the potential narrative energy of a large communication community and supported by complementary forms of discourse that give it factual credibility, is one of the most powerful avenues of greased communication between the story and the reader/viewer. Figure 6.2 represents the multistranded nature of news discourse and suggests how distinct conflict discourses are related to news events in the media, feeding off of them, in a sense, to develop the narratives that elicit alarm and narrative energy from the communication community members who sustain the discourse in their verbal and nonverbal behavior. Typically, the news community member is not totally committed to a single CDS, but seeks to balance the mix to achieve a multidimensional sense of reality.

A local news story in the *Honolulu Advertiser* in July 1996, illustrates a typical—I think universal—intertwining of distinct conflict discourses with an event in the news media. That is to say, the intertwining is universal, although, as in this case, the nature and mixture of the discourses can be very local. The precipitating event was a serious and dramatic accident during the construction of an elevated freeway segment. It was serious in that it resulted in severe injuries to three workmen and also because it caused added delay and expense to an already controversial project. The event was dramatic in that it involved a 240-ton segment of the roadway, "larger than a tennis court," as one news story graphically put it, crashing to the ground with four construction workers on top of it. The first of the *Advertiser* stories, by staff writer Kim Murakawa under the headline "Four workers hurt when H-3 girders fall," ran the morning after the accident. As is typical of news stories, the first article explicitly stated a set of facts that would serve as the anchoring structure for the extended narrative that would eventually comprise an evolving series of stories, letters, and editorial comment. Murakawa (1996) established the "What, When, Who, and Why" of the event, and the opening paragraphs are studded with facts such as precise dimensions, ages, and time that establish the linkage of the news story to objective reality:

> A 40-foot by 120-foot section of concrete girders collapsed under the H-3 freeway yesterday, injuring four workers.
>
> Three of the four men—ages 40, 49, and 53—were in fair condition yesterday at the Queen's Medical Center. A 41-year-old was treated and released. The men were airlifted to Queen's by helicopter after the 8:30 a.m. accident.
>
> Police said yesterday they did not know what caused the collapse, which occurred just makai of a historic site known as Luakini Heiau in Halawa Valley. The site is mauka of H-1 near the city's xeriscape garden. (*The Honolulu Advertiser*, 28 July 1996, A21)

The specification of ages, places, times, and physical measurements establishes the essential grounding that will allow a variety of conflict discourses to link themselves with reality. The use of the directional terms "mauka" and "makai," Hawaiian expressions for "toward the uplands" and "toward the sea," which is common practice in everyday conversation in Hawai'i, gives the story a particularly local purchase. While a news story itself need not explicitly suggest every possible way of interpreting the event within competing frameworks, it often does introduce the most likely ways in which the event might be used to confirm the basis in reality of a conflict discourse system. The follow-on paragraphs in Murakawa's piece set up two very different interpretations of the accident:

> State officials, including the Occupational Safety and Health Division, were called to the site, where there have been deaths since construction began.
>
> A foreman died in 1990 and three workers were hurt when a 47 ton girder they stood on collapsed.
>
> A carpenter died in 1995 when a concrete wall, weighing several tons fell on him in a muddy stream. That accident resulted in the levying of a $5000 fine against the general contractor, Kiewet Pacific Co., for unsafe conditions at a work site in the North Halawa Valley.
>
> The project has been criticized by many native Hawaiians.
>
> "There's been numerous accidents in the course of this highway construction," said Mahealani Cypher, a Hawaiian researcher concerned about the treatment of significant religious sites in the area.
>
> "They have to be careful when they go into an area where it's filled with Hawaiian sites," she said yesterday. "They have been very disrespectful to these sites. They go right in and they bulldoze it before they have had proper consultation."
>
> Hugh Ono, state Highways Division administrator, said yesterday evening that he had not been informed of the accident and could not comment. Attempts to reach officials at Kiewet were not successful. (*The Honolulu Advertiser*, July 28, 1996, A21)

An accompanying photograph shows the broken roadway, and the caption under the photo is the quote, used in the body of the story, from Mahealani Cypher about there having been numerous accidents in the course of the highway project. Perhaps this photo caption tips the story toward an interpretation of the event as supernatural revenge, but the writer is careful to attribute that reading to a spokesperson, preserving the reporter's position of apparent neutrality. Using spokespersons for such purposes is traditional in US journalism (see Arno 1985), and the technique is so important in maintaining the objective, factual mood of the news story that the reporter in this story even mentions two other unsuccessful attempts to obtain alternate interpretations. As it stands, however, the story elaborates only the more unusual—for many, bizarre—conflict discourse system competing for the reader's allegiance. The reader is invited to believe that the reported incident confirms the reality—in real life events—of a system of identities and beliefs that posits revenge by ancestral Hawaiian spirits as a plausible cause of the accident. Two alternatives, which remain largely implicit in this story, are much more mainstream discourse systems that often support one another in the quest for readers' belief. Both start from the basic definition of the event as an industrial accident—not a paranormal, twilight zone phenomenon. References to worker safety, the government agency in charge of regulating the workplace, and previous fines paid by the contractor all point to an interpretation of the event as an instance of conflict between worker and management or, more abstractly, labor and capital. The other frame of reference and explanation system is that of science and engineering. Details about the weights, lengths, design details, and so on, invoke the basic conflict of humankind against the natural world and the role of technology in securing a human victory over nature. These two systems of thinking and talking about conflict—which might be labeled for present purposes the socialist and the scientific—are not always in agreement, but they come easily to an accommodation in explaining the underlying threat to the reader that makes this particular event news. And they contrast strikingly with the alternative, spiritualist definition. Science and social welfare discourse systems sometimes struggle against each other to define conflict situations and power relations, but they are united against the supernatural. Thus, the contest of discourse systems recognized by the reporter and editor lines up as pitting "worker versus management" and "human versus nature" on one side against "human versus supernatural forces" on the other, in depicting the basic news value. There may, of course, be other competing systems of explanation of which the journalists are not aware, but journalists are specialists in detecting such systems in their reading community. They know that among the readers, some few are firmly committed socially and psychologically to one or more of the three identified discourse systems; such readers think of themselves, and they are identified by others, as scientists, liberals, or spiritually attuned individuals. But most readers are not so committed; they are open to and might repeat in conversations with others—with greater or lesser conviction—the arguments and interpretations of all three systems. Getting the readers to talk about the story among themselves is the key problem for journalists. Once that part of the news process gets in gear, there will be demand for more articles about the same issue.

It is now Sunday morning and readers are leafing their way through the *Honolulu Advertiser/Star Bulletin* Sunday edition; the accident took place early on Saturday and the story begins its life as news today. Where will it go from here? Editors and reporters have to decide how to play it—which discourse systems or a mix of them will engage readers for a few more days. If they go with the supernatural revenge angle, ignoring the commonsense, dominant paradigm of science and welfare capitalism, will they begin to look like a supermarket tabloid filled with Elvis sightings and alien landing stories? On the other hand, is there any reader interest in the engineering, human versus nature angle? And given the local and national rightward drift of political discourse, will the exploitation of workers excite enough outrage—that is, generate enough narrative energy—to sell papers? As a point of potential methodology, I should mention that my analysis of the editors' decision-making process is merely conjectural—I am starting from the content of the stories and working backward. Clearly, analysis of actual conversations among the editors and reporters would be valuable—with the caveat that people are not always consciously aware of their own intuitive processes of decision making.

Somehow Hawaiian ancestral spirits win out, and the story continues on Tuesday with a large headline at the top of the first page, all the way across: "H-3 work halted after accident: Union wants construction site blessed again." Staff writers Greg Barrett and Jennifer Hong (1996) continue:

> Work on the H-3 freeway in Halawa stopped indefinitely yesterday, as teams of engineers began to investigate Saturday's mysterious collapse of concrete girders.
>
> There is no obvious evidence of why four 120-foot concrete beams collapsed, said Patrick Stinson, vice president of Kiewet Pacific Co., the general contractor for the Halawa portion of the freeway.
>
> "It makes me nervous—especially nervous of the unknown," said Stinson, looking at the long cracks running through the 240 ton concrete section lying in the grass and the mangled steel wiring poking through the remaining girders.
>
> Meanwhile, the 7,600-member Hawaii Carpenters Union wants construction on the freeway to be blessed again by a priest—complete with ti leaves and holy water.
>
> "We want a Hawaiian priest to bless that site," said union head Walter Kupau. "And we're suggesting they bless it on a monthly basis."
>
> Kupau, a 39-year veteran of construction in Hawaii, said he's not superstitious man—but there are some things that can't be explained by engineers. (*The Honolulu Advertiser,* 30 July 1996, A1–A2)

At this point in the article, the writers shift gears and begin to reinforce the factual, objective character of the story by referring again to
the accident itself, mentioning facts and numbers, such as "8:30 a.m.,"
"larger than a tennis court," "16-mile," "$1.37 billion," and "[t]hree re-
main hospitalized in fair condition at the Queen's Medical Center; one
was treated and released." After this brief excursus into factuality, the
story returns to the spiritual interpretation, although with both general and specific attribution to others, thereby avoiding commitment to
this explanation by the reporters themselves. They write, for example,
"[p]rojects such as H-3 that disturb sacred grounds are said by some to
incur supernatural wrath," and they then go on to quote two spokespersons for the spiritualist discourse system. The reporters do note, as
an unattributed fact, that during previous construction the project "has
been blessed many times by Hawaiian priests," which seems to challenge
the idea that a priestly blessing would be effective to prevent future accidents. John Keola Lake, identified as an expert in Hawaiian culture,
however, is quoted as observing that "[t]he [previous] blessings were
at different junctions—and after the fact," which explains their failure
to prevent this accident. The testimony of another spokesperson, Mark
Erwin, "a 45-year-old carpenter foreman on the project," counters another possible objection to the spiritual interpretation—namely, that
the accident was simply caused by unsafe working conditions. According to the article, Mr. Erwin "said Kiewet is 'by far' the safest contractor
he's worked with during his 25 years of construction." The authors close
with a direct quote from the foreman: "[i]t's a scary thing that happened—Hawai'i is a spiritual place and blessings never hurt."

At this point in the newspaper's coverage of the story the slant toward
the spiritualist discourse seems rather extreme, but a photograph on
the front page, where the story starts, emphasizes the mechanical nature of the incident by showing the girders—one still in place and the
others on the ground. While the story continues on the second page
with the spiritualist leaning headline, "H-3: Girder collapse a mystery,"
that page also features a large, very clearly set out graphic depicting the
engineering aspects of the accident, with a scale drawing of the entire
segment of the roadway including two close-up enlargement balloons
that show in exact detail how the girders were joined together. In other
words, the newspaper is providing material for a materialist as well as
a spiritualist interpretation, but it is clear that the editors think a realist story alone would not be enough to warrant much attention. The
editors are counting on the spiritualist angle to give the story narrative
energy in the community, and they are probably right to assume few
readers are going to spend their coffee breaks talking about details of

engineering. On the other hand, there is also a possibility that the readers will not be interested in talking about ghost stories either, with the result that the news item will die, and the paper will have wasted its time and injured its reputation.

Undaunted, the *Advertiser* editors move the story along, three days later, with a photograph about six inches square, inside a box on page A12 headed, "Troubled worksite blessed." The photo shows the late Rev. Abraham Akaka, who specialized in such blessings and was very well-known and respected in the community, standing on the "troubled" roadway segment. Wearing Christian vestments, he is gesturing in priestly fashion and appears to be speaking. The caption, in large boldface type, recounts the facts of the accident—sprinkling in plenty of numbers as a reality hook—and notes that although "[t]he controversial $1.5 billion, 16-mile project has been blessed several times in the past," the "7,600 member Carpenters Union asked for a new benediction after the most recent accident." It adds that "[c]ritics say that the roadway has been cut through land sacred to Native Hawaiians."

At this point, the cynical realist reader of the *Advertiser*, who is not even tempted to credit the supernatural interpretation of the accident, must begin to feel that whatever news value the story might have had has been exhausted and the paper is merely dealing with folklore and entertainment. The editors, however, have not given up, and in their next contribution they manage to strike a nerve of conflict in the community and deliver another jolt of narrative energy to the news item. On the following Sunday, August 4, they run another story about the accident on page one, with a color photo. The headline this time is, "Troubles on H-3 strengthen beliefs in power of supernatural wrath," and the photo shows Professor Lilikalā Kame'eleihiwa, of the then Center for Hawaiian Studies at the University of Hawai'i. A well-known advocate of Native Hawaiian sovereignty and passionate critic of the American cultural, religious, and political presence in Hawai'i, Professor Kame'eleihiwa's inclusion in the coverage makes the connection—heretofore only implicit—between the accident story and the most fundamental conflict issue in the state: Hawaiian Sovereignty. The photo by itself sets up Kame'eleihiwa as the antithesis of the Rev. Akaka, who was shown blessing the site a few days earlier. In his photograph, Mr. Akaka was on the on top of the roadway, while Professor Kame'eleihiwa is shown standing on the ground under it, as it looms overhead. He is wearing Christian vestments, chasuble and stole; she wears a Hawaiian robe and a long traditional lei of green maile leaves. He is bestowing a blessing on the freeway, and she, according to the text, is pronouncing a curse on it.

The article, written by Greg Barrett, provides a number of Hawaiian construction industry ghost stories as related by Glen Grant, who teaches American Studies at the University of Hawai'i and is identified in the article as a historian and author who has studied Hawaii's supernatural traditions for "25 years" (a quantifiable fact!). Grant tells of workers excavating a tunnel on the H-3 project who were terrified by a seven-foot-tall ghost in a *malo*, or loincloth, who "came right out of the rock" and floated toward them. An eerie detail was that "[h]e didn't have any feet." In another story attributed to Grant, workers setting enamel tiles in a tunnel were frightened by the sound of a traditional Hawaiian conch shell trumpet, which "came from a thick mist that crawled slowly through the tunnel and then dissipated." Other workers told Grant about seeing a bulldozer rise off the ground. The reporter also interviewed Walter Kupau, head of the Carpenters Union, about supernatural accidents during construction at the Hilton Hawaiian Village hotel in the 1960s. Kupau is quoted as saying that they had "150 accidents in the first 120 days on the project ... [g]uys were hit on the head with two by fours, stepping on nails, everything." The rate of accidents slowed, however, after the Rev. Akaka—using a kou-wood calabash that had once belonged to Kamehameha the Great, the revered late eighteenth-century warrior chief who unified the islands and established the Hawaiian monarchy—blessed the site.

Although the article is shot through with details that encourage the angry ancestral spirit interpretation of the conflict—including hoped-for miraculous effects of Kamehameha's calabash—the Rev. Akaka himself does not participate in that form of explanation. On the contrary, his own quoted comments represent an accommodation between religion and science that are typical of modernist Christianity. A large box, inserted at the top and center of the body of the story as continued on the second page, presents this quotation in large, boldface type: "You can't wave a ti leaf at them and guarantee safety. Blessings come when people connect with God like light bulbs connect with power." In the body of the story, Akaka is quoted indirectly as follows: "[a]ccidents, such as fallen freeways or bumps on the head are perhaps elements of self-fulfilling prophecy, Akaka said. Worried workers, he said, are not focused on their jobs."

This nod toward a possible accommodation between the materialist and spiritualist lines of discourse, however, is not the thrust of the article that will go on to generate narrative energy and get people in the community talking about the story. Instead, it is the dramatic contrast set up between the two prominent Native Hawaiian spokespersons,

Kame'eleihiwa, the activist professor and supporter of traditional Hawaiian religion, and Akaka, the then pastor emeritus of Kawaiahao Church, which is the premier traditional Hawaiian Protestant congregation in Honolulu. As elsewhere in Polynesia and the Pacific Islands generally (see Engelke and Tomlinson 2006), Christianity is well integrated into contemporary indigenous culture in Hawai'i. At the same time, traditional beliefs and reverence for ancestral presence are also highly respected. In terms of conflict discourse system analysis, one could say that the ways of understanding and dealing with conflict implied by the two systems of spirituality—Christian and Traditional—have developed a mutually reinforcing alliance, parallel to the mainstream accommodation between science and religion expressed in Rev. Akaka's attributed statement. The contrast that the news story's text plays upon, then, is complex rather than clear-cut within the readership community.

The reporter, Greg Barrett, seems to pull back slightly from the tabloid ghost stories with which he opens the piece when, in the fifth paragraph he comments, "[f]act or fiction, what appears to be folklore to some is serious religion to others," and he goes on to quote Kame'eleihiwa, who expresses anger over "the desecration of our sacred grounds" (*The Honolulu Advertiser*, 4 August 1996, A1–A2). At this point, the contrastive counterposition of the Rev. Akaka is introduced with a large boldface subheading, "Prayers for Safety." The text then continues:

> The Rev. Abraham Akaka, pastor emeritus of the Kawaiahao Church, prayed last week over the fallen section of freeway. As he has many other times, Akaka, 79, waved his 175-year-old calabash over troubled construction.
>
> He prayed for comfort of the injured and for safety, asking for blessings from above.
>
> "When you take the generations of people past, you don't know what you are walking on," he said last week. "Something God has made has turned to dust ... It is best to revere that dust at all times, at all places. Not just at graveyards."
>
> In 1990, when the H-3 paved on and around the ancient Kukuiokane heiau—one of the largest temples in Windward Oahu—Kame'eleihiwa was there to protest.
>
> She chanted and prayed and placed a curse on the highway.
>
> A team of highway engineers approached her, unfamiliar with the Hawaiian tongue. She stopped and said flatly, "I have just cursed your freeway. And I hope the worst happens to you." (*The Honolulu Advertiser*, 4 August 1996, A2)

Apparently confirming editorial judgment, these comments did ignite a surge of narrative energy in the community, turning the story that started out with the construction accident into a genuine news story—something that threatened the interests of enough members of the community to get them to talk about it. Evidence for the extra-textual vitality of the story is seen in a group of four letters to the editor, printed four days later, on August 8, under the subheading, "Associate professor's comment inappropriate." The letters actually include criticism of the H-3 project and the *Advertiser* as well as Kame'eleihiwa, about whom a 12-year-old letter writer says, "she blew her conch shell too loud this time!" (Ortiz 1996).

These letters set up the last large piece on the issue, which takes up a bit more than half of the op-ed page the following Sunday, August 11. Under the headline, "H-3 story: 'a great injustice'," there is a reaction essay signed by Professor Kame'eleihiwa, coupled with a large version of the photo, used earlier, of her standing under the H-3. The photo caption is: "Lilikalā Kame'eleihiwa chanting under the H-3 freeway: 'I have never wanted any innocent person to suffer ...'" In her op-ed article, Kame'eleihiwa attacks the newspaper and the reporter who wrote the August 4 story. She says that Barrett did "a great injustice" to her and to Hawaiian religion and used four comments—quoted out of context—from a two-hour interview. She goes on to explain several points about Hawaiian religion, emphasizing the idea that *hewa*, transgressions, are punished by angry, *akua*, ancestral gods. She recounts the interview as one in which she, as a Hawaiian woman with a duty to protect ancestral burials and sacred sites—"especially those dedicated to female Akua"—had great difficulty in getting the essential ideas across to Mr. Barrett, "who has just arrived in Hawaii," and who "writes from the bias of a non-Hawaiian and a devout Christian." Such a person, she argues, "cannot see the terrible affront caused by a Hawaiian Christian minister blessing an American military freeway that destroys sacred Hawaiian ancestral grounds." She writes:

> It is a sign of settler racism that the H-3 freeway, built to connect two bases of illegal occupying American military, will be opened with 100,000 people in a "fun" run over the bones of my ancestors.

> Hawaiians are powerless in this situation because we choose to renounce violence, but the hewa makes our hearts heavy, and it is pono [right] to pray for the end of such hewa. (*The Honolulu Advertiser*, 11 August 1996, B3)

She concludes with another strong criticism of the newspaper, which, she says, should hire a Hawaiian reporter to provide depth and understanding to Hawaiian issues. Until it does so, she states, "The *Advertiser* will continue to be a racist settler rag."

In response, the editors have placed a box to the right of the op-ed piece with the heading "Kame'eleihiwa transcript." In it, with an explanatory editor's note, are short segments of transcripts of the tape-recorded interview discussed in the op-ed piece, with the quotes that were used in the original article shown in bold type. In these sections of the transcript, Kame'eleihiwa explicitly rejects armed revolution not only because "we would never win," but also because "we really don't want to kill anybody," although she is grateful to the Akua for taking care of it.

The letters section on the same day includes a satirical attack on the *Advertiser* by Garry P. Smith of Ewa Beach, who writes in part:

> I must congratulate The Honolulu Advertiser on its routinely fine investigative reporting of "trouble on H-3." Rather than make the effort required to truly investigate what must be safety and engineering related accidents, The Advertiser lets the contractor and state off the hook by lending credence to the ghosts and goblins theory of construction accidents. (*The Honolulu Advertiser*, 11 August 1996, B3)

As if chastened by this rebuke—unlikely as that may actually be—the editors end this series of stories on the construction accident with an almost purely materialist, engineering oriented article on the front page the following Wednesday, August 14. The headline is "H-3 Girder collapse attributed to heat," and the story sets forth a mechanical, "thermal expansion" scenario in which hot weather caused one girder, which was temporarily constrained so that it could not expand length-wise, to buckle and roll over, knocking the other three off as it did so. This final article provides an almost operatic denouement in which the characters come forward to put the conflict issue to rest. The reporter is again Kim Murakawa, who wrote the first story and introduced the "mystery" theme. Kiewet Pacific, the contractor, is absolved of blame—poor design or workmanship are "ruled out"—and the state and the contractor assure the public that the freeway will be safe when completed. Walter Kupau, the union leader, "said that the expansion theory sounded reasonable and that the extra braces were sufficient to ensure workers' safety." The state Transportation Director, Kazu Hayashida, is quoted as saying "that the state has 'accepted Kiewet's theory that thermal expansion of one of the girders' caused the collapse." It is reported that work on the freeway has resumed, and the last sentence is: "[t]he injured workers have been released from the hospital." The only thing missing is a statement from the seven-foot floating ghost also agreeing with the thermal expansion theory.

What I have called the supernatural revenge discourse—and I choose this somewhat slighting term rather than, say, "spiritual" to indicate the tone of the articles—in this series of newspaper articles and letters illustrates something of the complexity and fluidity of conflict discourse systems in general. The way this theme was handled by reporters indicates that the target audience might have included many readers who found it engaging at the superficial level of colorful folklore or "chickenskin" local ghost stories. The Civic news media grade card I proposed earlier, based on modernist values and the marketplace of ideas model of journalism, would record a low grade for this series. As one critical letter writer put it, it put forward a "ghosts and goblins" theory that obscured the serious issues. In terms of the momentous re-ordering of the hierarchy of cultural identities taking place in Hawai'i, however, the story takes on considerable gravity. In the intervention of Professor Kame'eleihiwa, one sees the unexpected depth of this supernatural discourse system and its associated identities—including the ancestral akua—from the perspective of indigenous religion and cultural identity in the context of the dominating issue of Hawaiian sovereignty. Many readers no doubt dabbled at the surface, perhaps attracted by the sacred dimensions of the talk but also repelled from it by the formidable defenses of the Enlightenment alliance of "reasonable" ways to talk about the events, while others had much deeper commitments to the spiritual CDS. For those members of the news community, whose numbers wax and wane partly in response to news media content, this way of framing and talking about conflicts can rise almost to the level of a total form of life, coloring every aspect of daily existence. Neglecting these deeply felt forms of conflict discourse, or failing to accord them due respect in political analysis, distorts the complex, living reality of the news community—a reality that is reflected, however, in news media narratives.

A Brutal Crime as a Message: But to Whom? From Whom?

The variety of distinct conflict management—or control communication—discourses that the news media orchestrate and bring to bear upon a particular conflict related event is richly illustrated by a very big news episode from the late 1980s in New York City. On the evening of 19 April 1989, a group of teenagers savagely beat and raped a woman jogger in Central Park. That is to say, these were the facts as taken in the "news reality" of the time. About thirteen years later, the story reemerged with a different focus—the uncertainty of justice—and different facts. But at the time, the attackers were identified in news accounts as teenage male African- and Hispanic-Americans from East Harlem, while the jogger was a 28-year-old European-American investment banker. Following an expectable pattern, newspapers in the city and elsewhere treated the incident as a message (see Arno 1985: 51–52). In addition to the who, what, where, and so on, of recognized "objective" reporting, the immediate questions posed by the news media were: what did it mean, who was sending the message, to whom was it addressed, and what should the answer be?

Over the course of succeeding weeks, the *New York Times* ran story after story on what came to be known as the jogger rape case. The full range of newspaper treatments, from "straight" news stories to specialized, in-depth analytical pieces, editorials, op-ed commentary, letters to the editors, and even advocacy advertisements were part of the multifaceted attempt to portray and interpret the event. Citing experts in many fields, stories in the *Times* presented the assault alternatively as a statement about relations between rich and poor, African/Hispanic and European-Americans, young and old, or male and female. Well-developed control discourses were invoked, including sociology, political science, anthropology, economics, law, feminism, traditionalist morality, and media studies.

For example, in the first front page story on the incident (Pitt 1989a) the writer sets out the facts of the case and then immediately poses the question of the meaning of the message. The story—initiating a theme that dominates the entire news episode—suggests that the meaning is unknown; it is a puzzle to be worked out. Perhaps the most obvious and literal way to start the search for meaning would be to inquire into the intentions of the attackers themselves, and they are quoted as saying that they were engaged in "wilding."

Of course, such a statement cannot in itself constitute a satisfactory answer to the problem of interpretation. New York City Chief of Detectives Robert Corangelo, interviewed in the story, says that, "it's not a term [wilding] that we in the police have heard before." He is cited as going on to touch on and discount several of what have come to be standard interpretive frameworks for decoding violent crimes as statements, indicating that the attack was not related to money, race, drugs or alcohol. "It's difficult to explain," he says, pointing out that the attackers had no criminal records, and stating that, "we don't see any evidence of drug use here." Furthermore, there was no evidence of a leader. In other words, the *sender identities* of *criminal, drug addict,* and *gang member* are not available to provide an easy answer to the question of meaning. It would seem from subsequent stories that the very meaninglessness of the crime, coupled with its extreme sadistic violence, accounted in large measure for the intense coverage it received. The extended series of articles constitutes a search for meaning much more than just a search for facts. A puzzle of this kind and magnitude in the news is an irresistible target for every conflict discourse system in the community. A week after the initial story setting out the preliminary facts of the case, the *New York Times* ran a piece headed, "New Yorkers Wrestle With a Crime: Whatever Role Race Had in Park Attack, It's Topic No. 1," that directly recognizes the opportunities that the case presents for interpretation by readers (Kaufman 1989).

A few days after the initial reports, a reporter (Marriott 1989) found people in the street in East Harlem who provided a sociological/psychological frame of interpretation. One argued that violent crime is a "function of hopelessness" among African-American youths. A group standing outside of a church are cited as saying that the pressures of life in the ghetto are great for young people and "some fall into despair and then into crime." If the event were to be construed in racial terms, the interviewees feared, it would "ignite smoldering racial tensions" in the city. In other words, they were afraid that the incident would be read by European-Americans in the city as an anti-white message, authored by "blacks" in general, and that it would be answered in kind with violence against African-Americans. This why the group outside of the church were concerned with advancing their socioeconomic and psychological gloss. As a sort of social science hybrid of conflict discourses, the proffered way of talking about the attack gives it meaning and suggests a way to manage the conflict it represents. The appropriate "answer" to the statement within the socioeconomic frame of interpretation would be an attempt to deal with economic and psychological problems through social programs—"better housing, education, and job opportunities," as the reporter puts it—rather than through counter-violence. But the continuing theme of difficulty in understanding the message is expressed by a minister who is quoted at the end of the story as saying that, "there is no simple set of reasons to explain why this happened."

Editorials and op-ed commentary were heavily employed by the *New York Times* in the search for meaning, and in typical journalistic fashion, that search took the form of allowing spokespersons to apply a wide range of conflict discourses. For example, a feminist, poststructuralist perspective is offered by an op-ed author (Chace 1989) who writes that, "nobody has convinced me that this is a racially motivated crime, and I don't think 'socio-economic crime' is helpful either. I think it has to do with fear of The Other." The writer goes on to say that "nobody is more Other to the adolescent male than a girl. She is a permanent, symbolic and real stranger." Elizabeth Holtzman (1989), in an op-ed piece appearing later in the extended coverage episode, also refers to the gender issue, and her essay illustrates an important discourse function of media news in that it combines several forms of institutionalized conflict communication, allowing them to reinforce one another. Holtzman brings feminism together with legal theory and mass media effects research by arguing that both law and television, as social practices, reflect the "distorted thinking about violence and gender" prevailing in society.

Another op-ed writer, who works with troubled adolescents and adults in the South Bronx, reports the social psychological perspectives that emerged from a group discussion among her clients, whose backgrounds were similar to—but in some cases more disadvantaged than—those of the attackers. One observed that although some of the attackers were from stable middle class families, "they still had a wolf in their belly. It's not a hunger for food. They are hungry for acceptance. They're raging because they are not accepted." The consensus of the group was that their worst deprivation is "being treated as outcasts in a society that calls itself democratic and egalitarian" (Sturz 1989).

Political analyst Tom Wicker (1989) explored the meaning of the crime for the New York mayoral election. Despite the fact that the crime does not lend itself to easy interpretation or stereotyping—because the standard political issues of drugs, the criminal justice system, and poverty were not obviously salient, given the facts—Wicker worried that the crime would be dragged into the campaign through racial demagoguery. He cited the intervention of financier and self-promotionist Donald Trump, who had placed full-page advertisements in the New York papers to vent his angry reactions.

The Trump ads raise what might be called a "law and order" control discourse, which is distinct from legal discourse. While Trump is concerned with punishing social deviants through the mechanism of law enforcement, other voices in the extended news episode place the event in context of legal procedure, commenting, for example, on the implications of the extensive press coverage for the possibility of a fair trial of the persons accused of the crime and the effects of publicity on police investigations (Pitt 1989b). Other stories followed the legal procedures and arguments at the early stages of the criminal justice process, such as bail hearings (Sullivan 1989).

Social/cultural anthropology as a conflict communication discourse was introduced in several interview stories. For example, a functionalist explanation asserted that the "attack may have emerged from several underlying currents in the community" (Kolata 1989). Philippe Bourgois, an anthropologist doing fieldwork in East Harlem, is reported as saying that the drug economy had shifted power to the teenagers in the community. It is argued that young men have to prove that they can be brutal in order to gain respect within the group. In the same story, another anthropologist, Ansley Hamid, provides a more cognitive approach in saying that "models of behavior come from the drug world" for the young men, even though the attackers may not have been on drugs. In the same "cultural" vein, rap music is cited as focusing on power and violence.

Although not mentioned in the Kolata article, the misogynist character of rap music has been widely commented upon, which in the present context—given the character of this particular case—is an example of the mutual reinforcement of two forms of conflict discourse: feminism and cultural anthropology.

Many other interwoven conflict communication discourse systems—some overt and others not—can be drawn from the present case, and not all can be discussed or even identified in this cursory account, but communication studies represents a particularly salient (given the topic of this book) example. In an interview article on May 2 (Goodman 1989), the reporter compares and contrasts the views of media scholars George Comstock, Neil Postman, George Gerbner, and Mark Crispin Miller. The specific question posed by the interviewer is the role of television in the attack. Postman and Gerbner express caution in assigning causal roles, suggesting that there is a critical lack of evidence for a connection between television and this particular crime. While they do not disagree entirely, Miller and Comstock are willing to state that they find such a connection entirely plausible. Apropos of this chapter, Gerbner is reported as taking the opportunity to criticize the *news* about the attack, characterizing it as catering to European-American middle class fear and exaggerating the real significance of the event in terms of the likelihood of the news consumers' being similarly victimized.

In terms of conflict management, the jogger rape case illustrates the characteristic function of news in turning a specific instance of conflict into a representation that bears on larger scale, societal conflict. The case also illustrates the way distinct forms of control communication are brought together, either as complementary or as alternative forms, within an extended news coverage episode encompassing many stories and other forms of commentary and also within the particular story.

Old News as History

When the jogger rape case resurfaced in October 2002, it was the same case—with some new facts added and some old facts discredited—but it was an entirely different news story (Dwyer 2002). A serial rapist, in prison for other crimes, confessed that he had committed the brutal Central Park rape, and he claimed that he had acted alone. DNA evidence corroborated his claim of participation, although it could not establish that he was the only attacker. Attorneys for the men who had been convicted of the crime—who had all by this time finished serving their sentences—demanded their exoneration. Prosecutors were granted time to go over the evidence from the 1989 trial, but they were able to find little support for the idea that the then teenagers had joined with the serial rapist in committing the crime. The convictions were reversed 19 December 2002 (Saulny 2002).

When old news returns to the media, it does so as history, not news. The return story was big news, but nothing like the original. Still, the exoneration story had several powerful inter-textual associations with ongoing contemporaneous themes in the news. A story about the uncertainty of justice is attractive to many conflict discourse systems in the news community, and its status as objective reality is enhanced by other stories in the news about, for example, the use of DNA evidence to overturn unjust convictions. People who are wrongfully convicted and sentenced to long prison terms or even to death are easily seen as the victims of a powerful and dangerous government. At the same time, the victim of crime is denied justice when the real criminal, in this case the serial rapist, is allowed to escape, and the rest of the community is put in peril of further attacks. Therefore both anti-government, libertarian discourse and pro-government law and order discourses found dramatic confirmation in the new stories. Also, in this story, the serial rapist confessed to having committed a similar rape two days before the April 19 crime, and he went on to commit other, particularly heinous assaults afterward. Investigators from different units had failed to put the information together that would have suggested a more fruitful search for the real culprit. From this perspective, government is too weak and inefficient to protect its citizens, and the news universe in 2002 included 9/11 stories about law enforcement agencies failing to coordinate information and letting perpetrators fall through the cracks. These inter-textual associations—DNA testing/unjust convictions, failure of communication among law enforcement agencies—among many current news stories gives further purchase to each of them as reality hooks for conflict discourse systems.

In chapter 3, I mentioned my stumbling when a colleague asked me how, if my theory of news were correct, one could find an implied threat in the headline "Man Walks on Moon." The threat was hard to see at first because when I thought of that story, it was as a part of history, and as history it lacked the essential elements of news. The news process not only evokes alarm, it is happening in the present, not the past. In context of the then present—the news present—the story "American Walks on the Moon" was saturated with the cold war threat. Of course, the valence of the story was different for the proponents of the United States and the Soviet Union, but the underlying energy was from the same threatening source. The original jogger rape story is still powerfully affecting, but in a different way than when it was news. In the introduction to this book, I argued that time, in the sense of the distinction between past, present, and future, is crucial to a theory of the news process. Miyazaki is concerned in *The Method of Hope* to create a methodological answer to the puzzle of dealing with the incongruity between the orientation to the past in academic knowledge systems and the orientation to the not yet realized future in the phenomenon of hope, and, crucially, he includes the active researcher in the picture by stressing method rather than theory. In contrast to hope, news is oriented to the present, and that presents another incongruity that demands a different methodological solution. Pursuing an analysis that combines an approach to news as narrative in a news community organized in terms of powerful, interacting systems of conflict discourse with news as media text represents a useful avenue of research.

Psychic Energy and Discourse Energy: A Freudian Perspective

What does it mean to say that a form of conflict discourse is powerful in society? The question must be approached, as I suggested in my methodological stereogram argument, from two interdependent levels of analysis, social and psychological. In terms of social analysis, a discourse is powerful if it is employed by people in powerful social positions to talk about and guide action with respect to conflicts. This could mean either that a power elite within a society or, in more democratic setting, a large number of nonelite members participate in that way of understanding and acting in regard to conflicts. Power, in the sense of Foucault's force relations distributed throughout myriad arenas of social interaction, can be discursively concentrated through hierarchical recursive links to elite social positions of authority, including in some societal settings reifications of public opinion. But structural configurations in social relations can only operate upon—channel, concentrate, or diffuse—energy from another level, having no endogenous source. Discourse energy is a reflection or appropriation of psychic energy, which has its source in the individual social actor. And, at the psychological level, a discourse form is powerful in proportion to how passionately it is held and asserted.

My argument is that news is in essence a nexus between the discourse dynamics observable in social space—the hegemonic waxings and wanings of conflict discourses, their competitive struggles and coalitions—and the psychic energy of the human actor that is the ultimate force that, aggregated, energizes the system. The attachment of psychic energy to, and concentration within, socially held discourses is a kind of discourse cathexis that converts psychic energy to discourse energy and distributes it in social space. *Cathexis* is Dr. Sigmund Freud's term for the process by which fundamental psychic energy is attached to objects or mental processes, and I think it is a useful idea in communication theory. Whether Freud's theories of psychodynamic processes have any therapeutic value or not may be an open question, but they can be read as theories of communication as much as of medical treatment. In his most important contribution to language and communication theory, *The Interpretation of Dreams,* Freud attributes psychic energy exclusively to the primary process, which he sometimes referred to as the *id,* and the primary process is defined as a pre-language form of representation in which mental images stand for—but are not rationally differentiated from—external reality. The secondary process, which Freud called the *ego* in other theoretical contexts, is the form of communication deployed as rationality, problem solving, and language. Freudian psychodynamics, then, is fundamentally based on the interaction of two forms of communication. The secondary process develops in response to the practical necessity of recognizing that an external reality exists and that it must be dealt with intelligently in order to quell the urgent needs that are felt—that is, psychically energized—at the level of the primary process. Narrative pleasure, as I have argued elsewhere (Arno 1993), can be understood as the reduction of tension, alarm, and fear, which are intensely, at times painfully, felt surges of psychic energy, by investing them in language. Here, the conflict character of news is seen to be essential to the process. News as an alarming report—a threat to individual interests—evokes a psychological tension that, according to Freud's pleasure principle, the person will seek to diminish. Narrative pleasure theory explains the motivation for the individual to place the highly cathected narrative unit—a scary news item—into an articulated form of discourse. The discourse, being a semantic system of interrelated elements of meaning and explanation, provides pathways for the distribution and consequent flattening out of the spikes of psychic/discourse tension produced by alarming news. This flattening out or bleeding off process, in that it reduces the psychological tension attached to the specific news event, is the mechanism of narrative pleasure motivating the news reader.

To avoid the fallacy of psychological reductionism, it is necessary to recognize that discourse energy, although it is ultimately derived from psychic energy, is *not* psychic energy. It is a force in its own right, at the Durkheimian level of social fact, with its own unique characteristics, and as such discourse energy has powerful effects upon psychic energy—the influence is far from being one-way. Part of the power of a form of conflict discourse is that it generates threats, which create psychological tension, as well as provide an avenue of release or resolution. If the cycle were as simple as that, however, the system would begin to wind down, losing both psychic and discourse energy. But historical events, capable of being encoded in various conflict communication discourses, provide needed impetus. For news, current events constitute the standing reserve in an economy of meaning, a renewable resource to be harvested as needed.

To take the jogger rape case again as an example, the description in words and especially in pictures of the brutal physical facts provides the raw energy of threat and fear. At the level of the primary process, the images are *real*, and evoke real time fear. The city resident easily imagines herself or himself as a potential victim and seeks the partial relief of an explanation. Among the many proffered lines of discourse, feminism is one that is plausible to many. It explains the attack as related ultimately to the institutionalized devaluation and domination of women. The reader who becomes a participant in the feminist control communication discourse—by voicing the categories, values, and goals of feminism as a way of explaining to oneself and to others the instant conflict event—now sees as much more salient a variety of other stories that otherwise might have been ignored. The discourse, having gained ground in the one news episode, now serves to elevate the news value of stories of spousal abuse or sexual harassment in the workplace, for example. The same dynamic is at work in each of the conflict communication discourses participating in news. Placing a news story threat into a conflict discourse frame does not solve the problem for the individual reader, but it may raise the hope of a possible solution. Merely recognizing and understanding the nature and origins of a threat immediately enables prediction and strategies of avoidance.

The psychodynamic system of threat and the discourse dynamic system of news circulation can be seen to be articulated by the mirror image relationship of their structures. The human actor needs to reduce the intense, painful tension of fear associated with a report in order to engage in rational problem solving without the distortion of excessive subjectivity. The raw fear evoked by the report of a brutal and physically proximate attack might lead to a wildly irrational or even dangerous response unless the report is embedded in a narrative frame that explains it in rational terms. Placing the reported threat in discourse context objectifies it and cools it off. But in the realm of social space occupied by discourse dynamics, the problem is not to dissipate energy, but to capture and concentrate it. Relatively innocuous stories with virtually no news value for the individual can be invested with threat by a conflict discourse frame, creating them as actual news and providing material for rational problem solving. A sensational news story focuses the energy of threat among the community. Each form of discourse tries to incorporate such a case within its own system of explanation because just as cathected psychic energy drains off into language, making more manageable the too-hot-to-handle-rationally cognition for the individual, the aggregated energy of threat surges into the discourse as individuals talk about the news story within specific frameworks of meaning, energizing the narratives within the social parallel in the news process. Talking about—and in the process explaining to oneself—anxiety may not have any effect on actual mental illness, but it does have an effect on the balance of normal mental states and their adjustment to external reality. Talking about scary news helps, and the total news process represents a communication cure to communication problems. In terms of the model of the news act presented in chapter 3, the event/reader side of the news triad foregrounds the issue of meaning, which is just as much a part of the total news process as truth (the correspondence between event and story from the reader's socially ascribed perspective) and communication (the reader's ability to understand the report as presented). Much of this definition of meaning, as I have argued, takes place off of the page, as news consumers discuss the story among themselves. But the meaning dimension is also explicitly addressed in what journalists refer to as *opinion* or *interpretation,* strictly distinguished from news and labeled as op-ed, editorial, and columnist text. In certain kinds of news—for example, a story about new legislation concerning personal bankruptcy—the news consumer may have little or no response until he or she reads what *New York Times* columnist and Princeton economics professor Paul Krugman has to say about it. So can one say that news and opinion are categorically different and independent? In terms of the total news process, meaning, stimulated by opinion talk and interpretation on and off the page, is a very central part of the news.

In the following chapter, I will explore further the event/reader leg of the news triad, approaching it from the intersubjective perspective of language philosophy rather than as a psychological question. My question is how news as a speech genre, a defined way of talking, manages to influence action—to move people to act in a specific way with regard to the issue reported on. After all, generally accepted news ideology insists that news is about what happened—what is—not what ought to be. Speech genres aimed at directing people's actions—telling them what they ought to do—are better identified as rules and policy talk. My argument is that rules and policy talk are inextricably embedded in straight forward objective description, a broad speech genre I will identify as *reportage,* taken to include not only journalism, but ethnography and the paraethnography of specialist discourses, such as the statement of facts by judges and legislators. A simple statement of fact, in the context of political or legal talk, has considerable power to influence action because it, as the core of policy talk, fleshes out the universe of application within which rules govern.

CHAPTER 7

Policy Talk

In Law, on the Street, and on Television

> Sing, goddess, the anger of Peleus' son Achilleus …
> —Homer, *The Iliad* (Richard Lattimore's translation)

Perhaps the most fundamental and longest debated issue in understanding communication about conflict in all of its forms is the relationship of *is* to *ought*. In legal cases, legislative processes, journalism, and in empirical social sciences, the rules, values, and goals that are invoked to manage conflicts are grounded in descriptive representations of social reality. A rule- or value-based statement of what people ought to do in conflict management discourse must, to make sense, be validated by actual social experience. While the *ought* of rule application may not be explicit in self-consciously objective, unbiased journalism or ethnography, straight description evokes a social reality, and goals and values are always part of social life. Rule or policy talk can then draw explicitly on the values and goals embedded in that reality.

Clearly, the path from *is* to *ought*, and from *ought* to *must*, runs through the terrain of discourse. That is, the movement takes place not just through language *per se*, but language employed in social, cultural, and political context. The classic problem of tracing that path continues to be important in the philosophy of morality and ethics, and the work of contemporary moral philosophers like Hilary Putnam (2002, 2004) suggests an affinity between philosophical pragmatism and discursive practice theory in mounting a fresh attack on the issue. David Hume's classic dichotomy of fact and sentiment posits an unbridgeable gap between the two, and Hume's logical positivist followers elaborated the idea in their efforts to insulate science from metaphysical "nonsense." In jurisprudence, Hans Kelsen attempted to construct a strictly formal, "pure theory" of law independent of the ideas of justice or ultimate values that are grounded in social experience (Kelsen 1967). Putnam, to the contrary, argues that in ordinary social life—and even in science—descriptions of fact and assertions of both ethical and aesthetic rules are densely entangled. How a discursive community proceeds from fact to obligation to law is central to the development of an emerging anthropology of policy (see e.g., Shore and Wright 1997), and discriminating between *rule* and *policy* as forms of talk is a challenging but useful step in addressing the problem. A third form of talk that I refer to as *reportage*—but in a broad rather than a narrow, disciplinary sense—is also implicated in understanding, to paraphrase Greg Urban (2001) again, how rules move through the world. Investigating rule, policy, and reportage as interlinked speech genres contributes to the broader study of the ideology of text and the ubiquitous metadiscursive practices that linguistic anthropologists Michael Silverstein and Greg Urban identify as *entextualization* and *co(n)textualization*—the extraction of a discursive segment from its context in ongoing social activity, the production of that segment as autonomous text, and the reinsertion of text into social contexts and co-texts with important cultural consequences (Silverstein and Urban 1996). Here again, law, whether in the context of a formal legal system or its functional analogs often studied by anthropologists in small-scale communities, offers a clear-cut example. The actual or hoped for facts of social reality are entextualized as legislative rule statements, co-textualized as part of code, and contextualized at sites of enforcement in ongoing social process. Journalism also entextualizes social life, turning reported news events into verbally formulated stories that reenter the life of the news community when the stories are read and talked about. Seen from this perspective, rule, policy, and reportage comprise a complex discursive unit of elemental significance in social ordering.

Both Mikhail Bakhtin (1986) and J.L. Austin (1975) make important contributions to the taxonomy of talk, and linking their theories suggests a way of understanding the relationship between rule and policy at the level of utterance rather than language. Austin's distinction between constative and performative utterances affords an approach both to the difference between and the essential dualism of rule and policy talk, while Bakhtin's dialogic perspective and his linkage of primary and secondary speech genres suggests a research program that connects policy/rule talk in everyday conversation, televised news, and legislative text. Further distinguishing, within the domain of policy, between insider and outsider addressed talk posits an expanded category of *reportage* that encompasses a variety of ways in which the general public, addressed individually or en masse, is brought into the rule/policy process. The distinction I am proposing is roughly this: insider policy talk is framed as "this is the policy," while reportage says, less reflectively, "this is the social reality that is the context of a rule." The one genre more openly evokes the entextualizing rule formation history of the performative reality, the other foregrounds the hoped for contextualizing aspect of application.

The Taxonomy of Talk: Rule, Policy, and Reportage

The rule, as a generic category, has received massive attention in anthropology, language philosophy, and jurisprudence. In his *Rules and the Emergence of Society*, Meyer Fortes argues that "the capacity and the need to have, to make, and to enforce rules are of cardinal importance for human social existence," a fact, he says, that has been well-known to, and much commented on by, "philosophers, scientists, moralists, men of affairs, as well as creative writers and artists throughout recorded history" (1983: 6). Ludwig Wittgenstein's discussion of rules and language in his *Philosophical Investigations* (1958) has inspired a lively literature of commentary in language philosophy about the social and cognitive nature of rules (e.g., Kripke 1982; Werhane 1992), and in jurisprudence H.L.A. Hart explains the nature of law in terms of primary rules governing social behavior and secondary rules governing the ways that rules legitimately become law (e.g., Hart 1961). These and many other writers in many other fields of social inquiry have investigated the basic phenomenon of the rule as a crosscutting constituent of social order that spans cultural differences and operates continuously on a scale of complexity from children's games, to the state, to world systems. *Policy,* on the other hand, while constantly talked about in public affairs and daily life, has not been so thoroughly analyzed, and the relationship between policy and rule is confusing. The confusion of terms is particularly intractable because at times the distinction between policy or rule as ideational or as a form of communication is not clearly drawn. When both are viewed as forms of discursive practice, that is, as dialogically linked instances of communicative interaction, policy and rule can be more clearly understood as distinct objects of study. Furthermore, the generalized speech genre of reportage can be understood by examining the interrelationships among the three kinds of talk—rule, policy, and reportage—at varying levels of generic complexity from everyday conversation to elaborated cultural forms mediated by print or electronic media, a contrast that Mikhail Bakhtin (1986) draws between primary and secondary speech genres. In default of a cover term in general use,

I am using *reportage* in its most basic sense as empirically based description of social reality that is addressed, often by way of print or broadcast media, to a wide audience outside the core process that produces the description. In this sense, for example, journalism and academic ethnography are related as forms of description grounded in fact and addressed to the public. Thus, policy talk can be seen as an overarching general category term that includes insider/outsider varieties when policy is contrasted with reportage.

In *The Problem of Speech Genres*, Bakhtin argues that the *utterance*, not the sentence, should be taken as the fundamental object of analysis in the study of discursive practices. This is an important definitional move because it focuses on language in use and not as an abstract system. An utterance is an empirical event that has an author, an audience, and imbricating contexts—both physical and notional—that frame intent or purpose. An utterance need not be a complete sentence, and it might even consist of a single word. Or, heading in the other direction on a scale of complexity, it might be a paragraph, a treatise, or a whole set of books. What marks an utterance as a unit is the speaker's turn in a dialogic sequence; it starts when the speaker addresses others in dialog and ends with the speaker's final *dixit*, "I have spoken," however expressed (Bakhtin 1986). As in any systematic study of a complex phenomenon, questions of taxonomy follow—what are the kinds of utterances that matter, how can they be identified, and how are they interrelated both in processual and in static, descriptive terms? Bakhtin suggests, consistent with his roots in literary criticism, that differences in thematic content, style, and compositional structure can be used to sort utterances into "*relatively stable types*" that "we may call *speech genres*" (1986: 60).

For Bakhtin, "language enters life through concrete utterances (which manifest language) and life enters language through concrete utterances as well" (1986: 63). "Primary" speech genres, which are the building blocks of "unmediated speech communication" such as the back and forth rejoinders of natural conversation, are "absorbed and digested" by "secondary" speech genres that "arise in more complex and comparatively highly developed and organized cultural communication (primarily written) that is artistic, scientific, sociopolitical, and so on" (Bakhtin 1986: 62). This primary/secondary distinction is important because it frames the theoretical linkage between, for example, the policy talk between a Norwegian bedside nurse and his or her patient, or between a nurse and a doctor, and the official policy documents of the hospital or the state regulatory agency (Hansen 1997). Each utterance must be understood in terms of an entire range of thematically interlinked utterances.

Bakhtin insists that the difference between primary and secondary utterances is to be "understood not as a functional difference" (1986: 61), meaning that a shared function can link the two. And indeed, Bakhtin sees tracing the linkages between primary and secondary utterances as essential to understanding speech genres. Examples of the two types that Bakhtin offers divide between face-to-face conversational rejoinders in everyday life as primary, and mediated cultural forms like novels and scientific treatises as secondary. Today, we could well add television genres, such as news, to the latter category. A major difference, then, is in the dimension of *addressivity*, which Bakhtin identifies as "an essential (constitutive) marker of the utterance," namely, "its quality of being addressed to someone" (1986: 95). Addressivity is far more complex, however, than a relationship between a speaker and his or her intended, present audience. Utterances, by definition, are linked in dialogic sequences that range freely through time and space, so that a televised press conference, for example, is attuned to everyday conversations as well as to legislative texts, past and future, through empirical chains of discursive events that are thematically linked.

J.L. Austin approaches the problem of speech genres from another direction, but his work can be seen to dovetail with Bakhtin's. As Dupré notes about classification in general, there is never any "uniquely best classification," because "classifications are good or bad for particular purposes, and different purposes will motivate different classifications" (2006: 30). Austin's project is to develop a classification of utterances based on function—a starting point that is orthogonal to Bakhtin's. In his *How to Do Things with Words* (1975), Austin begins by distinguishing two categories of utterance, *constative* and *performative*. Constative utterances refer to a reality outside of language and can be said by some criterion or another to be true or false. The other genus, the performative, establishes the reality that it speaks, and rather than being true or false, can be said to succeed or fail to accomplish what it attempts to do. As Austin points out, citing conversations with his friend and colleague H.L.A. Hart (Austin 1975: 7n1; and see MacCormick 1981), the law has a long tradition of recognizing the performative or "operative" utterance as establishing, in and by its own necessary pronouncement, the social reality of legal rights and duties. At law, performative utterances can sometimes be implied in fact—that is, accomplished by conduct other than speaking—a doctrine of interpretation that Austin sees as suggesting a broader relationship between performativity and ritual.

Along with establishing the performative as a distinct form of utterance, Austin's major contribution to the taxonomy of speech genres is his seminal discussion of the illocutionary act. To recapitulate the discussion of Austin's theory in chapter 2, all utterances, including constatives and performatives, have three kinds of force as acts, *locutionary, illocutionary,* and *perlocutionary.* The locutionary is simply the act of producing a properly formed, meaningful utterance, and the perlocutionary force is the effect of the utterance on the person addressed. The illocutionary dimension of the utterance, on the other hand, opens to the Bakhtinian analysis of the utterance in that it centers on conventionally understood purpose or intent, implying that the utterance is addressed to a someone in dialog. For example, Austin says that for a performative utterance to work, "the particular persons and circumstances in a given case must be appropriate for the invocation of the particular procedure invoked" (1975: 34). The classification of illocutionary utterance types is functional, not stylistic, although stylistic devices such as tone of voice, and so on, may be used to signal different functions. For example, "shut the door" may be voiced as a command, a grant of permission, persuasion, and so on, depending on pitch, cadence, and stress, as well as to whom it is addressed and in what circumstances. Austin states, "I shall call the act performed" by the utterance "an 'illocution' and shall refer to the doctrine of the different types of function of language here in question as the doctrine of 'illocutionary forces'" (1975: 100).

Austin's generic distinction between the descriptive, constative dimension and the power infused performative potential of an utterance is useful in mapping the close but contrastive relationship between rule and policy as well as the generic kinship of policy and reportage. Bakhtin's approach to speech genres, especially his emphasis on addressivity, dialog, and the linkage of simple and complex forms of utterances, allows the analyst to trace discursive manifestations of policy in diverse social, cultural, and media settings. Although both philosophers firmly address themselves to the utterance as a concrete instance of language use, Austin's analytical approach remains more inclined to a grammatical or system orientation and looks for continuity and generalization, while Bakhtin focuses more on the unique circumstances that frame specific spheres of communication and foster creative reformulations of speech genres. Isaiah Berlin (2000) notes the macro dialogic pattern of alternation, in the communication sphere of Western social analysis since the eighteenth century, between system seeking Enlightenment argument and the Romantic celebration of the unique. Clearly, both of these lines of argument and explanation are important parts of the "echoes and reverberations of other utterances " to which both Austin's and Bakhtin's utterances are "related by the communality of the sphere of speech communication" (Bakhtin 1986: 91) represented by academic language philosophy. Both shared conventions and a potential for creative difference are essential to any language or language-like form of human communication, and in this case, both approaches point to the need to investigate speech genres such as rule and policy in the usages of ordinary language, including the working language practices of politics and law.

Policy Talk as Ordinary Language

The first question posed by an investigation of policy talk is, what is policy? Philosophers influenced by the ordinary language tradition typically frame questions of this sort by asking "What do we mean when we say *X*?" Locke argues—counter to Aristotle's idea that natural kinds are distinguished by objective differences in their essential natures discoverable by observation—that humans can never know real essences and must classify on the basis of nominal essences constructed by language use (Jolley 1999). The determinancy of nominal essences and their cognitive reality is particularly clear when language practices themselves are the objects of classification (Sinding 2004). Harry Frankfurt (2005), for example, in seeking a definition on which to build his theory, reviews the differences in the ways we use the terms *bullshit, humbug,* and *lying.* Like Willard Van Orman Quine, Frankfurt defers to ordinary language usage, but he does not shrink from clarifying its inherent confusions in order to better understand its basic import. Quine finds irony in the fact that "those philosophers most influenced by Wittgenstein" are the very ones most prone to reject such clarifications, "failing to recognize that it is precisely by showing how to circumvent the problematic parts of ordinary usage that we show the problems to be purely verbal" (1960: 261). As an anthropologist, my first reaction to any analysis beginning with "what do we mean when we say …" is the counter question "who is *we*?" When the object of study is policy, however, the answer is clear. *We* are all who are subject to the influence in our lives of contemporary state or trans-state instrumentalities of power. As George Marcus's seminal essay on ethnography "in/of" the world system (1995) makes clear, *we* is becoming more and more inclusive for students of social reality, encompassing the communities of the ethnographer, the people studied, and the reader when a topic like policy is being investigated (Brenneis 2005; Marcus 2005).

So, what *do* we mean when we say *policy?* Departing temporarily from the ethnographic imperative of using real data instead of made-up examples, let me put it this way: if one returns merchandise to a department store, what would be the difference between the clerk's saying "our policy is to require a sales slip," as opposed to "our rule is to require a sales slip"? "Policy" seems a more polite way to put it, but why? While *rule* foregrounds the command aspect of the interaction, *policy* implies a reason—and therefore at least some attempt at persuasion or placation. The answer to "please explain your rule" might be "what part of 'no slip, no return' do you not understand?" "Please explain your policy," on the other hand, would likely fetch a reason that might make submission to the rule more tolerable.

A real example of *rule/policy* usage corroborates this basic observation. In a *New York Times* story published 6 September 2005, *rule* appears in the headline, but *policy* is used instead throughout the story. The headline is "Traumatized by 9/11, Fired Over Drug Rule," and the story is about a New York City fireman who, suffering post traumatic stress disorder after extensive, gruesome duty recovering body parts at the site of the 9/11 attack on the World Trade Center, was fired on the basis of the Fire Department's "zero tolerance policy on drug use" (O'Donnell 2005). *Rule,* in the headline, suggests the possibility of a harsh, untempered action in which a traumatized fireman is denied consideration of significant extenuating circumstances. Certainly this scenario is a legitimate reading, among others, of the situation, and it engages reader interest right at the start. The body of the story, however, never uses the term *rule,* but instead refers fourteen times to the Fire Department's *policy.* The story, having initially posed the possible injustice of unreasonable rule enforcement, sets out to explain the rule—to make sense of the department's action. The reporter, Michelle O'Donnell, writes that, "policy was tightened after a spike in reported drug abuse within the department's ranks after 9/11 and a series of embarrassing incidents including an accident last year in which the driver of a fire truck was found to have had cocaine in his system." In this sentence it would seem to make sense to say that the *rule* was tightened, but the recounting of the justification makes *policy* an appropriate word choice. O'Donnell continues, "the policy stipulates that firefighters caught once using drugs are fired unless they come forward to report their problem" and "the Fire Department says the policy, and a decision last year to do random testing, are sensible, necessary measures to protect the safety of other firefighters and the public." A department spokesman is quoted as saying that, "there was a consensus that drug use had no place in an occupation that is so dangerous." Is the department's "decision" that random drug tests will be performed—and that those testing positive will be fired—a rule devised to enforce the policy, or is it the policy itself? Are rule and policy the same, or are they distinct aspects of a complex social reality? My argument is that rule and policy constitute a linked discursive pair, and each makes sense in context of the other. Rule is a statement of command; policy is a justification that takes the form of describing a situation in which the rule will have a desired effect.

Rule and Policy in Legal Usage

Rule and *policy* seem to be used almost interchangeably in many language use situations, such as the news story just cited and in everyday conversation, but even so, the distinction I am suggesting often underlies what appears to be mere stylistic preference or polite indirection. In law, however, the difference between the two is more sharply defined. A legal *rule* is a specific formulation of words that creates particular rights, duties, or opportunities, while *policy* is a representation of the social goals or purposes that justify and explain the rule. Justice Antonin Scalia makes this difference clear in his opinion, joined by three other justices, announcing the decision of the US Supreme Court in *Rapanos v. United States,* a 2006 case construing the Clean Water Act. Justice Scalia concentrates on the specific language of the act, particularly the meaning of "waters" and "the waters" of the United States in deciding whether the wetlands owned by Mr. and Mrs. Rapanos are covered by the act. Dismissing the dissenting opinion in the case, written by Justice Stevens and joined by three other justices, Justice Scalia calls it "an opinion long on praise of environmental protection and notably short on analysis of statutory text and structure" that therefore offers a "policy-laden conclusion" (547 U.S. 715, §VI (2005)). Here, environmental protection as a public purpose is the policy of the act, while operative language like "navigable waters of the United States" enunciates the rule.

Although Justice Scalia disparages the authority of policy talk not specifically supported by the language of the rule, it is clear that in legal discourse, the cover term *law* demands an account of both rule and policy. The relationship between the two is illustrated by the debate in jurisprudence between H.L.A. Hart and Ronald Dworkin. Hart, an influential member of the Oxford ordinary language movement in philosophy, viewed law as a deployed language system rather than as a system of abstract ideas, but he did not agree with the pragmatist, legal realist position that law is an utterance defined entirely by context (Hart 1961). That is, the legal realists hold that law is what the judge says in a particular case, whereas Hart, as a legal positivist, argues that law as a generally formulated rule has meaning in itself and that it is not in essence an utterance addressed to individuals, such as parties to a case, but rather to general categories of people, including those who formulate the rule. For Hart, then, law can best be described as a tiered system of rules, consisting of primary rules that govern substantive actions and secondary rules specifying the way primary rules must be enacted in order to be recognized as law. Dworkin, an American who succeeded Hart as the Professor of Jurisprudence at Oxford, argues that Hart's legal positivism, being rule focused, is inadequate to explain law because it leaves out standards, such as principles and policies, that are not enacted in accordance with secondary rules, but that lawyers and judges use to decide hard cases (Dworkin 1977; 1985). For Dworkin, "a policy is that kind of standard that sets out a goal to be reached, generally an improvement in some economic, political, or social feature of the community (though some goals are negative in that they stipulate that some present feature is to be protected from adverse change)" and, by contrast, a principle of law is "a standard to be observed not because it will advance or secure an economic, political or social situation deemed desirable, but because it is a requirement of justice or fairness or some other dimension of morality" (1977: 43).

In the analysis of policy talk on US television, I will use the term *policy* in a wide sense to include both of Dworkin's nonrule legal standards, policy and principle. Further, because I want to discuss policy talk in a wider arena of discourse—not just among lawyers and judges in the context of court cases—I include any references that purport to describe the rule's universe of application, that is, the social reality in which it will take effect. Susan Philips (1998), as part of a brilliant microethnographic study of the way judges use language in legal hearings, provides an analysis of the ways that judges directly address criminal defendants in guilty plea proceedings. Philips found a striking difference in the ways judges with contrasting legal ideologies implement a state law that, with the explicit public purpose of insuring procedural fairness and justice, requires the judge accepting a guilty plea to make sure that the defendant is acting voluntarily, with full knowledge of the legal consequences, and that he or she really is guilty. Philips shows that the legal ideologies she uncovered—using participant observation and transcript analysis—and labeled *procedure-oriented* and *record-oriented* correspond to political ideologies that fit the general categories of *liberal* and *conservative* on the basis of differing assumptions about the relationship between the state and the individual. Record-oriented judges talk to defendants in a way that is strongly addressed to an indirect but crucial audience, the appellate judges who will review the record and may vacate the ruling. They are careful to ask all of the required questions in a way that avoids confusing, complicated answers that may muddy the record. Procedure-oriented judges are more concerned with addressing the direct audience—the defendant him or herself. They want to make sure, as they explained to Phillips in interviews, that the defendant really does know what is going on and what will happen to him or her if the plea is accepted. To accomplish this policy goal of the law, the procedure-oriented judges try to create dialogically a more precise representation of the lifeworld of the defendant, asking specifically and probingly about background, education, and social circumstances. The one type of judge is more rule focused, and the other more policy focused, but both are engaged in what I call policy talk in that they are discursively creating an account of the point of contact between the rule and its local impact in social reality. When judges, lawyers, legislators, and philosophers talk to one another about policy—often in print—they refer explicitly to abstract public goals and purposes, including procedural principles of fairness. When they address the public, either by mass media or in one-to-one spoken interaction with defendants, however, they may also attempt to create—either monologically or dialogically—a representation of the lived social reality that the rule attempts to bring about. The linkage among rule, social and moral goals, and world picture is a strong one because specific shared perspectives on the limits of social reality, generally talked about as ideologies, are defined by their embedded policy purposes.

Logically, the result in an actual case, understood in terms of salient system goals and purposes, is the practical embodiment of the policy dimension of the rule. As judges use a rule to decide individual cases, they are defining, in the medium of social reality, the precise scope of the policy involved. As they do so, they may also employ policy talk as a way of explaining the social purpose of the rule in order to justify the result and guide future conduct. From the perspective of discursive practice, it is this kind of policy talk, rather than policy as abstract ideas or categories, that is the object of policy study.

The Word as the Minimal Unit of Policy Expression

In an important sense, the very language of the rule is an incipient statement of policy because the words that make up the rule must make reference to a reality that the rule addresses, and social goals and purposes are inherent in social reality. But the words of a rule divorced from the context of actual application are equivalent to the words of a sentence that have dictionary meaning in the abstract, but take their specific meaning from the context in which the sentence is used (Voloshinov 1986). Meaning in rule/policy discourse is both stratified and nested.

The two distinct strata of meaning are referential (constative)—the words refer to a universe of application in social reality—and performative, in the sense that the rule as pronounced in context accomplishes some modification of social reality. By *nesting* I mean that there are concentric levels of specificity involved. A single element of the articulated rule/policy, for example the word "drug" in a statement of the New York Fire Department's zero tolerance policy, has referential meaning at an extremely broad, nonspecific level. As included in the rule/policy statement, however, the component word reaches a much more specific level of referential meaning because semantic interaction with the other elements of the syntagm focuses it on a narrow part of the range of its potential meanings. It is at the level of enforcement in a particular case that referential meaning of the rule/policy reaches its full extension, however. At this point, "drug" refers to a specific chemical compound, in a specific quantity, as indicated by specific testing procedures, and in the sampled fluid of a particular person. Looking at the other stratum of meaning, the isolated, individual word has virtually no performative meaning, except that it may alert the hearer to the potential for regulation, given one's social experience. That is to say, "drug" has become a loaded word in that its range of meanings has been skewed—by the frequency and emotional energy of its usage—to foreground associations in the domain of the illegal and dangerous. As included in the formulated core language of the rule or the extended explication of policy, the word reaches a much higher level of performative efficacy. People who read or hear about the rule/policy may very well alter their conduct because of it. The ultimate level of performative force or meaning is reached when—just as in the referential stratum of meaning—the rule is enforced in a specific case. Policy talk, then, does not actually supply the concrete contexts in which the rule will apply, but it does provide, by elaborating, extending, and limiting the terms of the rule statement, a rhetorical representation of the universe of the rule's application, and that representation can be evaluated in terms of accuracy, given shared perspectives that have been established politically.

Selective Ambiguity in Rule and Policy Talk

Although policy and rule are a linked discursive pair, and neither makes sense without the other, one or the other can recede from explicit articulation—situations that cause confusions in usage. An unenforced rule, with its policy only sketched out by dictionary definitions of its terms, is one example of uneven salience between the pair, but policy talk can also exist without an explicit rule statement, as when the command dimension is being expressed directly in action. In volatile regulatory situations, the coherence among specific instances of application may be so loose—perhaps because of countervailing political factors—that formulating an explicit rule may be difficult, and references to general policies have to serve in place of a rule. Jack Bilmes' pioneering ethnography of regulation, which focused on discussions among Federal Trade Commission lawyers, demonstrates situational prominence of policy in regulatory discourse (Bilmes 1985; Bilmes and Woodbury 1991). As Bilmes shows, in the 1970s and 1980s, references to a discursive policy world based on free market ideology were an important part of policy talk at the Federal Trade Commission (FTC). At the level of public announcements rather than of in-house negotiations, Jeremy Stein (1989) has analyzed the Federal Reserve Board's strategy of making imprecise policy statements in order to manipulate expectations in the financial community without revealing its policy goals in detail. Precise information about policy goals would entail a loss of discretion in the timing of rule-dictated action by the Board.

The foreign policy of a nation is often a prominent example of a rhetorical imbalance between policy and rule. A country may declare a "doctrine" of unilateral pre-emptive intervention in stated kinds of situations, for example, but then it may act on that doctrine selectively. Rather than admit to an ad hoc strategy, statespersons tend to talk in terms of policy or doctrine, with the implication that the rule dimension is too complex to conveniently state. As Wittgenstein argues, however, an unexpressed rule is actually an oxymoron in discursive practice (1958: §§201, 202). An observer watching a purportedly rule bound activity may object at some point by stating, "you violated the rule," but if the rule has not been openly stated, the actor can always reply, "Not at all. It's just that the rule is more complicated than you realized." At a micro level in law, judges routinely cover the inevitable changes in a rule, as it applies to divergent circumstances, with policy talk to rhetorically establish continuity, if not fixity, in the law. Justice Stevens, dissenting in the *Rapanos* case mentioned above, uses talk about the public purpose of environmental protection to explain an asserted extension of the words "navigable waters of the United States" to include not only adjacent wetlands, but even intermittently wetlands that have an ecological impact on "waters of the United States." Also, in many regulatory situations, legal decision making may be fast and furious as administrators close to the action in their fields adapt to changing circumstances. In arenas like this, participants, for example, a social worker and client, often refer to the regulation as policy or as *decisions* rather than law. In reality it is administrative law in action, and the rule (command) dimension is co-present.

Another major area of policy/rule talk selective ambiguity is often seen in mass mediated policy talk, such as televised news conferences of legislative and administrative officials. A rule, as a discursive event, has innumerable sites of performative impact in society, many quite divorced from one another, and policy talk can be used to invoke the social reality of the rule selectively, emphasizing one site and ignoring others.

Mass Mediated Policy Talk

Because mass mediated policy talk is a form of rhetoric employed to explain and either to justify or to discredit a legal rule, an improvement or a degradation of a shared cultural reality is at least implied to be at stake, and any effort to specify the meaning of the rule's constituent language by creating a representation of social reality can be an attempt to serve the persuasive ends of policy talk.

As one moves away from the explicit, monological form of policy talk among lawyers to the more open, negotiated version of policy talk addressed to a mass media audience, precise reference to the empirical realities and shared goals—practical and moral—addressed by the rule often gives way to more oblique forms of persuasion. In this context, I am using *monological* to refer to talk in which lawyers, among themselves, use terms of art that have been more or less precisely defined in law, as opposed to *dialogical* talk in which meaning is more actively negotiated (Neuman 2003). The following examples are taken from C-SPAN broadcasts in which the mass media audience is either a primary or secondary addressee of policy talk. My concern is to critique the televised policy talk as an attempted representation of social realities—reportage—applying some of the standards that anthropologists and journalists have set for themselves in their own versions of this enterprise, namely, academic ethnography and news reporting.

Austin's observation that performativity may be accomplished in rituals by nonlanguage acts suggests the parallel question of the accomplishment of constative, referential policy communication through nonlanguage modes in ritual settings (Arno 2003). The ritualistic nonlanguage dimensions of televised policy talk in the US, including the indoor or outdoor settings, the "look" of the participants, and other visual details draw on the aesthetics of everyday experience and capture some of the emotional energy of interpersonal speech genres. The locutionary aspects of the language used, such as the strategic droppin' of g's to achieve a folksy sound, also draw on aesthetic motivation. At a deeper analytical level, Hirokazu Miyazaki's (2004) analysis of the discursive production of hope in ritualized interactions suggests the ethnographic salience in televised policy talk of strategic displacements in time and agency in representing a desired social reality. The temporal scales and powers to influence events attributed to business corporations and to individual folks of mainstreet America are representational resources drawn upon in the following examples. In this regard, Carol Greenhouse's (1996) discussion of temporal improvisation and political legitimation—for example, in the invocation of the scales and semantic textures of social time and individual biography in televised confirmation hearings for supreme court appointees—is clearly central to analyzing many different forms of televised policy talk, including press conferences and committee hearings.

Examples of televised policy talk taken from C-SPAN telecasts of congressional hearings and press conferences illustrate some of the rhetorical techniques that US politicians have adopted in policy formation and exposition. Some of these techniques are parallel to those employed by anthropologists in the related genre of academic ethnographic writing and to journalists' depictions of social reality in news reporting. The first example is a press conference held outdoors in bright sunlight on the grounds of the capitol building. It took place on 24 October 2001, and the general political economic context was the aftermath of the 9/11 attacks and the ongoing economic stagnation. The purpose of the press conference was to advocate proposed legislation produced by the House Ways and Means Committee called the "Economic Recovery and Security Act of 2001" (H.R. 3090). The text of the bill, of course, was highly technical and could be read and fully understood only by highly specialized corporate tax lawyers. But the aim of the press conference was to put a human face on the proposed legislation and to build support for the bill in public opinion. Clearly, the politicians do not expect a large television audience on C-SPAN, but they can hope that a few colorful, entertaining phrases will be picked up by the commercial press for later use on network or cable news shows. Perhaps more important, they are modeling talking points that the members of their party can use in more direct communications with their own constituents in portraying the party's response to economic concerns and in countering attacks from the other party on the sponsoring party's purported pandering to business interests. In other words, the politicians seem perfectly aware of the dialogic linkage between primary and secondary speech genres discussed by Bakhtin.

The speakers at the press conference are all Republicans, mainly middle-aged European-American men with lawyerly suits and haircuts, but the lineup also includes party members representing racial, gender, and age diversity. I think it is not overly cynical to surmise that the apparent diversity is not accidental. To simulate a dialogic form of communication, that is, a way of talking that is characterized by the speaker's "attunement to the attunement of the other" (Rommetveit 1992), the message is delivered by a group of politicians selected to mirror the audience. If the assemblage appears to the audience to be "folks like us," arguably a presumption of mutual attunement is established. As they form a line facing the cameras before starting the press conference, the politicians appear to be in high spirits, laughing and settling into position, looking more like students posing for a class picture than a group of powerful politicians. They are modeling in their manner the hopefulness they will attempt to construct by this press conference. The ritual is opened by a few remarks from the Speaker of the House, Dennis Hastert:

(This transcript and the following ones are taken from videotapes of C-SPAN broadcasts. I represent the speech as I hear it, rather than as corrected, to the extent that it seems to make some communicative difference. Deleted material is indicated by brackets, [ ], a pause not articulated as a full stop is indicated by three periods, ..., and heavy stress by underlining.)

G'morning ladies and gentlemen. 'Preciate everybody being here this morning. First of all I'd like to introduce a gentleman we have with us, Mr. Cham Patel, who is ...he works for Econolodge out in Fairfax ... who really'll be one of the people who receives the benefits of this package, this economic stimulus package, as well as people investing and getting the economy going again. [ ]

Speaker Hastert goes on to introduce Congressman Bill Thomas, the Chairman of the Ways and Means Committee, who has reported the bill. Mr. Thomas thanks various people including the president, commenting that the "administration statement of policy" supports the bill because:

[ ]when you examine the particulars in the package you find that about forty cents of every dollar goes to individuals, low income and moderate income, to assist them in continuing the consumer demand portion of our economy's engine. About sixty cents of every dollar goes to the machine that creates jobs ... oftentimes it's called business or corpora-

tions, but there tend to be negative reactions when you say you're gonna provide some money to corporations or businesses. But if you say you're gonna provide some money to the machines that create jobs, then you understand what the stimulus package is about.

The next speaker is Congressman Richard Armey, the Republican Majority Leader of the House. He speaks in a genial and somewhat ceremonious way:

We call on everybody, in Congress, in this government. Put aside your partisan efforts, your parochial interests, and focus on the well being of this great nation. We want jobs for the American people. We have constructed in this committee a package that does spend a large share on individuals' tax incentives for work and rewards for work. Tellin' Mr. and Mrs. America if you have a job you will keep a larger share of your pay ... as what we all treasure the most, your take-home pay. But also, for investors. Investment is the driving engine of the economy and investment is on the business side of the ledger, and anybody who understands what it takes to make an economy grow must only applaud what this committee has done to tell investors, if you take the risks, if you build the opportunity to put people to work, you will receive a return on your investment, and you will have the opportunity to retain the return on your investment. Simple analytic of human activity.

The next to speak is the Republican Conference Chair, J.C. Watts. In contrast to the previous speakers who, as graying European-Americans, look very much like the Republican party as the business party, Mr. Watts is young, African-American, and, as a former college football star, athletic. He said:

Norman Vincent Peale made millions of dollars by tellin' us the obvious, and I'm gonna repeat the obvious here this mornin' that the strength of America is our people. And the hopes, the dreams, the ideas, the ambitions ... and we've seen back in April 19, 1995, in Oklahoma City, we saw on September 11 of this year, in Washington, here in D.C., and in Virginia and Pennsylvania, and in New York City, we've seen that, uh, the American people's goodness. We've seen how we respond in tragedy, how we respond in the difficult times, and I think that, you know, we have our role to play as government. All of us standing here believe that it's important that we pass legislation, we pass a plan that will help the American people. And anybody that believes that this plan is about Republicans or Democrats, or it's about numbers, they're wrong. This plan is about the American people. Helping the American people have more money to do what they need to do with it, buyin' their kids clothes, buyin' food, helpin' to pay their rent. This legislation is about more than just havin' a check in the mail, it's about havin' a job. I think the American people are wanting jobs. They're itchy about the economy. As has been said already, the economy is soft. We're trying to do some things to spur this economy, to create economic security, to move this economy along. I commend the Ways and Means Committee, Chairman Thomas, I commend all those that've had a hand in this to get us to this point that we can vote on this plan today to help the American people, and, and make no bones about it, if this legislation is about nothing more than helping the American people accomplish the things that they want to accomplish in their lives. And getting them ready for Christmas. We've got Christmas, two, two months away. You know, people are wondering how they're gonna pay for Christmas, so the things that we're doin' in this plan will assist American families, the single moms, single dads, the moms and dads that have financial responsibilities. So again I commend Chairman Thomas and the Ways and Means Committee. And a person that's had a role in getting' us to this point is a lady I want to introduce. My colleague from the great state of Connecticut, the gentlelady from Connecticut, Ms. Johnson.

Representative Nancy Johnson speaks with great enthusiasm and energy:

[ ]That's stimulus, that's enlightened tax policy! We're gonna drive this economy up and help those people who are having an unusually hard time both because the economy was soft and because of the catastrophic impact of September eleventh, and we're proud of this legislation!

At this point, a reporter is given the opportunity to ask a question, which turns out to be about the differences between the House bill and the version that is being written in the Senate and the compromise that might result. Before anyone can respond, however, Representative Watts again takes the microphone:

Before the whip answers that question, I want to make a couple of introductions. Mr. Cham Patel, that the Speaker mentioned, and Mr. Zack, uh, Borges who's here. They are both small business owners, they're small business owners. They operate, uh, hotels. So we appreciate you all being with us today to actually put some faces behind what we're doin' here this morning.

The last remark was addressed to the two guests, who, from a position off to the side, nodded and waved briefly. A few more questions were asked by reporters and the press conference ended. The notably perfunctory character of the participation by Mr. Patel and Mr. Borges, including the speaker's failure to complete the introduction of the men that required Congressman Watts' repair work at the end, points at their role as human props. Physical props are commonly used in presentations seen on C-SPAN, often with intentionally humorous effect, by congresspersons to make a point visually and to key their messages to the purported social reality addressed by their policy arguments. For example, in a debate that concerned funding for border security after the 9/11 terrorist incident, one presenter appeared with a large orange traffic cone, which he introduced as the guard on duty at many points along the US/Canadian border during off hours.

The use of human props, that is, simply bringing individuals to a media event to serve as indexical and iconic signs for the policy being advocated, may have been stimulated by what many US politicians perceived as the effective and innovative use of them by former President Reagan, who punctuated his state of the union addresses with such introductions. Generally, the technique is, at an appropriate point in a televised speech, to introduce a person by name and tell his or her story briefly while the camera registers a close-up of his or her face. There is great potential for this device to be employed badly, and some rhetorical energy has to be spent in fending off the lurking idea that the person is being exploited. A negative disposition of the audience toward the policy idea being thus grounded in physical reality will create resistance to this persuasive technique, but the practice is widely used by politicians of diverse ideological positions. In my viewing of C-SPAN policy talk by legislators and executive branch spokespersons over the last few years, I noted, for example, the display of an elderly couple who could not afford to buy prescribed medications, a group of young Central American women garment workers whose wages and working conditions were described as appalling, and several appealing young children who were NOT destroyed as fertilized embryos.

In text, human props are often represented by quotation—for example, by reading from a letter received or recounting a story that the speaker has been told—with the source being quite explicitly identified along salient lines such as name, age, class, ethnicity, residence, and so on. But do anthropologists and journalists make use of what I am calling human props in their ethnographic representations of social reality? The answer, of course, is yes. Precisely grounded quotation is one of the more powerful techniques of ethnographic writing, and as such it subjected to strict scrutiny. The telling use of quotation—and in a somewhat less developed way, the use of photographs and video—is an effective way of evoking a sense of the reality that can never be completely represented, whatever the medium. The actual words, the actual faces, and so on, engage the imagination of the audience, and they, accurately or not, intuitively fill in the blanks and reconstruct the absent lifeworld. Not only individual informants, but also languages can be rhetorical props in this sense, and anthropologists often insert vernacular words in descriptive texts. Use of the vernacular term implies precision of reference, hermeneutic authority, and it constitutes a scientific gesture in opening the data to the scrutiny of those who do speak the object language. At another level, however, the vernacular is inserted not because some readers will understand the word, but precisely because most readers will *not* understand it, underlining the difference between that reader's own and the ethnographic reality that the entire ethnographic text as a whole must address.

My argument is that there is a rhetorical continuity between the representation of Mr. Patel in the Economic Recovery Act example and the Mr. Patel who might appear in an ethnography of hotel management written by an anthropologist. In ethnography, authors, readers, and critics pay serious attention to the problem of allowing the informant to be heard, and anthropologists have cultivated a critical awareness of the impossibility of completely closing the gap between voice and representation of voice as well as the difficulty of making the empirical connection between the quoted individual and a larger group, and between the quotation and the larger questions at issue (Marcus and Fischer 1986; Clifford and Marcus 1986). Mass media policy talk by elected officials and legislators is just as important—to say the least—as academic ethnography, but too often it escapes critical attention from those who produce it as well as from its audience. At times, it becomes a game in which rhetorical devices are foregrounded instead of being eclipsed by the substance of the debate. At other times, however, televised policy talk can be extremely compelling. In the following example the speaker, far from being a mere prop, is a genuine witness who tells his own story in such a direct and powerful way that awareness of rhetorical technique is erased.

The setting of the example is a hearing of the House Government Security Subcommittee, chaired by Congressman Christopher Shays, that took place in November 2003. The topic is federal government funding for ongoing health and medical research programs aimed at understanding and treating illnesses derived from the environmental and psychological impact of the 9/11 attack on the World Trade Center

in New York. A major element of the political context was the contention that the federal government had not lived up to its commitments to
support New York City's recovery from the terrorist attack. Among the
many witnesses who appeared was a construction worker, David Rapp,
who testified in support of a Mount Sinai Hospital program whose funding was in question. After introducing himself with his name and labor
union affiliation, Mr. Rapp continued, reading his prepared statement
in a steady but slightly raspy voice and pausing at times for breath:

I was at ground zero for near five months including three days of the
first week of the terrorist attack. I hope my testimony is goin' to make
everyone aware of what we experienced at ground zero, and what I and
others are going through now. I viewed, smelled, handled things that you
cannot imagine. Although I worked twelve hours a day, seven days a week,
I looked forward to heading back for another shift. I started experiencing
health problems like dizziness, shortness of breath and skin rash while I
was still working down there. Although we accomplished what we set out
to do, which was keeping the slurry wall from collapsing as the debris
was removed, our job was installing tiebacks while being exposed to who
knows what. My job was completed in March of two thousand and two at
ground zero. I went to my next job at Kennedy Airport driving piles for
American Air Lines, where my ability and stamina had diminished. I was
laid off the first week of April and have not worked since. I'm a forty-two
year-old dock builder that normally could do as much as a twenty-two
year-old—and more. I could carry a hundred and fifty pound tank of oxygen or acetylene a half a block to a rough job site. But now I can't even
take out my household garbage. I'm also a mechan'—auto mechanic with
five certifications. After a long day of dock buildin' I could still come
home and install a two hundred pound transmission on my back, off my
chest. Now I can't even change a flat tire. There's a lot of fear in my life
now. I've had several emergency visits, several short stays in the hospital.
I rely on oxygen at night to sleep, and I still wake up sometimes gaspin'
for air, tryin' to stay calm. Sometimes I feel like I'm under water. I've
had a sore throat for fifteen months now. When I cough I can feel the
outlines of my lungs. I sleep on a recliner, straight up. I can't go out in
the humidity or breathe cold air. I need to keep my house at a sixty-five
degree temperature where my wife sleeps with a quilt. I'm on steroids
which have caused weight gain. I've put on fifty pounds since I've stopped
workin' in April of two thousand and two. Which probably doesn't help
my condition, but the steroids do help. I'm on twelve other, different,
uh medications, plus three types of inhalers. And I carry an oxygen tank
wherever I go for assistance to breathe. I can't tell you how hard it is livin'

like this, my fear of not being able to get my next breath is unbearable. I'm goin' to two different doctors at this time, one is a Dr. Leo [ ] and the other is Mount Sinai, Health for Heroes. Mount Sinai has been great to me. They've been helpin' me since November, two thousand and two. They helped me get immediate benefits from workman's compensation. Most importantly with the medications that I rely on to breathe. All their staff has been compassionate and expressed real concern for my future. They always make sure I have enough medication. I'd like to end this with I have a beautiful wife of twenty seven years and two sons in their twenties that fear for my future as well. Thank you very much.

Mr. Rapp's brief testimony vividly evokes the lifeworld of a skilled mechanic, proud of his technical know-how and physical prowess, and this context frames the devastating impact of his debilitating illness. For public policy purposes, the cause and effect connection between illness and the lingering environmental impact of the terrorist attack is an essential question that is not addressed by individual experience alone. That part of the puzzle was spoken to in the hearing by expert public health and medical witnesses who presented their interpretations of the science involved. In terms of Bakhtinian speech genre analysis, how does the complex, secondary genre of the televised policy hearing absorb and draw energy from the primary genre of everyday talk, thereby engaging, as in a face-to-face interaction, the personal involvement of the viewer?

At the primary level of generic complexity, habitual differences in utterance may define a particular person's distinct style of expression, which may seem below the threshold of genre analysis, but an author may use invented dialog to index the character and personality of an invented speaker in a novel or drama. Greenhouse's (1996) penetrating discussion of the ways that narrated personal life history engages with social temporality suggests that in televised, individual testimony, style and substance can index implicit personality genres that are fundamental to cultural interpretation. Paul Friedrich and James Redfield explore the general idea of speech as a personality symbol in a close rhetorical and linguistic analysis of the quoted speeches that Homer used to convey the particularly striking mentality and volatile emotional constitution of Achilleus as distinguished from the other heroic characters in his *Iliad* (Friedrich and Redfield 1978). Thus, the complex genre of Greek epic poetry has "absorbed and digested," as Bakhtin puts it, not only the reported genre of classical Greek political rhetoric, but also the subgenre of individual style (which by implication indexes a culturally salient personality genre or temperament) that the reader understands in important part on the basis of his or her own experience of primary speech genres in everyday life. In a parallel sense, the anthropological author, as well as the journalist, also uses quoted speech—not invented but selected and edited—to convey a personality dimension that breathes life into an account of real life social action in ethnography and in news writing.

When Achilleus addresses Agamemnon in an assembly of chiefs, accusing him hotly of greed and obsessive profit-mindedness, the primary, face-to-face dimension of addressivity is paramount, but even at this "undigested" level of reality, his words address (in the sense of being in dialogic attunement with) countless previous as well as future generations of speakers who employ the cultural genre of Classical Greek political rhetoric. The vast, diachronic cultural dimension of talk, which Bakhtin insists is empirical and utterance linked, not abstract, is then foregrounded by Homer in the secondary genre of poetry, which itself in each utterance addresses the vast array of past and future participants in poetic discourse. But ultimately Homer's poetry draws its life and force from Achilleus's anger, which, although imagined, is understood by listeners in terms of real utterances experienced directly and indirectly in the contemporary cultural community. As Homer invokes the muse of poetry to sing the anger of Achilleus, the congressional committee invokes the generic conventions of television to represent the devastation of a rescue worker's life as a key element of policy talk.

Truth in Policy Talk

Both policy talk and ethnography/reportage—and here one can cite the professional ideals of journalism in particular—share an absolute commitment to two distinct kinds of truth. Reports of events—observable things that happened, what people said or did—have to be supported by conventionally accepted standards of verification. It is not okay to invent those telling details because they are the anchors in a reality beyond interpretation and perspective. But interpretation and perspective—which includes selection of events to report, emphasis, and so on—constitute the other kind of truth essential to both policy talk and ethnography. Dialogic or co-generic logic, which arguably is the basis of meaning and communication in human interaction (Neuman 2003), insists that the observer's position is an integral, nonreducible dimension of meaning, and communication inevitably involves a negotiation of perspective among the parties. *Event truth* and *perspectival truth*—or, in terms of Jürgen Habermas' validity claims in the ideal political speech community, *truth* and *sincerity* (Habermas 1984; 1987)—are ultimately similar at a basic ontological level, being based on a difference that makes a difference *to* someone (Neuman 2003; Bateson 1972), but they are sharply differentiated in discourses of modernity and rationality by different standards of proof. In televised policy talk on C-SPAN, the key issue of perspectival truth—that is, the honest representation of the speaker's perspective frame and the attempt to evoke a sympathetic attunement in the viewer—is often foregrounded, with competing perspectives being highly emphasized.

The Republican press conference on the Economic Recovery and Security Act of 2001 (H.R. 3090), discussed above, was countered by a Democratic press conference in which a senator and a congressman attempted to discredit the sincerity of the Republicans' claimed perspective and to present their own interpretations. The disputed perspective can be identified briefly in terms of labor versus corporate welfare. The Republicans, in an open although very general way, had stated the bill's intended benefits to business, but they emphasized the goal of job growth and presented a picture of main street America in which "Mr. and Mrs. America" could enjoy their take-home pay, and in which "single moms and single dads" could get ready for Christmas.

In the answering Democratic press conference, Congressman John Spratt, adding a comment after Senator Kent Conrad's initial response to a reporter's question about the proposed legislation's potential to create jobs, addressed the perspective issue directly:

Could I respond further to that? One component of this bill, as I said earlier, is a corporate tax break for the multinational finance and insurance firms...holding companies. The revenue impact of that is twenty-one billion dollars. By contrast, the CBO estimates that the impact, cost impact, of the unemployment provisions in this bill, Ways and Means Committee bill, will come to about three billion dollars. So ask yourself, which will help the economy more? A meager three billion dollars of unemployment benefits, or a twenty bill ... twenty-one billion dollars for foreign multinational firms? I mean, shows you what I was just saying, they bend over backwards to help corporate taxpayers, but they won't even stoop, or hardly stoop, to help hardworking Americans who are about to lose their jobs. Or have lost their jobs. Now, the headline for this bill maybe, in some of your publications will say "House Extends Unemployment Benefits for Thirteen Weeks" but the small print will say "this applies to those who lost their jobs after September eleventh, or after the effective date of this bill, and who are in states where the unemployment rate has gone up by thirty percent." That's why this bill is woefully inadequate in dealing with the hardships this recession will create, but also in providing a stimulus to the economy. When it makes choices like that.

In his just previous remarks, Senator Conrad had not questioned the sincerity of the Republicans' concern for workers directly, but instead challenged the wisdom of the bill on technical, economic grounds:

> You know, unfortunately I think the house package, if it were ever to pass, would actually hurt the economy. And I believe it would hurt the economy because the markets would see we're not serious about long term fiscal discipline. And that would put upward pressure on interest rates. And that would unravel all the good of the fiscal stimulus provided in that package. In other words, monetary policy would be at odds with fiscal policy. That is exactly what Chairman Greenspan warned us against. That is exactly what Secretary Rubin has warned us against. That is precisely what we should not do. And, to do a reality check, I just invite you back to the day the president announced after a bipartisan meeting at the Whitehouse that he recognized the importance of maintaining long term fiscal discipline and how that would have an effect on interest rates. You immediately saw the bond market rally. You saw interest rates come down. And it was attributed directly to the president's recognition that we needed to maintain fiscal discipline. This is the key part of our message here today. Yes, we need stimulus in the short term, but we need to couple it with fiscal discipline in the long term so we don't put upward pressure on interest rates. So we don't undermine the lift to the economy provided by short term fiscal stimulus.

What I would like to point out about this last statement, which represents a prevalent variety of policy talk in televised congressional events, is that the policy world that it constructs and addresses—that is, the social reality in which the proposed rule will take effect—is not at all the main street reality that Congressman Pratt or Watts tried to evoke. Instead, it is a metaworld of abstract economic entities and forces, congruent with the technical language of the bill. It is, however, a lived reality for economists and large-scale business professionals. In a Durkheimian sense, fiscal policy, monetary policy, and so on, are specialized collective representations that constitute constraining social facts in the business world.

The multiplicity of policy worlds, each constructed in policy talk with the presumption that it represents a lived reality, becomes apparent not only when technical realms are invoked, but also, very importantly, when the social worlds of the cultural other are represented. In other words, participants in policy talk may in some cases portray first-order, lived realities—not abstract metarealities of technical disciplines—of people other than themselves. In the domestic policy scene, this disjuncture can take place when rules are created to deal with criminal or other subcultures that are not deemed worthy of being given a voice in the process. Foreign policy formation also often provides examples of this discursive situation, as in the following example, which is taken from an October 2001, C-SPAN broadcast of a Senate Foreign Relations Committee hearing on anti-terrorism. The immediate political context is the US invasion of Afghanistan in response to Al Qaeda's 9/11/01 attack on US targets. The witness is Secretary of State Colin Powell. The late Senator Paul Wellstone, after Secretary Powell's opening statement, begins a criticism of the government in Uzbekistan:

> On Uzbekistan, passed an amendment yesterday that just called for reporting on our money and how it's spent with security in that country. We need them. They're part of our coalition. My simple point is ... and you're very sensitive to this ... my simple point is this is also a government that <u>crushes</u> people because they practice the Islamic faith. And we've made it clear that we're not at war with people who practice the Islamic faith. So some ... there's some kind of way in which we need to make this distinction of ally but not uncritical support of this government in the way it just crushes it's own people. We can talk about it.

Before Secretary Powell can reply, another committee member, Senator Sam Brownback, responds, presenting his own version of Uzbek political reality:

> Ah, if I could first say, ah, I wanna be a little contrary to my colleague from Minnesota about the Uzbeks. Uh, the foreign minister you noted was just here and, uh, is in town, I think would meet with any members who would like to, uh. Uzbekistan has I think been stand-up straight with us on, uh, taking on a very difficult situation, now getting a lot of pressure from people in the neighborhood, ah, that they're in. And I, ah, I hope we work real close and carefully with them. I know that, I know that you will. At the same time, we press them forward on our set of issues we believe in. We don't move off of democracy, human rights, religious freedom. Those are key things for us, but I think there's clearly a way that we work with people, and at the same time that our values get seeded with them over a period of time, and that we'll work carefully doin' that, and I would hope we would work over a <u>long</u> period of time with, with a number of these countries in Central Asia that I think are going to be critically important

to us in this, clearly in this campaign. And on into the future. These are just…they're gonna be in a central role. So, I just wanna add that as a side comment. I don't know if you have any thoughts that are any different?

Secretary Powell responds:

Oh, I agree with you. We have had tremendous cooperation from the Uzbek government, and the foreign minister and I speak regularly on the phone. And I know that when, when you invite us in and you want us to have a friendly relationship with you, we bring our values. And we believe our values are not American values, they're universal. So we'll always speak up for tolerance and for human rights, and, uh, individual liberty, and practice of religion.

Following a brief discussion of a US request that Russia not bomb Chechens in Georgia, Senator Brownback continues:

I wanna, ah, take up a comment that you made in the opening statement that, uh, I've heard a lot of and I, and I heard it from Mr., ah, Mussa, the other day … head of the Arab League…about the watching of the Arab street. And, ah, that there's only kinda so much that be, uh, can, can be taken on because of the reaction that might take place on the Arab street. And I really wonder if the issue here is a lack of, of other ways to express in the Arab street. Uh, if uh, uh, my, my fundamental point here is that I think we gotta push everywhere in the world for democracy, human rights, uh, uh, ability to be able to express freely, religious freedom. That's including in places in the Arab world as well, and as we go forward in Afghanistan, hopefully post-Taliban shortly, that we're gonna continue to push there and in the rest of the world for … look, in Afghanistan it's gonna be democracy, including women havin' the right to vote, uh, and participating in the society … we passed an amendment on that yesterday … that as we press forward in this campaign that we press a region of the world that at times I think we've been a little timid on, pressing just the basic things that we stand for. That's gonna be a difficult issue for ya in keeping the coalition together, but I, I think it's just paramount for us to do that.

Secretary Powell Responds:

It, it's a tricky issue, but I think you've absolutely right, Senator, because, ah, many of these … nations … the leadership does not represent the street. Ah, democracies represent the street. You all are here, sitting, behind that green table, because you represent the street. And the day you all stop representing the street ... you're outta here. Ah, more so with your colleagues in the other, the other side. [laughter] Uh, but nevertheless ... unto dust thou shalt return. The day you stop representing the street. But when you don't have a free democratic system, where the street is represented in the halls of the legislature and, and in the executive branches of those governments, then they have to be more concerned about the passions of the street. It, it's almost ah, it, it's you know, a ... it, it's not what you expect. You'd think if you don't have, ah, a democratic system you have greater authority, but in some ways you may have greater power, but it's not clear that you have greater <u>authority</u> in the sense that you're operating with the authority of your people. And, ah, I have started to raise these issues and talked to some of our friends in the region and said, you know, in addition to sorta criticizing us from time to time, in terrible editorials about us in your newspapers, better start takin' a look in the mirror.

In this example, to borrow Secretary Powell's metaphor, the policy makers are viewing the object world of their proposed policy in the mirror of their own values. Absent any serious attempt to portray the Arab or the Central Asian lifeworlds in realistic terms, the participants are content to discursively construct policy worlds defined negatively in terms of a purported absence of US values. Acknowledgement of problematic gaps between the lived realities of the US, Arab, and Central Asian "streets" enters the interchange only by negation, grounded in an asserted universality of US values. The topic of the discussion foregrounds a limit to cultural relativity that anthropological debates have also acknowledged, namely, a situation in which the intellectual goal of understanding the other is complicated by the accomplished fact of intervention and a perceived necessity to act in a way guided by one's own ethics. The point I would like to make is not the obvious lack of fit between the constructed policy worlds and the object worlds, but rather the vigorous attempt at constructing an encompassing moral community. The assertion of moral community, discursively constructing a policy world from which entextualized rules putatively emerge and can effectively reenter and move around in, is one of the basic tenets of text ideology that defines policy talk.

Further Research

The speech genre I am calling *reportage*, defined as an empirically grounded narrative description of social reality framed by a text ideology of objectivism and addressed to an audience external to the process of the description's production, presents an important avenue of further investigation. As thus broadly defined, it is ubiquitous and often appears with an unstated, implicit rule dimension. While anthropologists may cringe at the assertion that journalism can be a form of ethnography, the fact is that the term has long since escaped the disciplinary enclosure. Construed as a "qualitative method," ethnography is being actively explored and adapted by all of the social sciences. Cultural studies has taken up ethnography and honed it as an instrument of critical commentary. Pierre Bourdieu argues that objectivist, social scientific accounts of social reality position the addressees as a "lay audience"—that is, outsiders to the production of the account—and that "these 'scientific' mythologies can produce their own verification, if they manage to impose themselves on collective belief and to create, by their mobilizing capacity, the conditions of their own realization" (Bourdieu 1991: 226). Jonathan Friedman cautions that Bourdieu may be taking a "dangerous next step" in the reflexive analysis of academic discourse by claiming that all objectivist knowledge encompasses a claim to legitimate domination (Friedman 1992: 112), but the fact remains that naturalistic, fact based accounts—whether in social science, journalism, or law—often do have a policy talk function.

In the arena of policy talk, the ethnographic dimension of judicial decision writing poses a compelling object of further study. For example, in the 2005 death penalty case *Roper v. Simmons* (543 U.S. 551), Justice Anthony Kennedy opens the Supreme Court's majority opinion with a rather chilling statement of facts in the case. Simmons, the seventeen-year-old killer, having detailed his plan for burglary and sadistic murder to two friends, persuaded one of them to join him in the crime. Then, Justice Kennedy writes, "Simmons and Benjamin entered the home of the victim, Shirley Crook, after reaching through an open window and unlocking the back door. Simmons turned on a hallway light. Awakened, Mrs. Crook called out 'Who's there?'" (543 U.S. 551, 557). There follows a graphic, economically crafted narrative account of the extremely disturbing torture and murder. The teenaged killers bound and gagged Mrs. Crook with duct tape, then tied her hands and feet with electrical wire before throwing her from a railroad trestle into the Meramec River to drown. What reader can resist an instinctive reflection on his or her own deadbolts and latches on being presented with the image of the remorseless killer's arm reaching through Mrs. Crook's rear window as she slept? This biting *noire* imagery is only a small facet of the opinion, but it sets up and emotionally grounds the court's nuanced legal discussion of *ius cogens* (although without using the term), the consensual origins of law in national and international moral communities.

In conclusion, my argument is that investigating the dynamics of interplay among three interlinked speech genres, rule, policy, and reportage, can illuminate the cogeneration of the *is/ought/must* discursive complex of social reality. The internal grip of the rules that orchestrate social order—that is, the voluntary agreement that motivates compliance with a rule—is in many circumstances more powerful than threats of coercive enforcement, and it depends on a discursive marshalling of fact and sentiment. The basis of a rule's internal purchase on individual psychology can range from specific critical reflection (Hart 1961) to an unquestioned ideological sense of natural order (Gramsci 1992), and policy talk, in its various subgenres, evokes the whole range. Based on usage in ordinary language, and particularly in legal and regulatory discourse, it appears that policy—whether as insider-addressed, technical talk or broader depictions of social reality addressed to the public in mass mediated news—is never merely an innocent observation or simple constative, but is paired with a statement of force relations, explicit or implied, of a greater or lesser degree of generality. Policy talk is an exercise in rhetoric, serving to justify a rule by invoking public purposes or standards of fairness that are seen to be imbedded in the social universe of the rule's application.

CHAPTER 8

Order, Disorder, and the News Media in Western Society

Whose Side Are They On?

Ever since very early times, bishops in dogmatic or other conflict with other bishops have sought the assistance of their Roman colleague who, on principle, always took the party of the petitioner ... He came therefore to acquire the prerogative and tradition of a decisive tribunal. Here, what might be called the sociological logic of the situation of three, of which two are in conflict, is developed in great purity and intensity in the direction of the tertius gaudens.
—Georg Simmel, *The Triad*

In the present disturbed and unstable state of politics in Europe, there are two schismogeneses which stand out conspicuously; (a) the symmetrical schismogenesis in international rivalries, and (b) the complementary schismogenesis in "class-war." Here again ... the progressive evolution of behaviour towards greater and greater differentiation and mutual opposition is evident, and our politicians would appear to be as incapable of handling the process as the schizoid is of adjusting himself to reality.
—Gregory Bateson, *Naven*

That Devil News

Politicians, bureaucrats, generals, and so on, are often shocked—shocked!—by the cheeky, oppositional nature of news coverage that always seems to focus on what goes wrong and can serve to undermine the efforts of those in power. For example, Ari Fleischer, former press secretary in the second Bush administration, says in his memoir, *Taking Heat*, "the overly adversarial nature of the press and the relentless quest for conflict are creating a divide between writer and reader, reporter and viewer, journalist and source," and he adds that, "bad news travels through the press with a greater velocity and intensity than good news" and "bad news stories can stretch for days and weeks," while "good news stories are often one-day events" (Fleischer 2005: 99). Public opinion surveys have steadily indicated over recent years that many among the general public echo those sentiments and yearn for bright, uplifting stories—good news, in other words—rather than gloomy, scary, pessimistic accounts of what is wrong with the world. This feeling may explain in part the fact that the news media are among the social institutions with the lowest credibility among the US public, with a historic low of 28 percent expressing full confidence in a 2005 Gallup opinion survey (*Editor and Publisher* 2005). One of the findings to come out of George Gerbner's massive, long term investigation of violence in mass media content indicates that people who watch mass media news on television develop an unrealistic view of urban life, believing it to be much more dangerous than it really is (e.g., Gerbner and Gross 1976). Although Denis McQuail notes some serious reservations about Gerbner's dangerous world hypothesis among media theorists, there is no doubt that it is highly plausible and resonates with popular opinion (McQuail 1987: 284).

Criticism of this kind is a valid expression of people's feelings—nobody likes to be contradicted, criticized, or made to feel depressed—and as a political critique, of course, condemnation of press negativity and preoccupation with conflict often makes sense. In a story in *The Honolulu Advertiser* on the court appearance of a man accused of raping an 8-year-old child, reporter Ken Kobayashi recounts the defense attorney's objection to the court's allowing news cameras to show the accused in shackles. Kobayashi quotes the lawyer as saying, "I think it's racist to show a Micronesian man in chains on the evening news, but they don't show any pictures of good Micronesians doing good work" (Kobayashi 2005). The impact of news media content on racism is of course an important question (see Henry and Tator 2002). But would a counterbalancing feature on "good Micronesians doing good work" be *news?* If not, how could it be related to news? That, I think, is a good problem for advocates of public journalism—the much debated, as yet undefined, kind of journalism that promotes a positive link between news and community problem solving—to work on (see Glasser 1999). Finding a good, workable mix of education and news is a great idea, but redefining news itself is like trying to rewrite human nature by fiat.

Pro-social news media, of the kind evidently yearned for by so many in power, are by no means unknown to journalistic experience. Such media support the established leadership of the community they serve and strenuously avoid stirring up divisive controversies that might threaten social cohesion or shake public confidence. In a recent ethnographic study of politics and the press in Ghana, Jennifer Hasty reports that "an editor for the state-funded *Graphic* ... stressed the importance of responsibility and the commitment of his newspaper to the national interests of unity and development," while "editors of the private newspapers dismissed the sycophantic journalism of the state press and voiced their own set of commitments to editorial independence, freedom of speech and human rights" (Hasty 2005: x). Hasty remarks that she "was fascinated by these two contradictory interpretations of the democratic functionality of the press" (2005: x). Historically, small town newspapers in the US have been highly cooperative in their relations with local power elites. Tichenor, Donohue, and Olien (1980) systematically studied the participation of television and newspapers at difference stages of public conflict in rural and urban settings, and they observed that newspapers "live with the most intense conflicts of their communities," but they "do not necessarily turn the conflicts into public issues," and in small communities they often "play these conflicts down or avoid them entirely" (1980: 20). In the ideal type version of this situation, the mayor, the sheriff, and the newspaper editor make sure that the town does not get a black eye in public opinion and that conflicts do not get out of hand. Chain owned as well as locally owned newspapers in such venues can settle into the same pattern of accommodation and conflict avoidance (Baily 2004).

On a larger scale, whole nations can opt for forms of journalism that emphasize social solidarity and minimize internal disruption. In a seminal book published in 1956, *Four Theories of the Press: The authoritarian, libertarian, social responsibility, and Soviet communist concepts of what the press should be and do,* Fred Siebert, Theodore Peterson, and Wilbur Schramm explore fundamental differences among politically motivated expressions of journalistic practice that have found varying degrees of institutionalization. In one extreme, the press in the former Soviet Bloc countries, for example, submitted to party discipline, leaving the definition of truth in news—that is, what should be reported and how it should be interpreted—to those in a position to know, namely, ideologists and political leaders. This is not to imply, of course, that liberal media are unconstrained. In an apocryphal, cold war era confrontation, the US journalist says to the Soviet, "You are not free. The government tells you what to write!," and the Soviet journalist answers, "You are not free. Corporate interests and big business tell you what to write!"

Soviet-style journalism represented an entrenched, national establishment, but examples of cheerleading, subservient journalism are abundant in the US tradition as well. Most recently, even arguably the most serious newspapers in the US, the *New York Times* and the *Washington Post*, have engaged in public self-reflection and self-criticism regarding their uncritical acceptance of government arguments, actions, and justifications leading to the 2002 war against Iraq. More openly partisan news media, such as Fox Cable News, along with the perhaps less partisan but almost equally subservient CNN, made hardly any pretence of objectivity, at least early on, in their enthusiasm and tireless support for the government's prosecution of the war in Iraq. Critical press scholar Robert McChesney (1999), along with critical journalists such as Bill Moyers (Sorkin 2005), call journalists who depend on cultivating good relations with those in power in order to get their stories "government stenographers," and that phrase clearly conveys the subservient relationship to government in much normal (no government blood in the water) news reporting. And no doubt foreign wars represent a special case. It is very difficult for the news media, just as for the population generally, to voice opposition to the commander in chief in wartime (or even pre-wartime) without appearing to lack patriotic spirit or even the common decency to support the troops. Still, there are times when the supine press snaps into an oppositional, watchdog posture. That potential is always there, and it is enshrined in journalistic ideology and self-image. How can one account for its persistence in the face of well-entrenched (and well-rewarded) habits of subservience to power?

Georg Simmel (1955), in his classic exploration of the sociology of three, when two are in conflict, uses the term *tertius gaudens*, "the third who rejoices," in referring to those acting as third parties in conflict. He observes that the Bishop of Rome, at first just one powerful bishop among many in Europe, became the Pope because the succession of Roman bishops consistently offered to side with any bishop who came to them for help in a dispute with another bishop. Soon no bishop could afford *not* to seek such help—both parties to the conflict came to present their cases, and the Roman Bishop became an institutionalized third party who eventually accumulated enough authority to claim the right to adjudicate—not just mediate—all such conflicts within the church. Becoming the tertius gaudens, according to Simmel, was the path to enormous power in the Roman Catholic Church. In a more mundane example, Simmel argues that the consumer is the tertius gaudens with respect to producers of rival products in the general economy.

In a previous book chapter (Arno 1984: 229–238), I argued that the press in the US takes the role of tertius gaudens in every kind of conflict it can discover. Over its history, US journalism has developed an explicit professional ethos of objectivity, which is a necessary quality in a third party. Major entities engaged in a public conflict in all arenas of US life—in politics, commerce, and even in sports—typically turn to the press to get their sides of the story out. Like the contending bishops of the Middle Ages, they rush to get the ear of a powerful, uncommitted ally. Of course, the press itself, again like the Pope in this metaphor, represents access to a higher power. Public opinion, represented by the readership and viewership that the press can deliver, is the ultimate authority. The news media, accurately or not, are seen as vitally important in the formation of public opinion. The Pope has the ear of God, and the news media have the ear of public opinion. Being a disinterested third party, then, is a path to power and respect, and the news media have a powerful motive to portray themselves as—and to actually *be*—unbiased. Conversely, a newspaper or televised news organization that is obviously partisan forfeits its claim to third party authority. In international conflicts (Arno and Dissanayake 1984), a national press is powerfully drawn to support its own side, and citizens in wartime or during natural disasters have often turned to outside media for information. A villager caught in the middle of a third-world war may very well discount his or her own government's assurances that the enemy has been routed and is in retreat and turn instead to the BBC World Service radio news to learn how close the fighting is actually likely to come (Dissanayake 1984).

When I first thought about the news media as a Simmelian *tertius gaudens*, it seemed to me a solid insight. It certainly helped to explain why the media are drawn to conflict. And all of the pious—but I think often quite sincere—talk about objectivity and unbiased reporting in journalism—values persisting in the face of the many obstacles to their accomplishment—made sense. The theoretical model unified personal and institutional motivations not on the basis of some kind of surface, altruistic idealism, but in terms of a deeper, largely unspoken drive. That deeper force in human affairs is a craving to be listened to with respect—a motivation at least on par with mere economic gain. Yet there must be something wrong with this argument as a total explanation. Otherwise, the news media would have inexorably moved toward completing the logic of the sociological conflict triad and, through the mechanism of competitive selection in the national playing field of social justice, become paragons of sober objectivity. Obviously, this has not happened. I still think the argument works in explaining a persistent dimension of press behavior, but there must be some equally or more powerful interfering structural factor that has prevented the news media from actually becoming what they aspire to be.

In the Iraq war, both in the run-up to, and the conduct of, the war and occupation, it became apparent early on that the US public was split down the middle and highly polarized in relation to government policy. In that kind of circumstance, the two opposing blocs of opinion tend to be highly energized and unsettled in the sense of being under attack. Gregory Bateson (1958), writing some forty years after Simmel, but in the same plane of abstraction about the dynamics of interaction in social conflict, described the processes by which two parties develop and intensify a schism, or a deepening divide between their positions. Bateson identifies two kinds of schismogenesis, "complementary" and "symmetrical." A pattern of complementary schismogenesis develops when one side attacks, and the other cowers, which emboldens the first to attack more vigorously, leading to more abject cowering, and so on, as the two sides grow more and more apart. But in symmetrical schismogenesis the gap widens in another way—the pattern is one of escalation, in which the two sides trade licks. Attacking one another with increasing ferocity, each side sharpens its own sense of identity in relation to the other and hardens its own position. Applying this analysis to the problem at hand, one can see that a highly polarized phase in a conflict situation can readily evoke the Mr. Hyde of the news medium's split personality. The Dr. Jekyll of the US press persona is the rational, unbiased mediator, but Mr. Hyde is ruthlessly partisan. When public opinion is sharply polarized, the two sides are not seeking an evenhanded mediator. Each side wants to hear over and over again that they are in the right, reinforcing their embattled positions. Now, for the news media, the interactional path to both making money and being listened to is not objectivity, but rather the reinforcement of one or the other side's threatened identity.

Both Simmel's and Bateson's approaches to conflict communication draw upon wide ranging social and cultural contexts, and neither emerges from the focused study of news. Their analyses do apply to news, however, as a cultural phenomenon, and anthropology has historically pursued the empirical investigation of the linkages among culture, communication, and conflict.

Crime and Politics

A frequent criticism of the news media, along with negativity and bias, focuses attention on unintended injuries that can result from news. Like all social institutions, news media can cause harm while at the same time serving a useful purpose. At the level of individual injury, popular media criticism deplores the invasion of privacy and exploitation involved when the reporter stabs a microphone at a distraught victim of a disaster and asks, "how does it feel?"

At a structural level, too, news can be unsettling and disruptive, but if the news media simply supported the legitimacy of the establishment—government or corporate—they could hardly serve the basic, defining function of the news act: to convey an alarming report, grounded in reality, that can constitute the first step in managing threat and conflict. News media organizations live off of disorder, and without it they die as news sources. Given the unquenchable demand for "bad" news, sources seen as government or corporate poodles are replaced by other channels of news that are in one way or another insulated from overt censorship. Historically, US news media have at times challenged the establishment, as in the reporting of the Viet Nam war and the Watergate scandal. In the long run, however, the news media cannot afford to destroy the way of life that they are a part of any more than they can afford to abdicate their share of power as essential elements of the establishment. Still less can they afford to be seriously at odds with the basic values, prejudices, and cultural biases—the "stereotypes" that Lippmann (1922) identifies as necessary to intelligent thought—of their readership. They may come close to going over the line at times, but to survive and preserve their own place in the ruling order they must always pull back.

Media cycles of challenge and pullback are probably best charted on a time scale of decades rather than day-to-day. In the 1970s and 1980s, the press challenged the political balance of institutional power in the US, and all parties, press, government, and public, have reacted adaptively. Taking a historical section of the media's evolving, adaptive catering to order and disorder allows a glimpse of the way social structure learns and changes—in this case involving adjustments of news producers, consumers, and those who seek to use the news instrumentally. Shortly before Christmas, 1985, in a courtroom in Nantes, France, three highly charged institutions of Western society, crime, state authority, and the mass media, became entangled in a way that illustrates one of the more disturbing confusions of the times. The event itself was dramatic. A man armed with a revolver and a hand grenade forced his way into the courtroom, disarmed the guards, and gave their weapons to two of the criminal defendants. Holding judge, jury, and observers hostage, the intruder and his confederates then demanded that a television remote crew be brought in to broadcast the event (Bernstein 1985).

The impact of the news event, which attracted worldwide attention, was not due entirely to any unique dramatic quality of the action itself. Twenty years later, for example, a prisoner wrested a gun from a guard in an Atlanta courtroom and shot and killed the judge and other people before fleeing, but the underlying structural conflict was not presented as it was in Nantes. Certainly, in both cases it was arresting to see the naked reversal of power between criminal and court. But in Nantes the intruder, self-described as a Palestinian guerrilla, was quoted as saying that the event was intended as "a slap in the face to the French state," and there was a strange fascination for the television viewer in seeing an accused armed robber lecturing the court while behind him his confederates displayed their weapons in exaggerated, almost choreographic poses (Associated Press Photo 1985). "You came here to judge others," one said, in deadly mockery of a prosecutor's speech, "and you find yourselves on trial."

Although the tables were turned, there was no fundamental change in the adversarial relationship between law and crime in society. Shootouts and armed confrontations between government agents on one side and forces of crime on the other are common content of news around the world, and perhaps especially in the United States. Individual criminals and police officers confront one another in episodes of ordinary street crime in every US city, high tech police SWAT teams move against organized criminal enterprises, and the FBI squares off in military style against entrenched militia or other armed cults. In the category of politicized crime—as contrasted with criminalized politics—tactics may have shifted during the decades between 1985 and 2005, with less airline hijacking and more suicide bombings, but the conflict remains constant. There is really no novelty in seeing guns in court, then or now. In the Nantes case, the guards were already armed, as usual, before the intrusion. Deadly force is always at issue, nearer to or farther from the surface of the specific interaction, whenever criminal deviance and law collide. What emerges in the Nantes incident as truly anomalous, however, is the position of the third force of social organization involved, the mass media. During the following twenty years, the relative positions of all three have evolved together, each affecting the other. The question posed for the mass news media is whose side are they on (Arno 1986)?

The role of the mass media in the "trial in reverse" at Nantes was not perceived entirely in terms of the event itself in 1985. A train of previous incidents, fresh in the minds of the public and the media personnel, formed a context in which the televising of the crime could be understood. Perhaps the most salient of these precedents had taken place only four months earlier, when terrorists held 39 airline passengers hostage for two weeks in Beirut. During the ordeal, the news media, specifically television, served repeatedly to disseminate terrorist messages, and the situation supported the argument that the emerging genre of international political communication through the seizure of hostages was predicated squarely on the involvement of the mass media. Media, government, and the public had to consider the possibility that without instant publicity and the opportunity to explicitly delineate the meaning of the action in their own terms, terrorists would abandon symbolic hostage taking as a form of expression. Given access to worldwide television audiences, terrorists can explain their actions as political grievance and demands for justice, rather than to allow the established order to define the events as criminal behavior. By contrast, the taking and gruesome killing of hostages during the current US occupation of Iraq seems more intended to terrify and demoralize than to present ignored demands. Still, because news media present events as messages to be decoded, the questions still arise: who is sending this message and what does it mean? If the answer provided by US government spokespersons—"it means they hate freedom and democracy"—seems inadequate, the perpetrators have succeeded in opening a political debate. The standoff at Nantes ended with the hostages being released and the terrorist arrested at the Nantes airport, which now strikes one as an almost civilized ending. In Iraq, terrorists have provided the news media with videos of hostage beheadings—but the news media have been selective in airing them because of their gruesomeness. In this attempted use of the news media, the terrorists seem to have stepped over the line, overwhelming the political character of their action with its criminality and forcing the US media to alter their own position in the structural equation.

In general, crime is intended as an act to be carried out in stealth and secrecy, and publicity frustrates it. News media reporting private crimes, such as muggings and burglaries, are not in any direct sense generating that crime. They are merely reflecting something that already exists in society, and, at the same time, by making potential victims aware of the dangers and by focusing political pressure on the authorities to take measures against it, they are acting to help suppress it. By contrast, political acts in open societies are public in nature and often depend on public opinion to be effective. Media involvement in politics, therefore, is participatory and actively encourages it to flourish. But what happens when crime and politics merge, throwing our understanding of appropriate media behavior into a state of confusion? As a form of politics, terrorism is amplified and encouraged by media participation, but as crime, it can be thwarted by the media spotlight. Citizen awareness is often cited as a countermeasure against terrorism.

Lippmann characterized the entire content of mass media news as a "pseudo-environment" (1922: 10), as contrasted with the real world of direct experience. More narrowly, Daniel Boorstin identified a particular kind of news item as the reporting of a "pseudo-event" (1962: 11–12). Pseudo-events represent a large segment of modern news media content, and they are defined as events that are planned, staged, and carried out specifically for mass media coverage. News conferences of those in power are examples, as are political demonstrations by those out of power. Boorstin rightly denigrates the authenticity of many pseudo-events as news, but they can also be real news at times, in the same sense that speech can constitute performative action—that is to say, when just saying something creates a new social reality. Terrorist acts, reported as news, illustrate with particular clarity the dual character of "real," criminal threat and "political" rhetoric. When John Tierney (2005) argued that suicide bombings in Iraq are not news after the first few events, he was making a distinction between "real" death and performative death as a political statement. That is, instead of "70 killed in Suicide Bombing," a headline might as well read "Insurgency Forces Said Again Today...," which would have little force as news. When death is defined as a political statement, it undergoes a profound category shift.

News and Death, Political and Personal

On 19 February 1998, Shokei Arai, a brilliant and popular maverick Japanese politician, hanged himself in a Tokyo hotel room. He had been accused of corrupt financial dealings and was under intense pressure from the media and prosecutors, who were reportedly about to arrest him. According to Miyuki Matsuo (2005), Arai was highly unusual among Japanese politicians in his public preoccupation with death. He was a devoted reader of the novelist Yukio Mishima, whose book *Hagakure Nyuomon* concerns the aesthetics of death and the code of the samurai. Another book, *Nihonjin no shishei kan* ("The Japanese View of Life and Death") by Toru Sagara, was found on the desk in Arai's study, with many underlined passages (Matsuo 2005: 122). Matsuo argues that Arai's idiosyncratic devotion to this archaic element of Japanese traditional culture—the samurai code of death—may have been related to his personal and political identity crisis as a prominent Japanese politician of Korean ancestry. In some ways, perhaps, he wanted to prove himself more Japanese than the Japanese. Whatever the psychological or political origins of his thinking, Arai expounded in his autobiographical writings—he wrote three books about his political and personal life—a concept of "political death." He initially opposed the 1991 US war against Iraq, led by the first President Bush, but he later supported it because he came to see that the deaths involved were politically meaningful and therefore acceptable. From that point on, he began to talk about death as an important political concept. According to Matsuo, Arai's phrase for political death, *seijiteki na shi,* is simply a literal expression in Japanese, not a cultural idiom. In his writings and conversations, Arai declared that asking citizens to die for their nation must be the last resort in politics and that politicians themselves must also be willing to die in the same context (Matsuo 2005: 32). Arai said that he would be willing to die for Japan and his wife, with whom he was deeply in love.

Although no US politician that I know of has so explicitly propounded a doctrine of political death, I think it is a concept of universal application. The politician or general, who as a private person exhibits the normal range of moral virtue and weakness, is able with clear conscience to give orders that he or she knows will result in many deaths. Priests who are exquisitely sensitive to abortion or even contraception—not to speak of euthanasia—as sinful killing, can support capital punishment and just war. In the most delusional extreme, a pro-life activist can justify killing doctors who perform abortions. Eric Rudolph, convicted of bombing a Birmingham abortion clinic and having confessed to bombing a crowded event at the 1996 Atlanta Olympics, a gay bar, and another abortion clinic in Atlanta, showed no regret for killing and injuring people and made a statement at his sentencing "angrily denouncing abortion and telling the federal court that 'deadly force is needed to stop it'" (Rahimi 2005). Some of these distinctions make sense when the victim is defined not as innocent, but as a person whose own behavior justifies political killing—that is, killing that is morally just and performed in the name of, and for the benefit of, the community. But war obviously requires expanding the justification for death beyond the personal culpability of the victim. Enemy soldiers need not be personally culpable, personal self-defense is not necessary to justify killing the enemy, and the unavoidable deaths of innocent civilians are at times held to be acceptable as collateral damage. Furthermore, one's own troops must be ordered to their likely deaths at times, and their deaths must be seen by their comrades, families, and fellow citizens as politically justified as well.

Raymond Kelly, in *Warless Societies and the Origin of War*, a remarkable comparative, empirical study of the origin of warfare in human society, argues that war, as contrasted with the capital punishment of a specific offender, arises when people organize their social world in terms of exclusive corporate groups. When people reach a stage of organizational integration in which one's identity as a group member subsumes one's individual identity, members achieve a moral equivalence, and for certain purposes, one member is perfectly substitutable for another. Internally, social identities may be sharply differentiated in terms of gender, seniority, political rank, and so on. But rights to key productive resources—material and cultural—are vested in a collective sovereignty, and access to the resources, however it may be regulated internally, is available only through membership. When a society's political economic organization is characterized by moral and legal equivalence among group members vis-à-vis nonmembers, warfare is possible. Kelly argues that "social substitutability" in the targeting of individuals for organized, socially sanctioned lethal violence represents the essential difference between war and other forms of morally justified killing, such as capital punishment (Kelly 2000: 7). The range of economic systems, population densities, historical eras, and so on, in which social substitutability arises is extremely wide, as Kelly demonstrates through cross-cultural ethnographic analysis. The inter-group situation in which an injury—such as a killing—to a group member is understood as an injury to all members, and conversely the liability for the injury is also collectively shared by every member of the perpetrator's group, is not at all rare. Blood feud and inter-group warfare, together with capital punishment, then, represent the institutionalization of political death on a wide scale in human history.

In modern societies, the mass media play an important role in representing the meaning of, and the appropriate response to, death in the community. The death of an accident or crime victim is personal, but it can have important political consequences as the news audience reacts and demands a collective response to any public issues, such as law and order, safety, and so on, raised by the death. It may be a politically significant death, then, but that does not make it a political death in the sense of being justified by social purpose. The execution of a criminal, on the other hand, is an example of political death because it is carried out by society and is understood to be for the benefit of society. While the legal system, not the mass media, is entrusted with the process of capital punishment, ambiguity as to the meaning of the death can be introduced by media coverage. Obviously, each death by legal execution or under military orders in war is both personal and political at the same time, but only the political definition is debatable. Personal death is final and unarguable for the victim and his or her survivors. Political death requires an official imprimatur in modern society, but that certification can be contested, and eventually political deaths can be decertified by counter interpretation. Layla Renshaw (2007) describes the strategic representation in the Spanish media of Republican civilian victims of the Nationalists in the Spanish Civil War whose bodies are now being exhumed from mass graves, identified, and reburied. Depicting the dead in personal terms, the *fathers* and *grandfathers* of living family members, deflects the overt opposition to the exhumation project from the powerful Spanish right wing, which would be provoked by identifying the dead politically as *communists* or *socialists*. The Spanish right, in the Franco tradition, strongly rejects the idea of memorializing the "enemy" dead from the Civil War. But as I have argued in previous chapters, virtually any news story can serve to energize sharply contrasting discourses. Leftist media consumers in Spain interpret the personalized Spanish Civil War deaths in the political contexts evoked by relatively recent media coverage of the "disappeared" victims of the dirty wars waged by right wing dictatorships in Latin America.

While a dominating coalition of US conflict discourses, including the very powerful one centered on the rule of law, support the meaning of legal execution as political death, other active narratives insist that capital punishment is only personal in character, amounting to "state killing." Because of its narrative flexibility and communicative accessibility to the mass audience, news has particularly powerful potential for supporting as well as for destabilizing the political definition of death in specific cases. Death—even a legal execution—as reported in the news media can be more concrete and closer to the reader's emotions than death as a legal order. In the case of capital punishment, the law itself, like the news media, allows the contesting discourses, pro- and anti-capital punishment, to display themselves and to seek recruits. If capital punishment is eventually discarded by the US legal system, on the basis of the constitutional "cruel and unusual punishment" arguments and perhaps the *jus cogens* doctrine of international law—that is, the recognition of an international moral community touched on by the decision of the US Supreme Court in *Roper v. Simmons* (2005)—it will represent a joint accomplishment of the law, the mass media news, and many distinct systems of social identity and values in the larger community.

The definitional negotiation of personal and political death can be especially volatile in wartime, if public opinion is divided, with the news media playing a major part in the process. In the latter stages of the Viet Nam war, for example, casualties represented on television news came to be viewed by larger and larger segments of audience as personal deaths, stripped of the political justification necessary to legitimate war deaths. The interpretation of death in personal rather than political terms is facilitated by factors related to the text and also to the cognitive state of the audience—that is, the balance of conflict discourse systems in the news community. Graphic visual images direct the viewer's attention away from the political and toward the personal reality of death, and nightly television coverage of combat death is widely credited with having eroded domestic support for the Viet Nam war. Nonvisual dimensions of the story can be powerful as well, however. As I argued in chapter 2, the plot structure of news narrative as an aspect of the reader/story leg of the news triangle can grease the communicative tracks of the story, and some basic storylines with strong hooks in popular imagination can overwhelm the political definition of the situation. For example, a particular suicide bombing in Iraq took place when the bomber—and one is strongly inclined to say "killer" in this case rather than "insurgent"—drove to where US soldiers were passing out candy to Iraqi children and exploded his device, killing himself, one US American, and 24 children. In a *New York Times* story, Kirk Semple wrote, "the attack, in a poor, predominantly Shiite neighborhood of eastern Baghdad, left a wrenching scene of bloodshed, anger, and despair. Children's colored slippers, pieces of flesh and shrapnel were strewn around the wide crater left in the street by the bomb. Women wailed and slapped themselves on the chest and face in a ritual of grief as bodies were placed in crude coffins and carried away" (Semple 2005). The last sentence was illustrated by a powerful accompanying photograph, presented in color and in enlargeable format in the online edition of the newspaper (Hadi Mizban/Associated Press photo 2005). This particular story, ironically evoking for many readers the culturally iconic images of WWII US GIs—the good guys in the good war—handing out candy to children in liberated Europe, offers complex readings that could support both political and personal meanings of the multiple deaths, and the highly polarized state of US public opinion at that stage of the Iraq war made its interpretation especially volatile. Atrocities fuel the sense of collective danger to one's own group and collective blame of the enemy, reinforcing the social substitutability that Kelly identifies as the structural logic of warfare. But, on the other hand, the accumulating weight of the personal narratives of war death can overbalance a weak (that is, contested by many powerful conflict discourse systems) political rationale for a conflict. Certainly the differences between WWII—the archetypal good war with noble purpose and victorious outcome—and the second Iraq war are sharply drawn by the incident.

Conclusions

Returning to the basic communication model of the news process suggested in chapter 3, event>story>reader, I would like to pose again the basic question I started with. What is news? A commonsense response from the perspective of the journalist or reader is that the *event* is the news. In one sense, this answer is obviously not right. Like a tree that falls when no one is around, the event that is neither observed nor reported is not news. News is a phenomenon of communication, not a question of ontology. In another, more important sense, however, the "event" answer is right on target. The event, the factual reality that something actually happened, is the only absolute factor in the news process. The other elements of the news are necessary, but they are defined by their relationships to the event. An event that is badly reported or misunderstood by the reader does not cease to have happened. The unreported fact retains its potential, at least, to become news. A biased or radically incomplete story, however, becomes less than nothing in terms of news—anti-news in fact, a lie or fiction—if it loses its foundation in fact. The last element of the model, the consumer of news, has been a focus of this book because I insist that news must be news to someone. Various species of non-news factual reports may represent *information, education, history,* or some other genre of communication, but news is most usefully defined, as I have argued, by its connection to a live, present threat to some interest of the reader. The news reaction can be mild, stimulating, challenging, startling, or scary depending on the proximity and seriousness of the threat. Good news can display a similar range of intensity depending on the underlying threat that it draws its meaning from. But here again, an actual event is key. Reaction to a false report is not part of a genuine news process. The *fact* of the mistaken reaction, as event, especially if widely shared or significant in some way, can be news, but the original report is not. If a reader or a body of readers reacts to reports that Martians have landed on earth (assuming it is not true!), something other than news has been accomplished. It may be a hoax, like the Sokal hoax discussed in chapter 4, and a report of the perpetration of the hoax may be news to those concerned with the fragility of truth in society's institutions of information flow.

There remains for consideration as news (or not news) the situation in which an actual event is reported but the reader's reaction of alarm is based on what others might see as a bizarre interpretation. For example, a report of a deadly new form of disease, such as an untreatable influenza, might be interpreted by members of a religious cult as an awaited sign of the apocalypse. Although offensive to scientific rationality and probably dysfunctional at personal and political levels, this kind of event>story>reader sequence can still be read as an authentic enactment of news. To disqualify this kind of event as news on the basis of unreasonable interpretation would be to insist that event and interpretation together constitute an indivisible unit of truth in journalism. But such a unit is inherently unstable because it encompasses the two very different kinds of truth. The event is subject to an empirical test of truth. It either happened or it did not, according to reliable, observational evidence. The type of evidence relied on depends on the news community, and empirical truth is always defeasible, but "actual event" represents a distinct kind of judgment. The interpretation of the news event, on the other hand, is measured by intersubjective, socially constructed truth, equally powerful in human affairs, but different from empirical truth. The third element of the communication model, the story, represents a mediation between the two forms of truth. The story represents the verifiable facts that constitute the event for the news process, but it selects elements of the event and presents them in ways that facilitate or suggest interpretation. As I have argued in previous chapters, news media that strive for journalistic objectivity routinely present material selected to evoke multiple interpretations. The facilitated interpretations are chosen by reporter and editor on the basis of the ideological slant—whether conscious or not—of the media enterprise or, more commonly on an informed estimate of the conflict discourse systems present in the news community.

If the two forms of truth essential to the news act—empirical truth of the event and relative truth of the interpretation—are merged in analysis, one standard or the other will be imputed to both. When one is selected, the other will be elided or infected by misreading. If the truth standard of empirical reality alone is applied to the news act, for example, the analysis devalues the rich dimension of identity work and the expanded perspective that "deviant," nonstandard interpretations bring to mass media news. Practitioners of news, both journalists and readers, who hold to this view will try to rigidly segregate opinion from news and may believe that reports couched in terms of conventional understanding are thereby objective and free of bias. Both are demonstrably mistaken.

On the other hand, if relative truth is the sole standard in news, respect for the empirical grounding of news is eroded, and the pragmatic function of news in public threat management is endangered. Clearly, both kinds of truth should be accommodated in a theory of news. In chapter 4, I argued that the concept of truth internal to the news act is a judgment by the reader, from his or her own perspective as a discursively positioned subject, about the correspondence between event and story. The reader asks, "if I were investigating this story, would I have asked these questions and come up with these answers?" This essential dimension of truth in journalism is clearly relative, but the pragmatic meaning leg of the news triangle that connects the reader and the event in the real world reasserts the nonrelative, empirical dimension of truth in news. In the end, if either dimension of journalistic truth fails, if the event did not happen or if no interpretation links it to the reader's interests, news does not happen. News finds its truth, empirical and interpretive, in the lives of its readers. Returning to the Koran flushing story discussed in chapter 5, the fact that, based on a failure of corroborative evidence, the reported event did not happen invalidates the story as news. It is not sufficient to say "it might well have happened" or "worse things than that did happen" or "it raised valid issues." Invented details, however effective in communicating a story, destroy it as news. Stories based on fictional events are rejected vigorously and categorically by the news community, because they attack the credibility of the whole genre. The 2003 Jason Blair scandal at the *New York Times,* and many similar invented news exposés, demonstrate how seriously journalists and readers take the issue of factuality in news. Reporters who fake the news are not simply regarded as lazy or incompetent, but almost as evil or disgusting. By contrast, the self-described fake news of a comedian like Jon Stewart, as long as it is pegged to actual political events, can function as commentary, media criticism, and even reporting in the news process.

Regarding the other part of the *Newsweek* Koran episode—the use of the report in inflammatory rhetoric that incited violence and death in Afghanistan—the speeches and deaths hold up as valid, verifiable events that provide a scaffold for opinion and perspective-driven interpretation. Moving from a mere correlation of rhetoric and death—the two happened together—to a estimate of proximate cause represents a narrative transition highly motivated by discursive subjectivity. For active readers positioned by an *anti-media, irresponsible journalism* coalition of conflict discourses, the story validates a sense of embattled righteousness in the face of attack by the liberal media, while the *media watchdog, government-critical* discourse sees an interpretive overplaying of the causal importance of the Koran flushing rhetoric, in context of the established political forces of the region, as an attack on press freedom.

Along with the question of how news usefully can be defined, I have also pursued in this book a delineation of the conflict management function of news and its relation to other conflict management institutions and practices. The broad question of media power has attracted scholarly attention for over half a century—from the works of Harold Innis (e.g., 1950) and Marshall McLuhan (e.g., 1964) to that of contemporary sociologists and political economists like John B. Thompson (1995) and Manuel Castells (1997). Nick Couldry and James Curran, in *Contesting Media Power* (2003), contrast two approaches to the question of media power. One approach, brilliantly explored by Castells in his work on networked society, is to view mass communication media primarily as just that—media. As such, they provide an arena in which contests of power originating in various sectors of social life—political, religious, ethnic, and so on—are played out. As a relatively transparent medium, then, mass communication can amplify or extend power that comes from other sources, but it has no endogenous power of its own. The other, complementary approach holds that "contrary to the illusion that media only 'mediate' what goes on in the rest of society, the media's representational power is one of society's main forces in is own right" (Couldry and Curran 2003: 3–4). The general form of this debate is familiar to legal anthropologists who have dealt with the more specific question of the role of language as either transparent or formative in disputes (Brenneis 1988; Arno 1993). In both settings—media power in general and language power in law and disputes—the most fruitful resolution is the recognition of both approaches in theory construction as well as in case analysis.

In this book, I have looked at the question of media power by narrowing the field of inquiry to a specific dimension of mass communication, the news media, and to a specific function of news, conflict management. Looked at from a cybernetic, systems perspective, the news media have tremendous power in their own right, but, at the same time, they are also substantively quite open and widely distributed in procedural operation. There is no body of uniquely *journalistic* answers to social problems; reporters and opinion writers draw on virtually every kind of knowledge and reasoning about conflict in society. The forums in which news "holds court" include the enormous range between individual conversation and legislative hearing. As an institutionalized form of communication about conflict, then, the news media offer an interesting formal contrast to the legal system.

In conclusion, I would argue that the news, as a total social process, is enormously powerful in social life, and it is by no means a passive, transparent medium. Like other fully developed forms of control communication that draw narrative energy from emergent conflict discourse systems in their communication communities, mass media news is a distinct institutional presence in social life with recognizable functional and professional boundaries. Modern technologies of information acquisition and dissemination have vastly amplified the reach of mass media news, but the ancient underlying function of conveying alarming reports as a first step in conflict management has survived intact. In the perspective on news that I have offered in this book, I place particular emphasis on the audience as participants in the kaleidoscopic tumult of conflict discourse systems in the news community. Although I have maintained a theme of criticizing media criticism, particularly concerning the myths surrounding issues of negativity and objectivity, it is clear that media criticism is essential to the news process. The news media can go wrong in many ways, including the mortal sins of lying and being the uncritical servants of established power. But in the end, it is the audience that deserves the harshest criticism. Ignorant, selfish, irrational news consumers deserve, and get, ignorant, dysfunctional journalism. Lacking background knowledge of history, cultural diversity, and basic science, many in the news community are unable to recognize important threats to their own long term interests and prefer to pursue superficial validation of their social personae by wasting their time on details of the latest "trial of the century" involving celebrity misconduct. Stories of that kind can be real news from the conflict discourse system perspective so long as the events reported really happened and readers see them as bearing on their own anxieties about social identity, but, in excess, they are not politically healthy from the civic news perspective. Richard Posner concludes that the "sliver of the public that does have a serious interest in policy issues" is well served by the news resources that are available (Posner 2005). That sliver needs to be greatly increased by major investments in the institutions and media of education and aesthetics that form the cultural context of the news community. The conflict discourse systems that govern public opinion in the parliamentary theater of news thrive on diversity and narrative energy. The cultivation of other information genre will never replace dedicated forms of conflict communication, but they can sharpen their contributions to society.

References

Agar, Michael. 2005. Local Discourse and Global Knowledge: The Role of Local Knowledge. *Language in Society* 34 (1): 1–22.

Amsterdam, Anthony, and Jerome Bruner. 2000. *Minding the Law*. Cambridge, MA: Harvard University Press.

Arno, Andrew. 2005. Cobo and Tabua in Fiji: Two Forms of Cultural Currency in an Economy of Sentiment. *American Ethnologist* 32(1): 46–62.

———. 2003. Aesthetics, Intuition, and Reference in Fijian Ritual Communication: Modularity in and Out of Language. *American Anthropologist* 105(4): 807–819.

———. 2002. The Politics of Incommensurability: Localism, Globalism, and Cultural Production in Fiji. In *Sights of Contestation: Localism, Globalism, and Cultural Production in Asia and the Pacific*, ed. Kwok-Kan Tam, Wimal Dissanayake, and Terry Siu-Han Yip. Hong Kong: The Chinese University Press.

———. 1993. *The World of Talk on a Fijian Island*. Norwood, NJ: Ablex.

———. 1986. Faut-il Fusiler la Presse? *Le Temps Strategique* No. 18: 75–83.

———. 1985. Structural Communication and Control Communication: An Interactionist Perspective on Legal and Customary Procedures for Conflict Management. *American Anthropologist* 87(1): 40–55.

———. 1984. The News Media as Third Parties in National and International Conflict: Duobus Litigantibus Tertius Gaudet. In *The News Media in National and International Conflict*, ed. Andrew Arno and Wimal Dissanayake, 229–238. Boulder: Westview.

———. 1980. Fijian Gossip as Adjudication: A Communication Model of Informal Control. *Journal of Anthropological Research* 36(3): 343–360.

———, and Wimal Dissanayake, eds. 1984. *The News Media in National and International Conflict*. Boulder: Westview Press.

Asato, Bruce. 1989. Troubled Worksite Blessed (Photograph). *The Honolulu Advertiser*, A12, August 2, 1989.

Askew, Kelly. 2002. Introd. to *The Anthropology of Media*, ed. Kelly Askew and Richard R. Wilk. Malden, MA: Blackwell Publishing.

Associated Press Photo. 1985. Gunman Frees Defendants and Seizes Hostages at French Trial. *The New York Times*, December 20, 1985.

Austin, J.L. 1962. *How to do Things with Words*. Cambridge, MA: Harvard University Press.

Ayn Rand Institute. 2005. Website http://www.aynrand.org/site/PageServer.

Bagdikian, Benjamin H. 2000. *The Media Monopoly*. Boston: Beacon Press.

Bailey, Gina J. 2004. Short-Circuiting Democracy?: The Paradox of Competition in Newspapering and Why We Can't Get "There" from "Here." PhD. Dissertation, Vancouver, B.C.: Simon Fraser University.

Bakhtin, Mikhail M. 1986. The Problem of Speech Genres. In *Speech Genres and Other Late Essays*, trans. Vern W. McGee and ed. Caryl Emerson and Michael Holquist, 61–97. Austin: University of Texas Press.

Barrett, Greg. 1989. Troubles on H-3 Strengthen Beliefs in Power of Supernatural Wrath. *The Honolulu Advertiser*, A1–A2, August 4, 1989.

———, and Jennifer Hong. 1989. H-3 Work Halted After Accident. *The Honolulu Advertiser*, A1–A2, July 30, 1989.

Basu, Rekha. 1996. 'Conspiracy' in a Gorilla Pit. In Editorials, *Honolulu Advertiser*, A8, August 26, 1996.

Bateson, Gregory. 1972. A Theory of Play and Fantasy. In *Steps to an Ecology of Mind*, by Gregory Bateson, 177–193. New York: Ballantine Books.

———. 1958. *Naven*. Stanford: Stanford University Press.

Baudrillard, Jean. 1988. *Selected Writings*. Ed. Mark Poster. Stanford: Stanford University Press.

Berlin, Isaiah. 2000. *Three Critics of the Enlightenment: Vico, Hamann, Herder*. Princeton: Princeton University Press.

Bernstein, Richard. 1985. Hostages Seized at French Trial: Gunman Bursting into Court is Joined by Defendants—Judge and Jurors Held. *The New York Times*, A9, December 20, 1985.

Bilmes, Jack. 1985. Freedom and Regulation: An Anthropological Critique of Free Market Ideology. *Research in Law and Economics* Vol. 7: 123–147.

Bilmes, Jack, and John Woodbury. 1991. Deterrence and Justice: Setting Civil Penalties in the Federal Trade Commission. *Research in Law and Economics* Vol. 14: 191–221.

Blackmore, Susan. 1999. *The Meme Machine*. New York: Oxford University Press.

Boorstin, Daniel J. 1962. *The Image: Or What Happened to the American Dream*. New York: Atheneum.

Bourdieu, Pierre. 1991. *Language and Symbolic Power*. Cambridge: Harvard University Press.

Bovard, James. 1995. No Accountability at the FBI. *The Wall Street Journal*, A20, January 10, 1995.

Bragg, Rick. 1996. Loved Ones Lost, Perhaps Never to Be Found: Inaccessibility of Bodies is Adding to the Pain of Grieving Families. *The New York Times*, A1, May 13, 1996.

Brenneis, Donald Lawrence. 2008. Telling Theories. *Ethos* 36(1): 115–169.

————. 2005. Thinking about Our Diverse Audiences and Their Transformations. *Anthropology News* 46(6): 8–9.

————. 1988. Language and Disputing. *Annual Reviews in Anthropology* 17: 221–237.

————. 1984. Grog and gossip in Bhatgaon: style and substance in Fiji Indian conversation. *American Ethnologist* 11: 487–506.

Brenneis, Donald L., and Fred R. Meyers. 1984. *Dangerous Words: Language and Politics in the Pacific*. New York: New York University Press.

Brison, Karen J. 1992. *Just Talk: Gossip, Meetings, and Power in a Papua New Guinea Village*. Berkeley: University of California Press.

Bronowski, Jacob. 1978. *The Origins of Knowledge and Imagination*. New Haven: Yale University Press.

Buckley, Jerome Hamilton. 1966. *The Triumph of Time: A Study of the Victorian Concepts of Time, History, Progress, and Decadence*. Cambridge, MA: Harvard University Press.

Burns John F. and Terrence Neilan. 2005. At Least 60 Are Killed in New Round of Attacks in Iraq. *The New York Times*, May 11, 2005. http://www.nytimes .com/2005/05/11/international/middleeast/11cnd-iraq.html/. Accessed June 6, 2005.

Castells, Manuel. 1997. *The Power of Identity*. Malden, MA: Blackwell Publishers.

Caughey, John L. 1984. *Imaginary Social Worlds: A Cultural Approach*. Lincoln: University of Nebraska Press.

Chace, Susan. 1989. Safety in the Park: In Women's Hands. *The New York Times*, A31, April 27, 1989.

Clark, Hugh. 1978. 51 Hilo Protesters Arrested, Demonstrations Shut Airport. *The Honolulu Advertiser*, A1–A3, September 5, 1978.

Clifford, James, and George E. Marcus, eds. 1986. *Writing Culture: The Poetics and Politics of Ethnography*. Berkeley: University of California Press.

CNN, Online Newsmaker Profile. 2001. John Walker Lindh: The Case of the Taliban American. CNN Newsmaker Profile. http://www.cnn.com/CNN/ Programs/people/shows/walker/profile.html/.

Coman, Mihai. 2005. News Stories and Myth—The Impossible Reunion? In *Media Anthropology*, ed. Eric W. Rothenbuhler and Mihai Coman. Thousand Oaks, CA: Sage Publications.

Conley, John M., and William M. O'Barr. 1998. *Just Words: Law, Language, and Power*. Chicago: University of Chicago Press.

————. 1990. *Rules versus Relationships: The Ethnography of Legal Discourse*. Chicago: University of Chicago Press.

Coronas, Sister Teresa Ann. 1996. Don't Fault Mrs. Clinton for Seeking Guidance. In Letters, *Honolulu Advertiser*, A12, July 2, 1996.

Couldry, Nick, and James Curran, eds. 2003. *Contesting Media Power: Alternative Media in a Networked World*. New York: Rowman and Littlefield.

Crawford, Cindy. 2005. Letter to the Editor. In *What the President Said About Iraq* (6 Letters). *The New York Times*, August 25, 2005. http://www.nytimes .com/2005/08/25/opinion/125iraq.html/. Accessed August 25, 2005.

Crawford, Peter Ian, and Sigurjon Baldur Hafsteinsson. 1996. *The Construction of the Viewer: Media Ethnography and the Anthropology of Audiences*. Brooklyn: Smyrna Press/Intervention Press.

Dawkins, Richard. 1989. *The Selfish Gene*. New ed. New York: Oxford University Press.

Dennett, Daniel C. 1991. *Consciousness Explained*. New York: Little, Brown and Company.

Dissanayake, Wimal. 1984. The Roles Played by the National and International Press in the Management of the Sri Lankan Insurrection of 1971. In *The News Media in National and International Conflict*, ed. Andrew Arno and Wimal Dissanayake, 167–181. Boulder: Westview.

Douglas, Mary, and Stephen Ney. 1998. *Missing Persons: A Critique of the Social Sciences*. Berkeley, University of California Press.

Dupré, John. 2006. Scientific Classification. *Theory, Culture & Society* 23(2-3): 30–32.

Dworkin, Ronald M. 1985. *A Matter of Principle*. Cambridge, MA: Harvard University Press.

———. 1977. Is Law a System of Rules? Chapter II of *The Philosophy of Law*, ed. R.M. Dworkin, 38–65. New York: Oxford University Press.

Dwyer, Jim. 2002. Likely U-Turn by Prosecutors in Jogger Case. *The New York Times*, A1, October 12, 2002.

Eades, Diana, ed. 1995. *Language in Evidence: Issues Confronting Aboriginal and Multicultural Australia*. Sydney: UNSW Press.

Editor and Publisher. 2005. Gallup: Public Confidence in News Media Falls to New Low. *Editor and Publisher Journal*, June 10, 2005. http://www.editorandpublisher.com/eandp/news/article_display.jsp?vnu_content_id=1000954852/. Accessed July 19, 2005.

Engelke, Matthew, and Matt Tomlinson, eds. 2006. *The Limits of Meaning: Case Studies in the Anthropology of Christianity*. New York: Berghahn Books.

Fairclough, Norman. 1995. *Media Discourse*. London: Edward Arnold.

Fallows, James M. 1997. *Breaking the News: How the Media Undermine American Democracy*. New York: Vintage Books.

Felsteiner, William L. F., Richard L. Abel, and Austin Sarat. 1980–81. The Emergence and Transformation of Disputes: Naming, Blaming, and Claiming. *Law and Society Review* 15(3-4): 631–654.

Fish, Stanley. 1996. Professor Sokal's Bad Joke. Op-Ed in *The New York Times*, A, May 21, 1996.

Fisher, Roger, and William Ury. 1983. *Getting to Yes*. New York: Penguin Books.

Fiske, John. 1996. *Media Matters: Race and Gender in U.S. Politics*. Minneapolis: University of Minnesota.

Fleischer, Ari. 2005. *Taking Heat*. New York: Harper Collins Publishers, Inc.

Flyvbjerg, Bent. 2001. *Making Social Science Matter: Why Social Inquiry Fails and How It Can Succeed Again*. New York: Cambridge University Press.

Fortes, Meyer. 1983. Rules and the Emergence of Society. Occasional Paper No. 39, *Royal Anthropological Institute of Great Britain and Ireland*. London: Royal Anthropological Institute.

Foucault, Michel. 1978. *The History of Sexuality, Volume I: An Introduction*. New York: Vintage Books.

Frankfurt, Harry G. 2005. *On Bullshit*. Princeton, NJ: Princeton University Press.

Frantz, Douglas, and Desmond Butler. 2002. Imam at German Mosque Preached Hate to 9/11 Pilots. New York Times, July 16 2002. http://www.nytimes.com/2002/07/16/international/europe/16GERM.html/.

Friedman, Jonathan. 1992. Review of Nicholas Thomas, *Out of Time: History and Evolution in Anthropological Discourse*. Pacific Studies 15(2): 109–118.

Friedrich, Paul, and James Redfield. 1978. Speech as a Personality Symbol: The Case of Achilles. *Language* 54(2): 263–288.

Galtung, Johan, and Richard Vincent. 2004. *U.S. Glasnost: Missing Political Themes in U.S. Media Discourse*. Cresskill, NJ: Hampton Press.

———. 1992. *Global Glasnost: Toward a New World Information and Communication Order?* Cresskill, NJ: Hampton Press.

Gayner, Jeffrey B. 1995. The Contract with America: Implementing New Ideas in the U.S. In The Heritage Lectures, No. 549. Washington, D.C.: The Heritage Foundation. http://www.heritage.org/Research/PoliticalPhilosophy/loader.cfm?url/.

Gell, Alfred. 1998. *Art and Agency*. New York: Oxford University Press.

Giddens, Anthony. 1979. *Central Problems in Social Theory*. Berkeley: University of California Press.

Gerbner, George, and Larry Gross. 1976. Living with TV: The Violence Profile. *Journal of Communication* 26(2): 173–199.

Glasser, Theodore L., ed. 1999. *The Idea of Public Journalism*. New York: The Guilford Press.

Goffman, Erving. 1974. *Frame Analysis*. New York: Harper and Row.

Goodman, Walter. 1989. Television and the Attack in Central Park. *The New York Times*, C20, May 2, 1989.

Gouldner, Alvin W. 1976. *The Dialectic of Ideology and Technology: The Origins, Grammar, and Future of Ideology*. New York: Oxford University Press.

Gramsci, Antonio. 1992. *Prison Notebooks/ Antonio Gramsci*. New York: Columbia University Press.

Greenhouse, Carol. 1986. *Praying for Justice: Faith, Order, and Community in an American Town*. Ithaca: Cornell University Press.

———. 1996. *A Moment's Notice: Time Politics across Cultures*. Ithaca: Cornell University Press.

Habermas, Jürgen. 1987. *The Theory of Communicative Action, Volume Two, Life-world and System: A Critique of Functionalist Reason*. Trans. Thomas McCarthy. Boston: Beacon Press.

———. 1984. *The Theory of Communicative Action*. Vol. 1 of *Reason and the Rationalization of Society*. Trans. Thomas McCarthy. Boston: Beacon Press.

———. 1979. *Communication and the Evolution of Society*. Boston: Beacon Press.

Hackett, Robert A., and Yuezhi Zhao, eds. 2005. *Democratizing global media: One world, many struggles*. New York: Rowman & Littlefield Publishers, Inc.

Hadi Mizban/Associated Press. 2005. Photo: The family of a 9-year old boy, one of the children killed Wednesday in a suicide bombing, mourned over his coffin at the family home in Baghdad. *The New York Times*, July 14, 2005. http://www.nytimes.com/imagepages/2005/07/14/international/14iraq .ready.html/. Accessed July 14, 2005.

Hall, Stuart. 1973. The Determination of News Photographs. In *The Manufacture of News*, ed. Stanley Cohen and Jock Young, 176–190. Beverly Hills, CA: Sage Publications.

———. 1977. Culture, the Media, and the Ideological Effect. In *Mass Communication and Society*, by J. Curran, et al., 315–348. London: Edward Arnold.

Halloran, James Dermot, Philip Elliot, and Graham Murdock. 1970. *Demonstrations and Communication: A Case Study*. Harmondsworth: Penguin.

Handy, E.S. Craighill, and Mary Kawena Puku'i. 1972. *The Polynesian Family System in Ka- 'u, Hawaii*. Rutland, VT: Charles E. Tuttle Co.

Hansen, Helle Ploug. 1997. Patients' Bodies and Discourses of Power. In *Anthropology of Policy*, ed. Cris Shore and Susan Wright. New York: Routledge.

Hardt, Hanno. 1992. *Critical Communication Studies: Communication, History, and Theory in America*. New York: Routledge.

Hart, H.L.A. 1961. *The Concept of Law*. New York: Oxford University Press.

Hasty, Jennifer. 2005. *The Press and Political Culture in Ghana*. Bloomington: Indian University Press.

Hays, Constance L. 1989. Park Safety: Advice From Runners. *The New York Times*, B3, April 21, 1989.

Healy, Patrick D. 2005. Senator Clinton Assails Bush and G.O.P. at Campaign Fund-Raiser. http://www.nytimes.com/2005/06/06/nyregion/06cnd-hillary .html/.

Henry, Francis, and Carol Tator. 2002. *Discourses of Domination: Racial Bias in the Canadian English-Language Press*. Toronto: University of Toronto Press.

Herzfeld, Michael. 2001. *Anthropology: Theoretical Practice in Culture and Society*. Malden, MA: Blackwell Publishers.

Holmes, Douglas R. and George E. Marcus. 2005. Cultures of Expertise and the Management of Globalization: Toward the Re-functioning of Ethnography. In *Global Assemblages: Technology, Politics, and Ethics as Anthropological Problems*, by Aihwa Ong and Stephen J. Collier. Malden, MA: Blackwell Publishing.

Holtzman, Elizabeth. 1989. Rape…The Silence in Criminal. *The New York Times*, A35, May 5, 1989.

Hoover, Will. 2004. Slain Elephant Left Tenuous Legacy in Animal Rights. *Honolulu Advertiser.Com* poster, August 20, 2004. http://the.honoluluadvertiser .com/article/Aug/20/In/In19a.html/. Accessed June 7, 2005.

Horst, Heather A. and Daniel Miller. 2006. *The Cell Phone: An Anthropology of Communication*. New York: Berg.

Innis, Harold. 1950. *Empire and Communications*. New York: Oxford University Press.

Jolley, Nicholas. 1999. *Locke: His Philosophical Thought*. New York: Oxford University Press.

Kame'eleihiwa, Lilikalā. 1989. H-3 Story: 'a great injustice'. In Op-Ed, *The Honolulu Advertiser*, B3, August 11, 1989.

Katz, Elihu, Jay Blumler, and Michael Gurevitch. 1974. Uses of Mass Communication by the Individual. In *Mass Communication Research: Major Issues and Future Directions*, ed. W. Phillips Davidson and Frederick Yu. New York: Praeger Publications.

Kaufman, Michael T. 1989. New Yorkers Wrestle With a Crime: Whatever Role Race Had in Park Attack, It's Topic No. 1. *The New York Times*, A1, April 28, 1989.

Keane, Webb. 1997. *Signs of Recognition: Powers and Hazards of Representation in an Indonesian Society*. Berkeley: University of California Press.

Keever, Beverly Deepe. 2004. *News Zero: The New York Times and the Bomb*. Monroe, ME: Common Courage Press.

Kelly, Raymond C. 2000. *Warless Societies and the Origin of War*. Ann Arbor: University of Michigan Press.

Kelsen, Hans. 1967. *Pure Theory of Law*. Trans. Max Knight, 2nd ed. Berkeley: University of California Press.

Kleinfield, N.R. 1996. T.W.A. Jetliner Leaving New York For Paris Crashes in Atlantic; More Than 220 Aboard. *The New York Times*, A1, July 18, 1996.

Kobayashi, Ken. 2005. Man faces charges in girl's rape: Judge overrules defense's objection to cameras in court. *Honolulu Advertiser*, B1, May 4, 2005.

Kolata, Gina. 1989. Grim Seeds of Park Rampage Found in East Harlem Streets. *The New York Times*, C1, May 2, 1989.

Kramer, Andrew E. 2007. 50% Good News is Bad News in Russian Radio. *The New York Times*, April 22, 2007. http://www.nytimes.com/2007/04/22/world/europe/22russia.html/. Accessed April 25, 2007.

Kreitzer, M. 1996. A Service Rendered? Letters in *The New York Times*, A28, May 23, 1996.

Kripke, Saul A. 1982. *Wittgenstein on Rules and Private Language: An Elementary Exposition*. Cambridge: Harvard University Press.

Lasswell, Harold. 1948. The Structure and Function of Communication in Society. In *The Communication of Ideas*, ed. L. Bryson. New York: Harper.

Latour, Bruno. 2005. *Reassembling the Social: An Introduction to Actor-Network-Theory*. New York: Oxford University Press.

Lazarsfeld, Paul, Bernard Berelson, and Hazel Gaudet. 1944. *The People's Choice: How the Voter Makes up His Mind in a Presidential Campaign*. New York: Duell, Sloan, and Pearce.

Lea, Henry Charles. 1967. The Wager of Battle. In *Law and Warfare*, ed. Paul Bohannan. Garden City, NY: The Natural History Press.

Lefebvre, Henri. 1991. *The Production of Space*. Malden, MA: Blackwell Publishing.

Lewis, Wyndham. 1957. *Time and Western Man*. Boston: Beacon Press.

Levi-Strauss, Claude. 1966. *The Savage Mind*. Chicago: University of Chicago Press.

Lippmann, Walter. 1922. *Public Opinion*. New York: The Free Press.

Lopez, Jose. 2003. *Society and its Metaphors: Language, Social Theory, and Social Structure*. New York: Continuum.

Lovink, Geert. 2008. *Zero Comments: Blogging and Critical Internet Culture.* New York: Routledge.

Luhrmann, Tanya M. 2004. Metakinesis: How God Becomes Intimate in Contemporary U.S. Christianity. *American Anthropologist* 106(3): 518–528.

Lule, Jack. 2005. News as Myth: Daily News and Eternal Stories. In *Media Anthropology*, ed. Eric W. Rothenbuhler and Mihai Coman. Thousand Oaks, CA: Sage Publications.

MacCormick, Neil. 1981. *H.L.A. Hart.* Stanford: Stanford University Press.

McFadden, Robert D. 1996. 109 Feared Dead as Jet Crashes in Everglades: Atlanta Flight was Making Emergency Return to Miami. *The New York Times*, A1, May 12, 1996.

Mackey, Eva. 1997. The Cultural Politics of Populism: Celebrating Canadian National Identity. In *Anthropology of Policy: Critical Perspectives on Governance and Power*, ed. Chris Shore and Susan Wright. New York: Routledge.

Mankekar, Purnima. 1993. National Texts and Gendered Lives: An Ethnography of Television Viewers in a North Indian City. *American Ethnologist* 20(3): 543–563.

Marcus, George E. 2005. What is Wanted from Ethnographic Fieldwork Today? *Anthropology News* 46(6): 9 and 12.

———. 1998. Ethnography in/of the World System: The Emergence of Multi-Sited Ethnography (1995). Chapter Three of *Ethnography through Thick and Thin*, by George E. Marcus, 79–104. Princeton, NJ: Princeton University Press.

Marriott, Michel. 1989. Harlem Residents Fear Backlash from Park Rape. *The New York Times*, B3, April 24, 1989.

Maslow, Abraham. 1970. *Motivation and Personality.* New York: Harper & Row.

Matsuo, Miyuki. 2005. As *Zainichi* or Politician: How Yomiuri Witnessed The Tracks of Arai's Political Career. M.A. Thesis. Honolulu: University of Hawai'i at Mānoa.

McChesney Robert. 1999. *Rich Media, poor democracy—Communication politics in dubious times.* Urbana: University of Illinois Press.

———. 1997. *Corporate Media and the threat to democracy.* New York: Seven Stories Press.

McQuail, Denis. 2003. *McQuail's Mass Communication Theory*, 4th ed. Thousand Oaks, CA: Sage Publications, Inc.

———. 1987. *Mass Communication Theory: An Introduction.* Beverly Hills: Sage.

Mead, George Herbert. 1934. *Mind, Self, and Society: From the Standpoint of a Social Behaviorist.* Chicago: University of Chicago Press.

Merry, Sally Engle. 2000. *Colonizing Hawai'i: The Cultural Power of Law.* Princeton: Princeton University Press.

———. 1990. *Getting Justice and Getting Even: Legal Consciousness among Working-Class Americans.* Chicago: University of Chicago Press.

McLuhan, Marshall. 1964. *Understanding Media.* Cambridge MA: MIT Press.

Miyazaki, Hirokazu. 2004. *The Method of Hope: Anthropology, Philosophy, and Fijian Knowledge.* Stanford: Stanford University Press.

Morley, David. 1996. The Audience, The Ethnographer, The Postmodernist, and their Problems. In *The Construction of the Viewer*, ed. Peter I. Crawford and Sigurjon Baldur Hafsteinsson. Højbjerg: Intervention Press.

Mosco, Vincent. 1996. *The Political Economy of Communication: Rethinking and Renewal*. Thousand Oaks, CA: Sage Publications.

Murakawa, Kim. 1996a. Four Workers Hurt When H-3 Girders Fall. *The Honolulu Advertiser*, A2, July 28, 1996.

———. 1996b. H-3 Gider Collapse Attributed to Heat. *The Honolulu Advertiser*, A1, August 14, 1989.

Nakaso, Dan. 1994. Elephant Rampage: 1 Killed, 13 Injured; Panic at Blaisdell. *The Honolulu Advertiser*, A1, August 21, 1994.

Navarro, Mireya. 1996. Hope of Rescue is Swallowed by Swamp. *The New York Times*, A1, May 13, 1996.

Neuman, Yair. 2003. Co-generic Logic as a Theoretical Framework for the Analysis of Communication in Living Systems. *Semiotica* Vol.144–1/4 (2003): 49–65.

Nightingale, Virginia. 1996. *Studying Audiences: The Shock of the Real*. New York: Routledge.

Nord, David Paul. 2001. *Communities of Journalism: A History of American Newspaper and their Readers*. Urbana: University of Illinois Press.

O'Donnell, Michelle. 2005. Traumatized by 9/11, Fired Over Drug Rule. *The New York Times*, September 6, 2005. http://www.nyt.com/2005/09/06/nyregion/06fdny.html/. Accessed September 6, 2005.

Ortiz, Matthew Kavika. 1996. Associate Professor's Comment Inappropriate. In Letters, *The Honolulu Advertiser*, A13, August 8, 1996.

Oshiro, Sandra. 1978. Young Turk Emerges at Con Con: Waihee Called Shots in Convention. *The Honolulu Advertiser*, A1, A3 September 20, 1978.

Osorio, Jonathan Kamakawiwo'ole. 2003. Kū'ē and Kù'oko'a: History, Law, and other Faiths. In *Law and Empire in the Pacific: Fiji and Hawai'i*, ed. Sally Engle Merry and Donald Brenneis. Santa Fe: School of American Research Press.

Parsons, Talcott. 1968. Order as a Sociological Problem. In *The Concept of Order*, ed. Paul Kunz. Seattle: University of Washington Press.

Pedelty, Mark. 1995. *War Stories: The Culture of Foreign Correspondents*. New York: Routledge.

Peterson, Mark Allen. 2003. *Anthropology and Mass Media: Media and Myth in the New Millennium*. New York: Berghahn Books.

Philips, Susan U. 1998. *Ideology in the Language of Judges*. New York: Oxford University Press.

Pitt, David E. 1989a. Jogger's Attackers Terrorized at Least 9 in 2 Hours. *The New York Times*, A1, April 22, 1989.

———. 1989b. Two Youths Indicted in Beating and Rape in Central Park. *The New York Times*, B3, April 27, 1989.

Posner, Richard A. 2005. Bad News. *The New York Times*, July 31, 2005. http://www.nytimes.com/2005/07/31/books/review/31POSNER.html/. Accessed July 22, 2005.

————. 1972. *Economic Analysis of Law.* Boston: Little, Brown.

Putnam, Hilary. 2004. *Ethics without Ontology.* Cambridge: Harvard University Press.

————. 2002. *The Collapse of the Fact/Value Dichotomy: And Other Essays.* Cambridge: Harvard University Press.

Quine, Willard Van Orman. 1960. *Word and Object.* Cambridge, MA: The Technology Press of the Massachusetts Institute of Technology and John Wiley and Sons.

Rahimi, Shadi. 2005. A Remorseless Rudolph Gets Life Sentence for Bombing at Clinic. *The New York Times,* July 18, 2005. http://www.nytimes.com/2005/07/18/national/18cnd-bomber.html/. Accessed July 18, 2005.

Raiffa, Howard, with John Richards and Davis Metcalfe. 1983. *Negotiation Analysis: The Science and Art of Collaborative Decision Making.* Cambridge: The Belknap Press of Harvard University Press.

Rapanos et ux., et al. v. US, 547 U.S. 715 (2006).

Renshaw, Layla. 2007. "The Iconography of Exhumation: Representations of Mass Graves from the Spanish Civil War." Chapter 12 of *Archaeology and the Media,* ed. Timothy Clack and Marcus Brittain. Walnut Creek, CA: Left Coast Press.

Rommetveit, Ragnar. 1992. Outlines of a Dialogically Based Social-Cognitive Approach to Human Cognition and Communication. Chapter 1 of *The Dialogical Alternative: Towards a Theory of Language and Mind,* ed. Astrid Heen Wold. Bergen: Scandinavian Press.

Roper v. Simmons, 543 U.S. 557 (2005).

Rorty, Richard. 1991. *Objectivity, Relativism, and Truth: Philosophical Papers,* Vol. 1. New York: Cambridge University Press.

Rothenbuhler, Eric W., and Mihai Coman, eds. 2005. *Media Anthropology.* Thousand Oaks, CA: Sage Publications.

Saulny, Susan. 2002. Convictions and Charges Voided in '89 Central Park Jogger Attack. *The New York Times,* A1, December 20, 2002.

Schiller, Dan. 1981. *Objectivity and the News: The Public and the Rise of Commercial Journalism.* Philadelphia: University of Pennsylvania Press.

Schramm, Wilbur Lang. 1988. *The Story of Human Communication: Cave Painting to Microchip.* New York: Harper and Row.

Schudson, Michael. 1978. *Discovering the News.* New York: Basic Books.

Scott, Janny. 1996. Postmodern Gravity Deconstructed, Slyly. *The New York Times,* A1, A22, May 18, 1996.

Seelye, Katharine Q. 2002. Regretful Lindh Gets 20 Years in Taliban Case. *The New York Times,* A1, October 5, 2002.

Semple, Kirk. 2005. Baghdad Bomb Kills Up to 27, Most Children. *The New York Times,* July 14, 2005. http://www.nytimes.com/2005/07/14/international/middleeast/14iraq.html/. Accessed July 14, 2005.

Shafer, Jack. 2005. Judge Posner's Incorrect Verdict. *Slate,* August 1, 2005. http://slate.msn.com/id/2123764/.

Sheng, Ellen. 2005. Nanotechnology Hits the Tennis Court. *The Wall Street Journal,* D1, August 26, 2005.

Shore, Cris, and Susan Wright. 1997. Policy: A New Field of Anthropology. Chapter 1 of *Anthropology of Policy*, ed. Cris Shore and Susan Wright, 3–34. New York: Routledge.

Siebert, Fred S., Theodore Peterson, and Wilbur Schramm. 1956. *Four Theories of the Press: The authoritarian, libertarian, social responsibility, and Soviet communist concepts of what the press should be and do*. Urbana: University of Illinois Press.

Silva, Noenoe K. 2003. Talking Back to Law and Empire. In *Law and Empire in the Pacific: Fiji and Hawai'i*, ed. Sally Engle Merry and Donald Brenneis. Santa Fe: School of American Research Press.

Silverstein, Michael, and Greg Urban, eds. 1996. *Natural Histories of Discourse*. Chicago: University of Chicago Press.

Simmel, Georg. 1955. *Conflict and the Web of Group-Affiliations*. Trans. Kurt H. Woolff and Reinhard Bendix. New York: The Free Press.

Sinding, Michael. 2004. Beyond essence (or getting over 'there'): Cognitive and dialectical theories of genre. *Semiotica* 149(1–4): 377–395.

Smith, Garry P. 1989. Kame'elehiwa's Comments were Ill Advised. In Letters, *The Honolulu Advertiser*, B3, August 11, 1989.

Sorkin, Michael. 2005. Speech at Conference Assails Right Wing. St. Louis Post-Dispatch. http://www.commondreams.org/headlineso5/0516-o1.htm/. Accessed June 4, 2005.

Spitulnik, Debra. 1993. Anthropology and Mass Media. *Annual Review of Anthropology* 22: 293–315.

Stein, Jeremy. 1989. Cheap Talk and the Fed: A Theory of Imprecise Policy Announcements. *The American Economic Review* 79(1): 32–42.

Stout, David. 2005. U.S. Presses Newsweek to 'Repair' Damage From Flawed Report. *The New York Times*, May 17, 2005. http://www.nytimes.com/2005/05/17/internationa/middleeaast/17cnd-koran.html/.

Sturz, Elizabeth Lyttleton. 1989. What Kids Who Aren't Wolves Say about Wilding. *The New York Times*, A1, A17, May 1, 1989.

Sullivan, Ronald. 1989. Bail Denied for 3 Youths in Park Attack. *The New York Times*, A30, April 29, 1989.

Taussig, Michael. 1993. *Mimesis and Alterity*. New York: Routledge.

Thompson, John B. 1995. *The Media and Modernity*. Stanford: Stanford University Press.

Tierney, John. 2005. Bombs Bursting on Air. Op-Ed, *The New York Times*, May 10, 2005. http://www.nytimes.com/2005/05/10/opinion/10tierney.html/. Accessed May 10, 2005.

Tichenor, Philip J., George A. Donohue, and Clarice N. Olien. 1980. *Community Conflict and the Press*. Beverly Hills: Sage Publications.

Tomlinson, Matthew. 2004. Memes and Metaculture: The Politics of Discourse Circulation in Fiji. *The Australian Journal of Anthropology*, 2004, 15:2, 185–197.

Unger, Roberto Mangabeira. 1986. *False Necessity: Anti-Necessitarian Social Theory in the Service of Radical Democracy*. New York: Cambridge University Press.

Urban, Greg. 2001. *Metaculture: How Culture Moves through the World*. Minneapolis: University of Minnesota Press.

Vincent, Richard C., B.K. Crow, and Dennis K. Davis. 1989. When technology fails: The drama of airline crashes in network television news. *Journalism Monographs*, No. 117.

Voloshinov, V.N. 1986. *Marxism and the Philosophy of Language*. Cambridge, MA: Harvard University Press.

Walker, Lucy. 2001. Profile: Timothy McVeigh. BBC News Online, May 11, 2001. http://news.bbc.co.uk/1/hi/world/americas/1321244.stm/.

Watson-Gegeo, Karen, and Geoffrey M. White. 1990. *Disentangling: Conflict Discourse in Pacific Societies*. Stanford: Stanford University Press.

Werhane, Patricia H. 1992. *Skepticism, Rules, and Private Languages*. Atlantic Highland, NJ: Humanities Press.

White, Geoffrey M. 1991. *Identity Through History: Living Stories in a Solomon Islands Society*. New York: Cambridge University Press.

Wicker, Tom. 1989. Making Things Worse: The Park Attack and the Mayoral Race. *The New York Times*, A25, May 2, 1989.

Wittgenstein, Ludwig. 1958. *Philosophical Investigations*, 2nd ed. London: Blackwell.

Wolff, Craig. 1989. Youths Rape and Beat Central Park Jogger. *The New York Times*, B1, April 21, 1989.

Zeleny, Jeff. 2007. G.O.P. Senator Splits With Bush Over Iraq Policy. *The New York Times*, June 27, 2007. http://www.nytimes.com/2007/06/27/washington/27cong.html/. Accessed June 27, 2007.

Index